THE BORZOI
HISTORY OF ENGLAND
VOLUME FOUR
1640-1815

The Borzoi History of England

General Editor
ARTHUR JOSEPH SLAVIN
University of California at Los Angeles

ANGLES, ANGELS,
AND CONQUERORS
Volume I: 400–1154
Joel T. Rosenthal
State University of New York at Stony Brook

THE COMMUNITY
OF THE REALM
Volume II: 1154–1485
Michael R. Powicke
University of Toronto

THE PRECARIOUS BALANCE:
English Government and Society
Volume III: 1450–1640
Arthur Joseph Slavin
University of California at Los Angeles

A CERTAINTY IN THE SUCCESSION
Volume IV: 1640–1815
Gerald M. and Lois O. Straka
University of Delaware

Volume V: 1815–the Present
J. B. Conacher
University of Toronto

THE BORZOI
HISTORY OF ENGLAND
VOLUME FOUR
1640-1815

A CERTAINTY IN THE SUCCESSION

ALFRED A. KNOPF   NEW YORK

GERALD M. & LOIS O. STRAKA

University of Delaware

To "Mutze"

THIS IS A BORZOI BOOK
PUBLISHED BY ALFRED A. KNOPF, INC.

First Edition
987654321

Library of Congress Cataloging in Publication Data

Straka, Gerald M

A certainty in the succession.

(The Borzoi history of England, v. 4)

Bibliography

1. Great Britain—History—Modern period, 1485.

I. Straka, Lois O., joint author. II. Title. III. Series.

DA26.B65 vol. 4 [DA300]   942.06   73–12987

ISBN 0–394–47952–1

ISBN 0–394–31771–8 (text ed.)

Manufactured in the United States of America

foreword

The volumes making up the Borzoi History of England spring from the desire the authors share to preserve for the present the excitement of the English past. To a somewhat smaller degree we also share a prejudice against the writing of a history unified artificially by an allotment of "factors" and "forces." We do not think a good consecutive history of England between the coming of the Anglo-Saxons to Britain and the British entry into the Common Market can be made by such stinting of work.

This is not to say that we dismiss the need for a concern over how five volumes by as many historians go to make one history. It is to say that we began by admitting the diverse character of our assignments. We recognized at the outset that what might be central to the history of Anglo-Saxon England might be eccentric, if given the same weight by another author, to a history of industrial England. Moreover, we began in agreement that our own gifts and interests, if followed in a disciplined way, could bring out of many volumes one book.

Professor Rosenthal's history of early English society employs a narrative technique around a political center. Yet his most basic concern is to give the reader a sense of the rudeness of life in Anglo-Saxon England.

Because Professor Rosenthal had so firm a base on which to work in Volume I, Professor Powicke agreed to concentrate his work in another direction. He set out to tell how the medieval realm was ordered. While not altogether abandoning traditional narrative, he thought it profitable to examine in detail the shape and character of the various communities that constituted the medieval realm—royal, ecclesiastical, urban, and manorial.

The aim of the medievalists was thus to establish and explain the institutions and culture in a broad way, while telling how they worked. Their working order was profoundly challenged over a period of time stretching from

Chaucer's age to that of Milton, or, reckoning politically, from Edward III's time to that of Charles I. It was my concern to describe and explain how a series of shifts in the social basis of politics led the English to reorder a turbulent commonwealth.

The efforts at establishing political, religious, and social stability undertaken by the Tudors proved more daring than durable. Professor and Mrs. Straka wished to deal with the undisputed establishment of political stability between the Puritan Revolution and England's wars to contain the expansion of revolutionary France in Napoleon's time. Where Volume III sought to base an analysis of government and society in the economic and religious life of the era, the Strakas thought it essential to tell how stability was achieved in terms narrative and political at heart. They felt they could build confidently on the descriptions already achieved in Volume III, just as Professor Powicke thought to thicken the texture of the society whose shape was defined by Professor Rosenthal.

This alternation was acceptable to all because we accepted in principle the existence of three great revolutionary situations in English history—that surrounding the Norman Conquest, another focused on the Reformation, and a third based on the transformation of a mixed commercial-agrarian society into an industrial one. It fell to Professor Conacher to take forward into our time the account of the revolution that made aristocratic England into the liberal, industrial democracy of the empire and the welfare state.

Hence this History has taken shape around two concerns: giving scope to narrative, where the story of change was itself dramatic in social terms rather than in dynastic ones; and allowing room for more analytical work, where this seemed to point to an understanding of why changes took place rather than merely what changed and how.

Our historical assumptions reveal a pluralism rather than the ideas of a "school." Our concerns and styles differ, and we hope this difference is appropriate to our problems. We felt we would work best if we marched to the drum each heard best, whether it was the steady one of ordinary people working the land and the common rhythm of factory pistons or the subtler one beating to political tunes in high places. It has been our hope thus to avoid the mere repetitious noise of texts cut to cover uniformly every aspect of society. Philosophers say nature does nothing by leaps. History, however, is constantly surprising; it is alive precisely because of its variety, its stubborn refusal of any lockstep.

Between the extremes of Alfred's tight little island and the august empire ruled by Queen Elizabeth I's heirs and successors, English history lies, a polyglot thing, nurturing our own civilization and its discontents. Since the time when Ranke spoke of national histories as a perfect guide to people's consciousness, the sense of history has profoundly altered. Yet narrative—description and analysis centered in political life as widely defined to make room for religion, economics, and popular culture—has not yielded its central place. We therefore offer this History: of a country bound in by her triumphant sea; a sepulchre for famous men; an often bleak workshop; a place that sent blacks into slavery in 1562 in a ship named *Jesus;* frankly political.

ARTHUR JOSEPH SLAVIN

Contents

LIST OF ILLUSTRATIONS

Introduction

The subtitle of this volume, *A Certainty in the Succession,* is drawn from the most monumental of English constitutional documents, the Bill of Rights of 1689. Following a hectic half century that began with bitter denunciations of royal policy (1640), England's political condition disintegrated into civil war (1642), then coalesced around a military dictatorship (Oliver Cromwell, 1653), and finally subsided into a pragmatic compromise that included the restoration of royalty (1660). Just before a second rupture between crown and people could occur, a handful of headstrong court figures hazarded a gamble that resulted in the Glorious Revolution of 1688. They deposed their legitimate liege, placed his daughter and son-in-law on the throne, and sealed their revolutionary expectations and any discussion of future heirs and kingship in the Bill of Rights "for preventing all questions and divisions in this realm by reason of any pretended titles to the crown, and for preserving a certainty in the succession thereof, in and upon which the unity, peace, tranquility, and safety of this nation doth, under God, wholly consist. . . ."

The matter of who sat upon the throne was of paramount concern in this era, and the Bill of Rights was meant to establish once and for all that such determinations should in the future be made by law, not merely by birth, conquest, or fortune. Other political certainties were also established during this era: the prime ministerial and cabinet functions jelled into something resembling their modern equivalents, as did a workable party system, religious toleration, and a basic regard for legal equality. All these, however, were then dependent on the stability of the presiding monarch; thus a certainty in the succession is a major theme in this period of English history, especially so prior to 1689 in Charles I's and James II's reigns (one king lost his head with the crown upon it; the other supposedly left the throne vacant by abdication), and even later during the unstable years of the American revolution, when Lord North headed the ministry.

At a more parochial level an undisputed succession also provided a rare sense of security and continuity for an increasingly unstable social structure. Besides two political revolutions (1640 and 1688), there were a wholesale re-distribution of land, a cultural revolution, an agricultural and industrial revolution, enormous redistributions of capital, a mammoth population in-crease and geographical shift, a hundred years' war (with France), the loss of one empire (the American colonies), and the conquest of another (Canada). Much change was only minimally detected at the center by court politicians. Across the length and breadth of the island most transformations went un-heeded or misread.

For coherence, the period covered by this text has been divided into two great epochs. Part One deals with the epoch of the landed aristocracy and gentry (1640–1714) and Part Two embraces the epoch of the merchant prince and the industrial pioneer (1714–1815). As misleading as these two designations might be, they are an attempt, with some justification, to emphasize the groups that wielded the most political and social power during each of the two epochs. Moreover, they separate the Stuart and the Hanoverian dynasties. Each part is introduced with a chapter describing the structure and dominant trends in society; Chapter One portrays England in its primary rural setting as it appeared just prior to the coming of industrialism; Chapter Six surveys the changes introduced by the machine in what is classically called the in-dustrial revolution. A final descriptive chapter (Thirteen) dwells on the intellectual history of the period and covers some of the major features of the English Enlightenment. With these exceptions the chapters more or less follow a period-by-period narrative

A word about the style: the reader of histories usually expects a rigidly encyclopedic certitude from his author. On the other hand, no author has a right deliberately to bore even the most serious reader. It is these authors' hopes that factual presentation and readable prose are not incompatible. This work is a broad depiction of an extraordinarily complex period. Nonetheless, whenever a no nonsense explanation is called for, we hope the reader will allow a style that may be prosaic; when a dramatic moment is inescapable, an idiom hopefully appropriate to the emotion of the moment has been employed. There are abundant quotations from sources, and only the most archaic of spellings and punctuation have been altered for the sake of readability. The authors have indulged in few personal observations (despite ulcer-inducing urges), and then only when obviously appropriate to draw a parallel be-tween inescapably meaningful events. The nature of tyranny, the cause and course of revolution, the problems of industrialization—these are his-torical factors that intrigue us as much as they intrigued those who lived in

1700 and 1800. But most of the parallels with today's events are left to the reader to draw.

There has been a purposeful avoidance of the battles that rage among historians. Needless to say, behind every seemingly simple statement of fact there lurks a catalog of disputed data. For the sake of keeping focus and not cluttering pages with historiographical haggling, emphases have been made sometimes where the consensus of contemporary opinion was lodged and at other times where present-day historians find most agreement. Should additional clarification on any period be desired, bibliographical suggestions at the end of the book will lead the reader behind the lines into the camps of the professional historical combatants who continue to struggle towards factual omniscience.

There are pronounced characteristics within the two large periods covered in this volume. The age beginning with the Revolution of 1640 and ending with the death of Anne in 1714 was decidedly constitutional and religious. The number of laws put into force is staggering and probably indicates a struggle between court and Parliament over the control of public policy. Each factional triumph signaled a statute embodying the victor's policy. But it was sometimes necessary to reissue the same law in a strengthened form (there were three triennial acts governing the holding of elections; there were three decrees of religious toleration and a toleration act within a twenty-year period). Behind nearly every constitutional maneuver, there lurked a religious motivation, and the number of religiously motivated laws is noteworthy.

After 1714 public concern switched to political and economic matters. Politics was played with a craftiness and precision never before known. Consequently there is much discussion of party personalities, electioneering, debates, and cabinet shufflings. The age being decidedly acquisitive, politics took on the trappings of a profiteering enterprise. Bribery and spoils systems, commercial booms and busts, excise laws, national debts, and economic reforms preoccupied even the would-be statesmen of the day. By keeping the primary preoccupations of the two periods in mind, and by trying, as historians must inexhaustibly do, to understand why these matters so absorbed contemporaries, the reader can comprehend the narrative and arrange it around some meaningful orientation.

A few technical points of information: inasmuch as there are frequent discussions of money—income, taxes, the national debt, food prices, capital investment—a rough gauge is needed of the pound's approximate worth two hundred years ago. Dr. Samuel Johnson estimated that an annual income of £30 kept one just above subsistence; £200 he regarded as affluence; £1,000 allowed one to live in "splendor." [1] In terms of dollars, if the classical

---

[1] Joseph Wood Krutch, *Samuel Johnson* (New York, 1944), p. 191.

nineteenth-century undevaluated pound is used ($4.87 to the pound), it works out that lower-class incomes were about $150 per year, middle-class affluence meant about $1,000, and "splendor" required nearly $5,000 annually. Of course, not nearly the same goods and services were then available. Housing and food were cheaper, luxuries were comparatively far more costly, and theirs was not a gadget-oriented economy. But some idea of what these incomes meant is given by Dr. Johnson's estimate that someone with merely £300 annually would not own a carriage. In other words, a family with a $1,500 income would not be likely to have the equivalent of a family car.

Social structure in the seventeenth and eighteenth centuries presents a greater problem for clarification. Like the colors in a spectrum, there were numerous and fine variations dividing king from pauper. However, three basic social categories were observed: the aristocracy (all titled, the head of the family usually sitting in the House of Lords); the gentle class (which narrowly corresponds to the twentieth century's middle class), and the laboring poor and paupers. Those of gentle birth included knights (but their title, "sir," did not allow them a seat in Lords), large landowners (squires), wealthy tenant farmers, merchants, artisans and craftsmen, and, infrequently, artists and musicians. To be a gentleman, then, was far more a condition of wealth than of birth, though it also meant being possessed of a broad education and a certain sophistication. Finally, it is interesting to note that in England, as opposed to Continental usage, the term "the people" was usually applied only to the upper two strata and not to the poor (the "mob," the "vulgar," or the "rabble"). Apart from these delineations class lines were blurred. As a writer observed in 1767:

In England the several ranks of men slide into each other almost imperceptibly; and a spirit of equality runs through every part of the constitution. Hence arises a strong emulation in all the several stations and conditions to vie with each other; and a perpetual restless ambition in each of the inferior ranks to raise themselves to the level of those immediately above them.[2]

The terms "Whig" and "Tory" fill the pages starting with Chapter Five. Customarily these designations denote the two major parties that emerged in Charles II's reign and would seem the ancestors of the present Labor and Conservative parties (though the Whig, or Liberal, party died a strange death of its own around 1930). Since 1929, when Sir Lewis Namier published his powerful study of eighteenth-century politics, *The Structure of Politics at the Accession of George III*, it has proven difficult for any succeeding historian to write as though these parties ever really existed. Namier's point is that

---

[2] [T. Forster], *An Enquiry into the Causes of the Present High Price of Provisions* (London, 1767), p. 41.

eighteenth-century politicians only used "Whig" and "Tory" in a vague symbolic sense, and that if one analyzes actual political performance in Parliament, it becomes clear that politicians merely followed self-interests without consulting any supposed platform, be it Whig or Tory. In other words, there were only politicians involved in power plays.

The reverse of what is called Namierism emphasizes what contemporaries thought to be true—that though party structures and platforms in the seventeenth and eighteenth centuries may have been unsophisticated, Whigs and Tories nonetheless existed, sometimes in periods of very pronounced partisanship, and always at least in a vague commitment to their party philosophies. There are two excellent discussions of the Namier approach, in Richard Pares's *King George III and the Politicians* (Oxford: Clarendon Press, 1953), and in the bibliographical note of Robert Smith's *Eighteenth-Century English Politics* (New York: Holt, Rinehart and Winston, 1972).

This work attempts to unite both schools so that Whigs and Tories may be understood as broadly defined philosophical camps, sometimes with definably opposed programs, but always with the qualification that they took their stands from self-interest groups dominant at any given time within the camps.

Other terms, such as "Presbyterian," "Independent," and "middle class," will be used as if they too were clearly definable. The reader should be aware that this is a mere device to allow a sustained chronological narrative. The finer points of detailed qualification can only be left to further pursuit among the bibliographical suggestions.

Finally, this major reference should be cited as a master bibliographical guide: Elizabeth Furber, ed., *Changing Views on British History* (Cambridge: Harvard University Press, 1966). It is a composite of articles describing the leading recent writings in every field of English history, and it is far more complete than the list of titles at the end of this book.

Part One

THE EPOCH OF THE LANDED ARISTOCRACY AND GENTRY

Chapter One
THE TWILIGHT
OF AGRARIAN ENGLAND

Wealth, howsoever got, in England makes
Lords of mechanics, gentlemen of rakes:
Antiquity and birth are needless here;
'Tis impudence and money makes a peer.

DANIEL DEFOE
THE TRUE-BORN ENGLISHMAN (1701)

In 1650 an astute observer noted somewhat wryly that "the gentry strive for land, the common people strive for land; and buying and selling is an art whereby people endeavor to cheat one another of the land."[1] It was a blissful dream of rural independence that drew countless speculators into the open land market, and for those who consistently produced a profitable yield, there awaited a golden twilight inhabited by fat squires, socially ambitious housewives, and indulged children whose rough edges were smoothed by dancing masters and French governesses. The about-face in farm life is put aptly in this little verse:

Old Style

Man, to the plough;
Wife, to the cow;
Girl, to the yarn;
Boy, to the barn,
And your rent will be netted.

New Style

Man, Tally Ho;
Miss, piano;
Wife, silk and satin;
Boy, Greek and Latin
And you'll all be Gazetted.[2]

---

[1] Gerrard Winstanley, *A New Year's Gift for the Parliament and Army* (London, 1650).
[2] Quoted in George M. Trevelyan, *English Social History* (London, 1943), p. 472.

English landowners reaped a bountiful financial harvest along with social elevation. The value of Norfolk's fields, for instance, soared ten times between 1730 and 1760. On the eve of the Industrial Revolution, agriculture produced the largest slice of the total national income—£66 million as compared to industry's £27 million and commerce's £10 million. That the general economy was still dominated by the land as late as 1815 is evidenced by the fact that business cycles were even then controlled by food prices. The economic fact was that only when harvests were good and bread was cheap could the public afford manufactured items.

Around 1650 the realm of England (so far as can be reconstructed from incomplete records) was made up of thousands of square miles of fields tilled on a semicommunal basis, much as they had been in the Middle Ages. The only major division of land was in its usage: the upland's rolling hills to the west and north nourished cattle on the abundant grasses; the lowland's gentle plains fostered various grains. In autumn, cattle drives, welcomed by each town along the way, descended on the London area. The townsmen purchased their needs from the herdsmen, salted and dried their beef, and made sausages to store for the lean winter months ahead. In turn, the lowlands shipped its surpluses to the west and north to tide over the depleted herds while the ground was frozen.

Since the upland's grazing and the lowland's farming rarely filled the stomach abundantly in the middle of the seventeenth century, shepherds often fattened their purses by working in quarries or mines or in the local cloth industries (particularly stocking weaving). One district, famed for its mittens, produced an excess that it sent on to London for export to Holland.

In the lowlands this diversification of labor was even more evident. Many of the farmers let the land lie fallow and leased out the fields in a new venture, that of fattening cattle and sheep. Oliver Cromwell was one who increased his wealth considerably by this means. Canvas and linen weaving, the growing of hemp and the making of rope, gave employment for spare hours and extra energies. But the most common financial increment for farm families was provided by the time-honored wool industry. Spinning wheels in the parlor were not mere decor but put food on the table. The more daughters to spin, the more financially blessed the man of the house.

The Market Town

For the exchange of the goods and services offered by these local farmers and craftsmen, the hundreds of market towns scattered over England acted as agents. Without them the country's economy would have remained stagnantly based on the isolated and self-sufficient manor units of old. As early as 1300 these village centers, at an estimated number of two thousand, flourished at river and road crossings, on the sites of Ancient Roman camps, and at the bases of castle walls. They were fostered by royal charter allowing at least one fair per year plus an open market each week. In return they paid an annual *firma*, or tax, to the government. The most prominent of these even sent two members to Parliament.

The market town layout became typical throughout the English-speaking world, identical in Boston, Lincolnshire, and Boston, Massachusetts. A single street, "Main," "High," or "Market," dominated the town. Byways led into more remote quarters, such as "Haymarket" Street. The focal point of town life was the market house or toll house or (if it had retained the earlier designation) the guildhall. This center of urban activity, usually open on all sides of the ground floor, contained an upper hall for the town meetings of councilmen and merchants. On market days goods for sale were brought to the "common beam" (a great oaken shaft fitted with counterweights) on the ground level of the market house to certify measurement. Once the town stamp was affixed, the goods were trundled to their proper stalls in corn market or beast market or to temporary structures called "pentices" (forerunner of the word "penthouse"), usually little more than hinged roofs propped up by poles. Sometimes "tilts" (awnings) were used. Fish and meats were taken to stalls with benches, "shambles," where they were cleaned and dismembered. The word has appropriately come to describe any jumbled mess.

During the bustle of the business day, four or five market officers ordinarily sauntered about enforcing the town's stringent conditions. They often encountered interlopers on the market's fringes, selling wares illicitly weighed on competitors' beams. The unofficial markets frequently undercut the legal markets with cheaper prices and less rigorous quality controls. These black marketeers were harbingers of the free traders of the nineteenth century inasmuch as they challenged the monopolies of the chartered towns by offering competitive rates. The towns lost the ability to control prices as more and more transactions took place far from the market officers' purview.

In its prime the market town engendered a type of human ecological balance. Wares produced by a thousand diverse talents were grown, refined, or manufactured in a thousand scattered cottages; they were brought to the market center's shops and shambles, sold, and taken from the town for use or consumption by the same thousand talents. The townsmen saw eye to eye with their country kin; and instead of the competition that has since come to exist between urban and rural areas, the two were complementary. Most market towns required their able-bodied citizens to close shop during harvest and help the district bring in the crops. A healthy countryside was equated with a healthy town life. Conversely, farm workers were lured by the advantages of residing near a town. In a typical newspaper advertisement of 1696, prospective tenant farmers for a large estate were informed that, as well as orchards and gardens in the area, "there are two good market towns a mile on each hand, to which post comes three times a week, and carriers as often, and coach to and fro every day."

It is easy to romanticize the harmonious balance between town and country —variety in produce and folk crafts, renewing of friendships each market day, the color and wares of the annual fair, a sense of belonging that apparently eludes most modern urban dwellers. These conditions made city life meaningful where there is now often hopelessness and despair. There were no slums in market towns. Each resident was necessary, each house used and cared for; thus urban renewal was a daily happening. Yet the ecological balance was not without flaw. If either town or country went into a specialized line of farming or manufacturing, the community then lacked its full range of amenities, and its people found themselves living less full lives.

The market town could also suffer from its agricultural dependency. Crop failures affected the entire community disastrously. Then too, the crude sanitation encouraged disease. As late as 1635 the plague carried off half the population of Newmarket. Competition also pushed other market towns off the map.

The life style, however amicable, tended to be narrow and cramped, with little for either townsman or squire to do other than truck and barter. Not until the early nineteenth century did the townsfolk enjoy such refinements as libraries, theaters, and coffee houses. A scathing lampoon written by Samuel Butler around 1670 says of the "bumpkin," or country squire:

> His homely education has rendered him a native only of his own soil, and a foreigner to all other places. . . . The custom of being the best man in his own own territories has made him the worst everywhere else. He assumes the upper end of the table at an ale house as his birthright. . . . The chief points he treats on are the memoirs of his dogs and horses, which he repeats as often as a holder-forth that has but two sermons. . . . The top of his entertainment is horrible strong beer, which he pours into his guests . . . till they confess they can drink no more. . . . He has old family stories and jests that fell to him with the estate and have been left from heir to heir time out of mind. . . . All the heroical glory he aspires to is but to be reputed a most potent and victorious stealer of deer. . . . He goes to bawdy-houses to see the fashions . . . to have his pocket picked, and the pox into the bargain.[3]

The country squire's manners and narrow interests were favorite themes for jest.

[3] "A Bumpkin or Country Squire," *Eighteenth Century Poetry and Prose,* ed. Bredvold, McKillop, and Whitney (New York, 1939), pp. 11–12.

Yet there were other writers who found the bumpkins' life style picturesque and jolly. The drudgery of the fields was, after all, punctuated by myriad colorful holidays, most inherited from the medieval past of saints' days and vestigial pagan observances. The countryman's new year opened with a heartily prolonged wassail ("Be thou well"). On Twelfth-night (the January 6 conclusion of the twelve days of Christmas), three kings were chosen by the community, and with their queens they entreated Robin Goodfellow and his band of sprites to grant a trouble-free year. St. Valentine's Day in February was more the gift-giving day than was Christmas. Spring was ushered in by Lent, highlighted by Mothering Sunday (when the scattered family rejoined to take communion); Good Friday's fast was followed by Easter with its feast of simnel cakes and decorated eggs. May Day, the most pagan of the observances, witnessed all-night revels:

> Some to the woods and groves, some to the hills and mountains, some to one place and some to another . . . spend all the night in pleasant pastimes; and in the morning they return, bringing with them birch boughs and branches of trees to deck their assemblies withal. . . . But their chiefest jewel they bring from thence is their May Pole which they bring home with great veneration . . . covered all over with flowers and herbs, . . . and then they fall to banquet and feast, to leap and dance about it, as the heathen people did at the dedication of their idols.[4]

The long summer meant steady toil with little respite, but then Sheepshearing and Haymaking Days followed in August.

Wife, make us a dinner, spare flesh neither corn,
Make wafers and cakes, for our sheep must be shorn,
At sheep-shearing, neighbors none other thing crave,
But good cheer and welcome, like neighbors to have.[5]

Next came the rededication of the parish church and an all-night vigil. Corn harvest ran up against Nut Day (usually September 1) and then St. Katherine's Day for apple gathering. Bracken Day (October 1) saw a community excursion into the wilds to gather brake (hardy ferns for thatch and bedding). By the time Halloween arrived, the harvest was nearly in, allowing a rest through November that replenished the spirits for the month-long celebration of Christmas, when a lord of misrule, usually the burliest prankster, was elected. He, with the lads of his court, played good-humored tricks on the neighborhood. Mummers and "Morris" (for Moorish) dancers prepared their programs. At last on Christmas Eve the lord of misrule was toppled (sometimes

[4] Philip Stubbes, "The Anatomie of Abuses," quoted in *Delightes for Ladies by Sir Hugh Plat*, ed. G. E. and K. R. Fussell (London, 1948), pp. lxxxii–lxxxiii.
[5] *Ibid.*, p. lxxxiii.

into the nearest brook) as a token of Christ's bringing order and love to mankind. Then it all began afresh with Twelfth-night and another annual cycle.

Jolly and picturesque, or commonplace and boorish, the country-town relationship was doomed whatever the case. Historians correlate its mortality to the collapse of the tenant farmer and the small freeholder, the yeoman. Their fortunes had mounted dramatically since 1600 as a crushing inflation forced a buyers' market on landowners. Because rentals netted fixed income insufficient for rising prices, estates were broken up and sold or leased under long-term contracts. The new farms tended to be "champion," growing a variety of crops and grazing herds as well. More land became available during the Civil Wars as confiscated estates were put on the block. All this tended to profit the small farmer and tenant—until 1660. The trend then reversed itself in favor of ever larger spreads that abandoned champion farming for specialization. Some say the proud, free yeoman was finished by 1700; others date his demise at 1760; in any case, overall statistics reveal that around 1600 27 percent of the population were landholders, large and small; by 1688 the figure was closer to one percent. Conversely, it is estimated that in 1600 landless farm laborers accounted for 25 to 30 percent of the population. By 1688 that figure had risen to 47 percent. By 1800 most arable portions of the countryside were no longer dominated by farm villages but had been pulled together into sprawling estates of hundreds, even thousands, of acres. These mammoth holdings were lucratively farmed on capital gleaned from the export of excess crops not locally consumed. The great houses erected during the eighteenth century's lush agrarian age are today's stately homes of England, tourist attractions furnished with the crafts of Chippendale, Sheraton, and Wedgwood, and their hosts of imitators.

The Agricultural Revolution: Some Beginnings

What has been called the eighteenth-century's agricultural revolution was actually the result of over a hundred years' experimentation and education. Even in Queen Elizabeth I's time farmers were urged to utilize their lands wisely and fully: the tiniest strips adjoining farm houses were planted in caraway, fennel, dill, or aniseed; hemp for rope was raised along the borders of grain fields; fruit trees were planted among the hedges; ashes from the innumerable fireplaces were saved and spread on the fields in spring. In *A Surveyor's Dialogue* (1607), John Norden argued that if these practices were followed, there would be no need to drain off surplus population to overseas colonies. By 1700 hardy new grasses for grazing had been introduced, fertilizers were available for every crop, and patterns of rotations to avoid soil depletion were advocated. Jethro Tull advised planting grains in straight rows to make continuous cultivation and soil aeration possible. This conserved far more seed than the old broadcast system (throwing seed to the wind). The new method allowed frequent weeding, providing maximum nutrition for the growing grain, and at the same time ensured a harvest relatively free of weeds. Tull's inventiveness was best displayed in a wheat drill that planted seed at a proper depth and in optimum amounts.

Lord Charles "Turnip" Townshend promoted crop rotation in what became known as the Norfolk system. If wheat, turnips, barley, clover, or beans were sown in a four-year cycle, there would be no need for fields to lie fallow a year at a time, and the turnips or clover could be used to sustain cattle that might ordinarily have been slaughtered for lack of winter feed.

Dr. Francis Home placed agricultural studies on a scientific plane. He analyzed crops chemically, isolating seedlings in pots and subjecting them to various conditions to determine the effects of soils. His *Principles of Agriculture and Vegetation* ran into numerous French and German as well as English and Scottish editions. Robert Bakewell spent nearly all of his seventy years experimenting with improving breeds, particularly those of sheep. By selecting animals with small bones and meaty joints and isolating them from their less well endowed brethren, he bred far sturdier beasts. His work lured lords and kings to the great hall of his farm, which contained the skeletons of prize animals and the pickled remains of shanks and shoulders. Through his work, meat became a plentiful staple for even the most humble table. Records indicate that by the end of the eighteenth century, even some poor houses were financially able to serve meat four times weekly. The success of selective breeding shows up in the average weight of calves sold at market between 1710 and 1795—up from 50 to 148 pounds. For beef the contrast 370 pounds in 1710 to 800 pounds in 1795; for sheep from 28 to 80 pounds. The English were becoming a nation of mutton and beef eaters.

Fad and fashion helped popularize the new agricultural findings. Dinner and salon conversation was likely to turn to the merits of one crop over another, one breed over another. More than a thousand journals, catalogs, and treatises on agrarian subjects were published, one with a subtitle fitting to all: *A New System of Agriculture; or a Plain, Easy and Demonstrative Way of Growing Rich.* The greatest of the popularizers of this literature was Arthur Young, founder of the Board of Agriculture (1793) and a friend of George III, the leading patron of the craze. Young traveled hundreds of miles in search of detailed information on the rural doings of the realm and published some 250 works of his own, as well as editing the popular periodical *Annals of Agriculture.* The king, who wrote articles under the name "Farmer George," is said to have kept a copy always beside him for occasional reading.

The farming mania was imbued with a philosophical base by writers exalting the "native simplicity" of rural life:

> The inhabitants of which are religious, the fair sex modest and every countenance bears a picture of the heart. What . . . can be a more elegant amusement . . . than to inspect the beautiful product of fields and gardens. . . . And it certainly redounds more to the honor and satisfaction of the gardener that he is a preserver and pruner . . . than it does to the happiness of the greatest general that he has been successful in killing mankind.[6]

By the eighteenth century, cultivated land, "a scene of beauty, hopes and profit and all,"[7] had necessarily come to be managed on a grand scale. All the new techniques stressed volume, leaving the marginal tiller behind as his stronger neighbor increased his holdings at the other's expense. The enlargement was done in one of two ways: by "engrossing," the outright purchase of contiguous lands, or by "enclosing," the forcing of tenant farmers into specialized farming by refusing the use of open fields for other than specific crop cultivation. The portion of an estate most easily enclosed was the commons, a wild stretch of land that made up an eighth to a quarter of the entire holding, a preserve shared by landlord and tenant alike for pasturage and wood cutting. Enclosing the commons resulted in a lower standard of living for all but the landlord. By the loss of a cow, the lack of a place to keep chickens, or the deprivation of firewood, building timber, thatch, and herbs, tenants were stripped of extra benefits granted to them for hundreds of years. It was not long before the landlord could buy up their leases for a fraction of what they were worth. Only a remnant of the displaced tenants were invited to stay on as servants, stableboys, or fieldhands. The balance straggled to nearby cities or to the metropolis of London, most often to find abject poverty.

There was nothing new about enclosure. It dated back to the thirteenth century but until now had affected only a small percentage of estates. Earlier it was primarily used to take advantage of sheep raising, the sale of wool frequently profiting the whole estate. Like as not, the tenantry requested the lord to enclose, even forced him into it. But eighteenth-century enclosure deserved its evil reputation because of the concomitant drive against leases. Landlords merely applied by petition to Parliament to change the use of the common lands, and by a simple majority vote, the way of life for entire estates was converted. Between 1700 and 1760 two hundred acts enclosed 300,000 acres; the last forty years of the century witnessed nearly two thousand acts enclosing 3 million acres. This wholesale disregard of tenant farmers prompted

---

[6] Quoted in G. E. Fussell, *More Old English Farming Books from Tull to the Board of Trade* (London, 1950), p. 26.

[7] *Ibid.*, p. 9.

Arthur Young to characterize their demoralization over the loss of the use of commons:

> For whom are they to be sober: For whom are they to save?... If I am diligent shall I have leave to build a cottage? If I am sober shall I have land for a cow? If I am frugal shall I have an acre for potatoes? You [landlord] offer no motives; you have nothing but a parish office [to evict me] and a workhouse!—Bring me another pot [of beer].[8]

Population Increases

However, the decline of the small farmer and diversified farming appears to have swelled England's growth generally. Between 1600 and 1700 there was a barely noticeable increase in population, from some 5 million to 5.5 million; by 1801 and the first official census, England and Wales numbered 8.8 million people. By 1811 this count had swelled to 10 million, not half of whom could have been fed by the outmoded farming practices of 1700. London mushroomed from a half million people in 1688 to one million by 1811, eclipsing Paris's half million, and making London the most heavily populated city in the world. In 1760 only one English city other than London, Bristol, could boast a population of 60,000 or more. By 1811 six English cities had attained this population; by 1830 England was equally urban and rural.

The population explosion was only partially due to the agricultural revolution. Whatever the main cause, the death rate declined markedly from 33.4 per thousand in 1730 to 19.98 per thousand in 1810. Life expectancy was lengthened; the mortality rate of children under six decreased. The steady demand for workers in the new mills of the midlands and the north meant improved working conditions, higher pay, and therefore earlier marriages. Arthur Young noted that "the increase of employment will be found to raise men like mushrooms." For a time, industry was able to absorb the displaced farmers.

Food habits changed. With bad harvests beginning after 1760 and continuing on and off through 1815, grain prices more than quadrupled. But at the same time that the staple bread was outpricing itself, the workman's wife found substitutes coming on the market. Cabbage, potatoes, carrots, beans, and peas came into abundance, and citrus fruits, once held to cause fever, were now available. In 1757 the Admiralty ordered all ships to stock citrus fruit, roots, and greens as a protection against scurvy.

The nutritional content of foods was beginning to be understood. Doctors were learning from such studies as those conducted by William Stork, who

---

[8] Quoted in M. Dorothy George, *England in Transition* (London, 1931), p. 90.

as a living laboratory subjected himself to hundreds of diets. In the process he destroyed his health and hastened his death, but his notes bequeathed valuable nutritional guides concerning the benefits of cheese, berries, honey, and a host of other foods. Cod-liver oil came to be a general elixir in 1780 and despite its miserable taste undoubtedly improved the general health.

A safe vaccine against smallpox was developed by Edward Jenner and used in his National Vaccine Establishment (founded in 1808). Even health faddists played a role in health improvement. A merchant trading to Russia, Jonas Hanaway, advocated general use of the umbrella against both rain and sun. He blamed England's tea drinking for the country's ill health and deplored the middle class's use of wet nurses (some of whom were diseased prostitutes), advocating the use of cow's milk instead. By 1769 London's Dispensary for Sick Children was following his advice, using the new "bubby-pot" (baby bottle). Opiates, popularly administered to quiet children, were being discouraged. At least in the London area, adults were also profiting from the new attitudes on health. In addition to a foundling hospital, seven general hospitals were established. These institutions borrowed knowledge from the renowned medical center in Edinburgh (founded in 1725). Even in such small ways as more frequent bathing and more balanced diet was the public health improved enough to stimulate population growth.

The Growth of the Peerage

As the total population expanded, so did the number of the wealthy and the titled. English society, while recognizably stratified, possessed few barriers to social mobility. England had never known a caste system. From at least the Wars of the Roses and the Tudors' penchant for beheading their enemies, the medieval aristocracy experienced perpetual decimation and steady replenishment from the ranks of the middle class. The early Stuarts sold titles (an earldom cost £20,000) or lavished them on favorites. By the end of Charles II's reign (1685), the peerage had swelled from 60 in 1603 to 181. Around 1714 the number temporarily leveled off at some 220, then soared beyond 300 at the end of the century. The road from obscurity to greatness was traversed by a variety of talents—any service to the crown could be so rewarded, though it usually took a fortune to complete the metamorphosis to lordship. The tremendously wealthy merchants of the East and West Indian trade sometimes found it profitable to make a gift or a loan to a government minister. A hastily contrived marriage to a teen-age heir or heiress could also intrude one into a fine family. (An unscrupulous parson in London made seventy-five pounds yearly by performing these marriages; another averaged 6,000 clandestine ceremonies annually.) The Marriages

Act of 1753 finally curtailed this traffic by requiring parental permission for minors and the publication of marriage bans in church on three successive Sundays.

Whatever the source of his fortune, in his next step up the social ladder, the gentleman sought to purchase as large a country estate as his purse would allow. Land in itself bequeathed political influence. Though a townsman could vote in parliamentary elections through his municipal corporation, rural landholders consulted no one and controlled their tenants' votes and occasionally those of nearby market towns as well. Only an estate owner could realize the highest achievement appointment to the House of Lords. So that time could be spent primarily on politics and hunting, the land would usually be tenanted (at an average rental of ten shillings per acre). Within a year, on proof of possession of either freehold land valued at £10 or £300 in movable goods, residence at Oxford or Cambridge (though no gentleman took a degree), good reputation, and financial independence, a gentleman could easily obtain a coat of arms from the College of Heralds. Next, a knighthood might be secured through military or administrative service, especially that of justice of the peace.

To ensure that an estate stay intact, inheritance was entailed through strict settlement that forbade selling off portions of the land. The eldest son inherited the bulk of the estate. His siblings were expected to seek employment in the army, navy, or church, or simply stay on as poor relations. The only specific obligation for the maturing of one's sons was the grand tour—a year or two of tutored traveling in the capitals of Europe, with the tacit condoning of wild-oat sowing. Membership in the House of Lords necessitated a townhouse in London, especially after 1714, when St. James' became the royal palace and the Hanoverians became an urban monarchy. The London season opened with a round of balls, boating parties on the Thames, opera and theater, and (hopefully) royal audiences. Discourse with the great might lead to powerful marriage alliances for one's offspring as well as to one of the hundreds of governmental sinecures conferring influence and a sweat-free income.

The Urban Influence: Life in the Capital

The seasonal descent of the aristocracy on the capital had raised London to its peak in national affairs. Though this influence waned markedly at the end of the eighteenth century, for the period 1640–1780, when no other English city approached its size and wealth, London led the country into most new ventures. It had generally supported the Civil Wars and the Glorious Revolution and backed the recurring wars against France. Largely because the bulk of the nation's surplus money was lodged in its banks, providing the government with a source from which to borrow, no minister dared embark on major policies without first consulting the "five companies": the Bank of England, the Royal Exchange, the East India Company, the South Sea Company, and the London Exchange Corporation. The capital sent four, rather than the usual two, members to Commons; its lord mayor had the right to demand audience with the king; the city government could present a case directly before the House of Commons. Many outsiders resented London's dominance, but in the long run the city presented opportunity for advancement through investment in one of its grandiose overseas ventures, intermarriage with its merchant princes, or, at the very least, by the enjoyment of its cultural offerings.

London was divided into twenty-six wards, within which some twelve thousand freemen elected an alderman from each to serve for life and two hundred common councillors who served a year at a time. The city seldom displayed a united opinion because no one group of merchants or bankers held sway over another. Furthermore, the commercial block in the upper house was frequently thwarted by the shopkeepers and craftsmen in the lower house, who did not always share the capitalists' dreams of empire. During the American Revolution the two houses split over American rights versus colonial trade and taxation. Despite dissensions and entrenched interests, some of the eighteenth century's most radical proposals and boldest schemes emanated from London.

Even after the Great Fire of 1666, London was still a city of graceful spires, the horizon dominated by Christopher Wren's rebuilt St. Paul's Cathedral. The water traffic was brisk. Travel by barge could be swifter than sedan chair or treading the narrow streets on foot. London regarded itself as a northern Venice. The Thames was full of small barks that were rowed upstream to Westminster (then a small village a mile or so from London proper) or downstream to the "pool" below London Bridge (where on any day some two thousand assorted ships could be viewed) or up the Fleet River into the heart of the West End. A walk from the Westminster area eastward into the city presented startling contrasts—the grand palaces of St. James and Leicester House, the middle-class homes of Bloomsbury, then the slum squalor where, as Dr. Samuel Johnson noted, "Falling houses thunder on your head."

Some of the slum lords made substantial incomes renting cubicles to transients at twopence a day. The ancient lure of the city had pulled a diverse humanity into its walls. Now the streets were jammed with every variety of day laborer and unemployed hands imploring work of gentlemen as porters, guides, deliverers, or servants. By the eighteenth century much of London's manufacturing had dispersed to the suburbs, and the city was one of trade and shopkeeping. Those who toiled in the few remaining industries—watchmaking, printing, coachmaking, laundering, tailoring—or as dockhands or silk weavers found themselves easily replaced by faster hands in the perpetually glutted labor market. What work existed was geared to the social season, leaving long, dull—perhaps deadly—summers of unemployment when the gentry had retired to their estates. The truly desperate joined bands of pickpockets and jades who preyed on the wealthy. Highwaymen gathered at the remote edges of the city, such as Hampstead Heath, drinking congenially with a traveler at Spaniards Inn, only to waylay him minutes later on the road. In a hit musical of 1728, John Gay's "The Beggars' Opera," colorful thieves and prostitutes rollick from glamorous escapade to escapade. But the desperate plight of the wayfaring robber driven to support his family by mask and pistol is better understood in the regularity of killings. Since hanging could be meted out for the theft of even a shilling handkerchief, the victim seldom survived to identify the culprit.

A life in the London underworld was by no means the lowest to befall the ex-farmer or ex-workman. Circumstances might send him to prison as a felon or, more likely, as a debtor. In 1716 some sixty thousand inhabited the jails for nonpayment of the paltriest of sums. All prisoners were expected to pay boarding expenses in these eighteenth-century holes; and since the debtor was without means, he might be confined to the foulest of dens, knee-deep in water or chained. Without a sponsor, a debtors' prison could hold a man for life. In 1729 a particularly grisly case involving the Fleet Prison and its murderous warden precipitated an investigation that led to the release of an astounding 97,000 debtors. This was a rare show of clemency, however, in an otherwise callous age.

The London worker, considering his twelve- to sixteen-hour day and the little diversion available for his scarce free time fared little better. Drinking became a universal escape. In 1722 the estimate of beer consumption in all of England averaged out at thirty-six gallons for each man, woman, and child per year. But the most pitiable example of the workers' need to elude reality lay in the peculiar ravages of the gin epidemic. The distilling of gin, which originated in the Netherlands, at first evaded the tax collector's eye. By 1733 there were probably 6,500 dram shops in London—in private homes and in butchers', bakers', and even candlestick makers' shops—each purveying its own chemically unsafe raw spirits that quickly dulled, sometimes blinded or even killed the imbiber. Wages were paid in gin; workers were solaced with gin; children were quieted with gin; household goods were pawned for gin. In 1736 the government's attempt to raise the duty and impose a selling license at fifty pounds resulted in riots. Effective curbs were not realized until the Gin Act (1751) ended the gin craze. Consumption dropped from $8\frac{1}{2}$ million gallons in 1752 to 2 million gallons in 1760.

The all too few reformers of the early eighteenth century were quick to blame the nation's lax morality on society's "betters." Daniel Defore, Jonathan Swift, and Henry Fielding were chief among those literary critics who castigated the rich for setting a licentious tone for the whole of society. Defoe, the author of *The Poor Man's Plea,* was convinced that there was little hope for the poor until the wealthy reformed themselves. Swift, in his *Gulliver's Travels,* concentrated on the hypocrisy of the titled and powerful who ostensibly ruled for the sake of the people while mercilessly plundering them. Henry Fielding flatly stated, "Pleasure always hath been, and always will be, the principal business of persons of fashion and fortune. . . . To the upper part of mankind time is an enemy, and . . . their chief labor is to kill it." There were charitable societies that endeavored to elevate public life: the Society for the Reformation of Manners, chartered by William and Mary, instigated an intensive drive against prostitution; the Society for the Promotion of Christian Knowledge established over thirteen hundred free schools. But beyond these peripheral efforts to uplift the gaming, cursing, drinking gentleman of Hanoverian England, little was attempted. As sentimental a humanitarian as Dr. Samuel Johnson expressed the century's pessimism over reform in a remark to Boswell concerning the prospects of a boy rowing them down the Thames: "Learning cannot possibly be of any use; for instance this boy rows as well without learning."

Yet, while some of the inhabitants starved, grandiose buildings, parks, theaters, and libraries increased in London. With them a unique public institution, the coffee house, came into the being. This attraction provided a variety of pleasures for even the modest purse, and though patronized largely by gentlemen, a democratic first-come, first-served rule was observed. Here no class barriers existed. The rich rubbed elbows with the poor; and while having coffee or punch, any guest might engage another, lord or beggar, in conversation. A corner was set aside for newspapers, pamphlets, books, and even the latest songs. The main attraction, however, was the richly diverse conversation, occasionally that of the great and the near-great, in which all patrons had the right to join. One could choose his subject: the Grecian was a gathering place for scholars; the Smyrna for musicians; Button's and Will's for writers; at Lloyd's, merchants auctioned cargoes "by the candle," the last bidder triumphing when the inch-high candle died. Choose your politics? The Whigs' plans were discussed at Button's while the Tories did their conspiring at the Cocoa Tree. In these free forums few rules were imposed, though swearing and quarreling were fined and the topic of religion was banned. For the spread of ideas the coffee house has no modern equivalent.

Its effect on public opinion is best gauged by the popularity it assumed. In 1660 there were but six; by 1710 some three thousand saturated London.

Once a city of shops and homes, London now boasted great buildings and public settings. The Mall, Hyde Park, Vauxhall Gardens, and Ranelagh offered such entertainments as gigantic masquerades, the music of George Frederick Handel and Franz Joseph Haydn, fireworks, boating, picnicking, and promenades among clipped hedges, avenues of trees, and sprawling lawns. Ironically, the outdoors had become glamorous, whereas for centuries the necessity had been to find shelter. When the elements threatened, those at Ranelagh could enter an enormous rotunda that seated a hundred diners in a great circle around an enclosed promenade, where they could enjoy an orchestra and organist in consort.

This was a pointedly social era, though not in the sense of being socially responsive to the needs of others. Although the streets of the largest city in the world teemed with the indigent, the displaced, and the outlawed, most pamphleteers seldom doubted that it was of the poor's own making since the rich "paid their way" by taxes and by the employing of others. Even the London season, for all its brilliance, was a part of the whole agrarian social syndrome, for London was to the squandering squires of Hanoverian England the market town of the world to which they repaired if their fortunes allowed. The fox hunts, the country festivals, and the enclosed fields that yielded comfortable incomes were the major ingredients of the eighteenth century's agrarian twilight. Even as this life style reached its apex, the commercial wealth drawn from India and America, the industrial fortunes made in iron, steel, coal, and cotton were already impinging upon the squires' dominion. Those who foresaw the trend sold out in time to invest in the new industries. Those who clung to the soil maneuvered Parliament into voting ever higher duties on imported foodstuffs. Then, in the middle of the nineteenth century, ever cheaper American and Canadian grain undersold native English corn, and protective tariffs were removed. After 1873 the meat market collapsed when refrigeration brought on an invasion of less expensive Australian mutton and New Zealand or Argentinian beef. By the start of the twentieth century, England was the only world power whose arable land had reverted to the forested cover it had known in Saxon times.

Chapter Two
THE GATHERING OF FORCES

Major Personages

Charles I, 1600–49; king of England, 1625–49
Laud, William, 1573–1645; archbishop of Canterbury, 1633–45
Pym, John, 1584–1643; leader of the royal opposition
Strafford, Thomas Wentworth, first earl of, 1593–1641; appointed Lord Deputy of
　　Ireland in 1632

CHRONOLOGY

1628	Petition of Right
1629	The Three Resolutions
1629–40	The Eleven Years' Tyranny
1637	Scottish rebellion against English religious reforms
1638	The National Covenant
1639–40	The two Bishops' Wars with Scotland
1640	The Short Parliament
1640–60	The Long Parliament
1641	Period of reforms including the Root and Branch Bill and the Grand Remonstrance
1641	Irish Rebellion
1642	King Charles I's attempted arrest of opposition leaders Nineteen Propositions Attempted seizure by the king of the Hull garrison

Since then the anti-Christian crew
Be prest and overthrown,
We'll teach the nobles how to crouch,
And keep the gentry down;
Good manners hath an ill report,
And turns to pride we see;
We'll therefore cry all manners down,
And hey then up go we.

The Round-heads Race, 1642

The Great Rebellion

About a hundred years ago the French historian Alexis de Tocqueville, in assessing his country's revolution, came to the still startling conclusion that revolutions are not violent breaches with the past so much as rapid maturing of latent institutions: people rebel not so much because they want to break with the present but because they want to retain and foster those structures that they believe to be seriously threatened. The dreamer and the visionary may want to destroy the evils of the day, but their revolutionary role is usually confined to galvanizing public sentiment against a tyrant. It is the men of affairs who guide revolution through traditional channels, changing adverse policies as they go but seldom abandoning the systems that have proved useful.

So it was for England in the years following 1640, the years of the English Revolution, or Civil Wars, or Great Rebellion, as it is also known. The orators who denounced King Charles rallied opinion behind the vision of a "new heaven and a new earth" intended to replace the old structures. But the majority of parliamentarians, lawyers, gentlemen farmers, merchants, and army officers, after listening to the revolutionary rhetoric, retained and strengthened the engines of state after king and court were gone, and made them more efficient and more sensitive to national need. By the end of this revolutionary era, the visionaries had become prisoners of these men of affairs. Oliver Cromwell's Commonwealth, though it changed the names, preserved the forms of the old system and strengthened its hold on the people to a degree undreamt of by Charles I.

Was the English Revolution then betrayed? Were democratic and liberal ideas only exploited to arouse emotional action? Cromwell, the ultimate victor, was accused of such a betrayal by critics, many of whom had been brothers in arms. But then, they never comprehended that the class of which the lord protector was a member had begun its crusade against Charles in order to safeguard the gains achieved under the Tudors. The Stuarts were frivolous; the middle class was provident. The Stuarts were unlawful; the middle class was law-abiding. The Stuarts were popish; the middle class was puritanical. The Stuarts were pawns of foreign courts; the middle class was patriotically English. The Stuarts were tax-oppressors; the middle class was concerned for its hard-earned wealth, anxious to do away with financial and commercial restrictions. Possibly, then, the revolutionary leaders who denied Charles his scepter and then his head felt pushed to extremes. They had not desired the overthrow of their king at the onset, but gradual disillusionment with autocratic policies destroyed their loyalty. Elizabeth had carefully nurtured the nation's resources and the people's good will. The men of 1640, many of whom had lived under Good Queen Bess, felt that there was nothing amiss with the establishment which could not be righted by replacing the royal incumbent. Most of the precipitators of the Civil Wars, then, were not revolutionaries in the utopian sense. They were timid, harassed men of good will who felt betrayed by their leaders and were bent on recovering their pride as Englishmen, as honest taxpayers, and as responsible subjects.

The English Revolution poses a major question: Why in 1640? Could it have occurred in 1540, 1440, or 1340? Equally, why was it not deferred to 1740 or 1840? Were other kings less autocratic than the Stuarts, more careful of their subjects' purses or their consciences? Was the generation that grew up under James I and Charles I, as the Royalist Edward Hyde, Earl of Clarendon, later charged, a generation of vipers, professional malcontents who would have destroyed even the best regime? Or was the accusation of the parliamentarian preacher John Goodwin, that no more devilish man than Charles I ever ruled so traitorously over his people, closer to the truth? Neither indictment was entirely valid. There seems to have been nothing unique about the society and monarchy of 1640.

Most political events, even those of the greatest magnitude, seldom disturb half a country's population for more than half their waking hours. During the Civil Wars the Royalists (or Cavaliers) and Roundheads (the term applied to the Puritans and parliamentarians) together with the Clubmen (a small group whose main purpose was to end the battling) constituted a minority.[1] Perhaps no more than a third of the populace was actively involved in the revolution, and then often only because their towns or country estates were threatened. As a national undertaking, the revolution was hardly

[1] The terms "Cavalier" and "Roundhead" were both originally intended as insults. The first term comes from the French for "knight," and the second was inspired by the close-cropped haircuts of London apprentices.

comparable to the American Civil War or Russia's Revolution of 1917. In neither fervor nor bloodshed did it approach the French Revolution. It was generally the upper- and the middle-class taxpayers who were involved— but few Englishmen then paid taxes. Religious convictions were at stake— but most Englishmen, though pious, barely knew their catechism. Questions of absolute sovereignty were raised—but few men in any age are philosophers. Most of England was concerned with the ordinary tasks of planting and harvesting and was bemused by the intrigues of courtiers.

It now seems that of those who took part in the Great Rebellion, the most active were a minority whose source of wealth or whose religious convictions were threatened by Charles I's policies. This group was a special category, for many men of substance and education remained neutral or simply lived abroad. Even those who did fight against the king issued parliamentary and military orders in his name throughout the war, thus denying an admission of treason. When a handful of men finally got around to executing Charles in 1649, their decision had to be forced on the majority of the parliamentary judges who sat at the king's trial.

The essence of revolution is that some drastic alteration, never before attempted, be made in a society. The fact that the Civil Wars were not a national undertaking or deliberately and consciously revolutionary does not detract from the truly revolutionary elements. For the first time, the initiative for lawmaking was taken out of the king's hands; religious toleration was encouraged; congregations dominated their clergy; military and naval operations, the ancient monopoly of the king and his feudatories, were managed by civilians; foreign policy became the game of businessmen, who used the power to wage trade wars. Most startling to contemporaries, a king was tried and executed for treason and his office abolished. These acts probably did more to announce the end of an old order of hierarchical dominion than all the others, for though the monarchy was restored in 1660, no Englishman could forget this ultimate precedent of political power.

Finally, the economic dislocation caused by the confiscation of the estates of the Royalists, who literally owned the kingdom, constituted a revolution. The crown's right to judge land titles was destroyed, and a free land market appeared, increasing the middle class's opportunities for land development. The knowledge that ownership would no longer be revoked by the king gave additional incentive to improve the fields. Agrarian capitalism, as well as commercial capitalism, flourished when the arbitrary Court of Wards (which allowed the crown to manage estates owned by minors) was abolished, royal interference on the behalf of courtiers and cronies ended, and antique feudal obligations, charters, and trade impositions were withdrawn.

The seventeenth century witnessed a revolution in some areas minimal, in others quite staggering. It was fought over the right to make law—religious, fiscal, commercial, judicial. The victors were the landed gentry whose estates comprised the wealth of England, whose lands lured capital from their town cousins whose riches came from trading ventures. In the course of the seventeenth century, the gentry came to control Parliament, the courts, the church, and the military. They regarded their rule, not as a class matter, but as a family concern, for they seldom recognized an identity of interest. They felt that acquiring and then maintaining an estate proved responsibility and entitled one to a "stake in society" regardless of private predilections. The unity brought about for the first time by the threat of Charles I's despotism lapsed as soon as that threat was defeated, and the gentry again became a factious clique, squabbling with neighbors over local boundaries and hunting preserves and debating political matters in London theaters, coffee houses, or their own great club of Parliament. Only when kings or overmighty ministers threatened to engross lawmaking powers did the gentry again present a semblance of unity. For the rest of the time, fox hunting, fortune hunting, and field enclosing occupied their days. Patronage to an occasional writer or artist, a parish living for a gifted nephew late from Oxford, a decorative wing built onto the manor house sufficed to prove a cultural awareness. Their world was one of rural retreat and a hearty love of zestful living.

The gentlemen summoned by the king to convene a parliament converged on Westminster that April of 1640 in a spirit of irreconcilability. Their old leader, Sir John Eliot, had shown them the way to bridle King James I in the Addled Parliament of 1614. It had been Eliot's genius that united the Commons and Lords in 1628. They had imposed the Petition of Right (guaranteeing parliamentary consent to taxation, the ending of obligatory billeting of troops, and forbidding martial law in time of peace) upon Charles I, who had attained the crown in 1625 on his father's death. But Eliot had died in the Tower of London while under permanent arrest "at the king's pleasure." Another thorn in James' side, the redoubtable Sir Edward Coke, drafter of the petition and champion of due process and civil liberty, had died in 1634. Thomas Wentworth, first earl of Strafford, had stood with the bold parliamentarians twelve years before the convention of 1640. He had seen his alternative to the Petition of Right defeated and had sold his conviction, so it was said, for an earldom and the lord deputyship of Ireland. The grievances were many, and there seemed no leader to stand for redress.

Of old account there was the matter of the king's illegal collection of tonnage and poundage and the taxes on wool that Parliament had denied the king in the petition. The ship-money tax, customarily levied for shipbuilding in wartime and then only on seaports, was now being collected in peace and from inland market towns. Numberless royal restrictions, not enforced for

more than a hundred years, had been revived to allow the collecting of fines—
for cutting wood in royal forests, for evicting under penalty those who
rented land on royal estates.

The Power of the Church

Not since the English church had been dominated by the
pompous Cardinal Wolsey of Henry VIII's day had good Christians witnessed the officious haughtiness practiced by the present archbishop, William
Laud. His ceremonialism, extravagant even to the more lavish spenders in
Parliament, was not only unseemly but to most betokened also a desire on
the part of the king (supposedly influenced by his French queen, Henrietta
Maria) to return the Anglican Church to Rome. The Ecclesiastical Court
of High Commission, which controlled religious law and publications, had
been utilized in Elizabeth's reign to protect the Reformation. It was now
employed by Laud to silence religious critics, and through Star Chamber
court to pillory and mutilate critical writers (Prynne, Bastwick, and Burton)
who were viewed as heroes by the populace.

Under Laud, church belief and practice had changed noticeably in two
other respects. The first concerned the theory of free will (man's ability to
attain salvation through his acts) as opposed to predestination (God's pre-
selection of the saved). Jacobus Arminius, an earlier Dutch theologian, had
upset churches in his own country with his theory that man is not predestined
by God for salvation but can attain that salvation through free will, since God
has granted him this power. English observers of a trial of Arminianism in
1617 returned from Holland with this doctrine, and Laud, then the dean of
Gloucester, was among those developing its basic tenet. To those who clung
rigidly to predestination, the Laudians were shockingly permissive in their
view of God's power—or lack of it. Even the majority of Puritans,[2] who felt
little kinship with Calvin's double predestination (God has decreed not only
who shall be saved but who shall be damned), agreed that Arminianism
seemed too close to Catholic theory. However erroneously, the average
Englishman, who adhered to the established Anglican (or Episcopal) Church,
held that unrestricted freedom of the will was a bolster to despotic government. In holding this belief one could set aside laws at one's discretion. If
that believer were an archbishop or a king, neither canon law nor common
law was safe.

In 1629 Sir John Eliot, in defiance of the king's order for adjournment,

---

[2] Those who, in the time of Elizabeth and the first two Stuarts, opposed traditional and formal
ceremonials because of their supposed Catholic content and advocated simpler forms of faith and
worship than those established by English church law.

had rammed the Three Resolutions through a turbulent parliament while the speaker was forceably held in his chair. (No business can be transacted once the speaker rises.) One of these resolutions declared, "Whosoever shall bring in innovation of religion . . . or introduce popery or Arminianism or other opinions disagreeing from the true and orthodox church [the Anglican Church], shall be reputed a capital enemy to this kingdom. . . ." For this rash act Charles had Eliot committed to the Tower. The resolution's effect upon the king was to foster a determination to do without Parliament, preferably permanently.

The second score against Laud had to do with his imposition of rigid uniformity in church services. While this was a more mundane matter, it directly affected everyday church life. He encouraged divine-rightist preachers who believed in absolute monarchy, refused to allow parishes to dispense with those parts of the service they found popish, and, though local option had become customary throughout England before the Reformation, denied congregations the right to determine their own ministers. Parish churches in the north had frequently retained those elements of the Catholic faith with which they felt comfortable, such as the high church liturgy. On the other hand, in towns that had acted as portals through which the followers of Calvin returned from the Continent in Elizabeth's reign, the congregations had removed their ornamental glass and the medieval stone and wood imagery, placed the altar among the congregation, and found themselves ministers who were experts in the new theories and techniques of sermonizing. The variety of religious observance in the pre-Laudian church must have been rich. But ironically, Laud, who believed in free will, was not about to allow anyone else to practice it. Whatever freedoms he believed in abstract, as bishop appointed by king and anointed by God, he would be obeyed in the absolute.

The Scottish Question

From 1629 to 1640 Charles maintained a tenuous peace, obviating the summoning of Parliament. His finances were so well managed that the extraordinary funds available only by parliamentary levy, such as those required to equip and sustain an army, were not needed. But rebellions in his Scottish kingdom, leading to an invasion of England in 1639, found his treasury flatly inadequate to engage the Scots, much less drive them out. The Short Parliament (April 5 to May 13, 1640) refused to grant the huge amounts necessary for such a force. When the Long Parliament (November 1640 to March 1660) met, it deferred the Scottish question indefinitely and passed quickly from reform to revolution, using the Scottish presence in the north as a means of intimidating the king and preventing its own dissolution.

Thus the initial fomentation of the English Civil Wars can be traced to Charles' worsening relations with his Scottish subjects. Though Charles had intended a just reform of church taxation, his reannexation of Scottish church and crown lands that had fallen into private hands had been done without consulting either the Scottish Privy Council or the Scottish Parliament. When he commissioned Laud to revise the Presbyterian church service, that had been looked upon as a final affront to the Scottish national faith. The new service, introduced in 1637, was greeted by riots. One minister was nearly lynched. A bishop read from the new prayer book while pointed pistols kept peace among his disgruntled congregation. Though the new service was Anglican, the Scottish Presbyterians, even more than the Puritans of the English Anglican Church, saw popery triumphant in Charles' endeavor to give Scotland a uniform service.

A group of commissioners appointed by the Scottish Privy Council formed a new government. To this action Charles foolishly remarked, "I mean to be obeyed," and refused to discuss terms with them. He soon found himself confronted with a most effective instrument of solidarity—the National Covenant (1638), copies of which were distributed throughout Scotland by the clergy and noblemen. Thousands, lairds and peasants alike, signed the document binding them to maintain the purity of the Presbyterian faith and to resist to the death attempts to modify the church or to introduce popery and tyranny. Ironically, the covenant also swore its adherents to complete loyalty to the king's authority. The covenanters would ultimately have to choose between their "kirk" (as the Scottish church is called) or their king, and, resolutely, they chose their kirk.

With Charles' prolonged bargaining, the suspicious Scots surmised correctly that the king was hoarding time to amass money and men for a punitive expedition. In the two short Bishops' Wars (1639–40), the Scottish leader, Alexander Leslie, easily marched a giant army into northern England, scattered disarrayed English militia, and forced the Treaty of Ripon (1640) on the monarch. With the small concession from the king that he would assume the Scottish army's daily bill of £850, the Scots forwent any further invasion of England providing that Charles would liberalize religious policies.

Even before this truce Charles had been counseled by the earl of Strafford, who had become his most trusted advisor, to summon the Parliament the king had sworn never again to convene. By exploiting ancient animosities, argued the earl, the king could maneuver the English Parliament into happily voting wartime taxes for a crusade to dislodge the barbaric Scots from home soil. Confident in his advice, Strafford returned to his post in Ireland to raise subsidies to be used against the Scots, as Charles, with some trepidation, convened the Short Parliament.

But the Englishmen who assembled in the summer of 1640 were hardly in sympathy with Charles' Scottish problem. Each delegate personally knew some tale of royal injustice. The patterns of suspicion and estrangement would inevitably have melded into outright hostility toward the king. However, though Charles had almost no following, no overt acts were then launched against him. Besides, many London merchants had floated loans with the government and wished to protect them from unstable times, and others possessed lucrative monopolies and trading privileges from the crown. (These men were the first to lose their posts in the city government when hostilities finally began in 1642.) Opinions were confusing and contradictory. Most older members of Parliament, incensed as they might have been with Charles' favoritism to courtiers or his blatant disregard for lawful rule, were held in check by a traditional belief in divine right monarchy and by convictions that God does command absolute obedience even to unlawful and unchristian monarchs. One of the judges of the merchant John Hampden, while finding him guilty as charged of neglecting to pay the ship money tax, declared that though kings had the right to tax their subjects, in all fairness they ought to consult with them about individual levies. But however mixed feelings were concerning the king, there was general rejoicing about his financial predicament.

Into the void of parliamentary leadership left by Eliot and Coke emerged "King Pym," member of Commons in the Short Parliament, John Pym. Before the elections of 1640 he had traveled tirelessly throughout England with the purpose of swaying the uncommitted, and, until his death in 1643, he campaigned incessantly against the king. Pym opened the session with a harangue summarizing the entire reign as one act of oppression, insisting that Parliament's grievances precede the king's business and that it refuse to vote army supplies to fight the Scots while England labored under the same conditions as did her neighbor. Parliament adjourned on May 13.

Throughout the summer Pym's message proved effective. The king's militia, called up to drive out the Scots, gradually dissolved into bands of rioters asserting their anti-Catholic sentiments by burning the communion rails that separated congregations from the altars and by chanting pro-parliamentary slogans. Strafford ill-advisedly taxed English towns for ship money. The Scots, cheered on by the English, formed an informal alliance with Parliament and allowed the coal supplies so important to London (which they had been holding back) to sail to their destination.

The Long Parliament

Charles' anger must have been something to behold. But so long as the monarch needed funds for his army, he must sooner or later allow

Parliament to reconvene. At the end of August 1640, the Lords, in the Petition of the Peers, called for a new election of their colleagues in the House of Commons with the purpose of reassembling Parliament. Browbeaten, Charles yielded, and in November the Long Parliament came into being with 60 percent of the Short Parliament's membership, including Pym, returned by the electorate despite Charles' efforts to exclude them.

The first wave of enthusiasm carried a host of measures designed to punish the king's Court and to demolish its political base. "Black Tom the Tyrant," the earl of Strafford, was impeached, but an able defense weakened each charge against him. Then the House of Commons revived the Bill of Attainder, which declared a man guilty by statute (rather than by trial) and ordered his punishment. Though hardly equitable, it was a prerogative of the victor, and Pym's remarkable legislative strategy succeeded where his prosecution failed. Strafford was executed for treason in 1641. However, the bloodletting stopped with his death, and England witnessed no headsman's terror, Laud, also impeached, lingered in the Tower of London until his execution during the Civil Wars. Other Royalists fled to France or the Netherlands, leaving the stage cleared of the court and allowing the reformers to recast the government.

In one of the most vigorous periods of legislation in English history, statute upon statute annulled the Stuart constitution. The prerogative courts, including the infamous Star Chamber, had allowed due process to be suspended and had been employed against the crown's enemies. These, as well as the church's Court of Ecclesiastical Commission, were abolished. Ship money was finally and forever outlawed. A tonnage and poundage act attached this tax irrevocably to Parliament's levy. The boundaries of royal forest lands were declared to be those of 1623, and the king was denied the privilege of ownership at will. The political power of the clergy was trimmed by refusing them seats in Parliament.

These statutes were negative inasmuch as they were abolitionist, which perhaps accounts for their easy passage. Men are generally more aware of what they dislike than of what they desire. A few laws aimed at positive reorganization were passed, such as the Triennial Act, ordering the summoning of Parliament every three years, and an act for a perpetual parliament, forbidding the king to dissolve the present sitting until the members should feel they had accomplished their work. But by August of 1641 the mood of accord had dissipated during debates on two key issues—the Root and Branch Bill and the Grand Remonstrance.

The first bill, introduced during the attack on Strafford and deferred because of his trial, lingered as unfinished business until the parliament had exhausted itself in the acts of repeal. In June 1641 it was reintroduced as a measure to rid the Anglican Church of its bishops, "root and branch."

While prelates were generally regarded as ecclesiastical tyrants during this period (largely because of Laud), there were those members of Parliament who still maintained that it was one thing to reverse unpopular policies and another to question the fundamental character of institutions. "No bishop, no king," James I had said of the issue during his reign, implying that if the hierarchical structure of the church were doubted, then all hierarchies, including the state's, were subject to question. He had outlawed all further discussion. Many of the members in the present House of Lords felt personally endangered in that Commons might transfer the analogy to them. Other lords thought Commons was going beyond its bounds in judging the fitness of noblemen, whether clerical or lay. Commons alone published the Root and Branch Bill, and the rift between the two houses widened.

The Grand Remonstrance was a broader matter. One of the lengthiest measures ever debated, the document, introduced in Commons, was as revisionary as all the statutes that had created the Reformation. In its 204 clauses the parliament began by placing the blame for England's problems squarely on the king and congratulated itself for rectifying them. The central portions authorized that body to undertake control of all taxes and church government. The conclusions called for parliamentary control of the king's ministers and his administration. More than a piece of legislation, it was a philosophy, a manifesto for reform. Had it passed both houses, it would have given to England the equivalent of a combined Declaration of Independence and national constitution. But because it was the creation of Pym's men, increasing numbers of parliamentarians, of both Lords and Commons, viewed the Remonstrance as a choice between rule by King Charles or rule by King Pym, and swords were drawn for the king. The November 1641 debates cracked the unity of both houses. The Remonstrance narrowly passed Commons by eleven votes, never coming to a vote in the House of Lords. Had it reached the king, he undoubtedly would have vetoed it.

Final Breaches

That same November, excited word came from Ireland that yet another portion of the kingdom was in rebellion. When Strafford left that country, the iron hand with which he had contained the mercurial Irish had relaxed. Land confiscations, domination over the Irish Parliament, and the disbanding of the Irish army with less than half pay were but a few of the complaints against English rule. Ireland had stuck tenaciously to Catholicism during the English Reformation and now viewed the English not only as conquerors but also as heretics. In that turbulent month of November, the Irish Massacre drove hundreds of English families into the English garrison at Dublin, and tales of the torture and slaughter of thousands reached London. A call to arms was sounded. Men had immediate second thoughts, however, as they wondered who would command the expedition and what would be the actions of such a force once it returned to England. Pym demanded that the army be put under Parliament's authority, hinting that the massacre had been inspired by the king as a diversion. This harsh accusation swayed opinion in Charles' favor. Had he remained aloof in Scotland, where he had gone in August of 1641 with hopes of mollifying the Scots, England might have witnessed a royal resurgence. But he chose to return during that crucial month.

In the first week of January 1642, Charles called for the arrest of Pym and four of his supporters. And he went in person, to execute his own command. The five rebels escaped by boat to sanctuary in sympathetic London, while the flustered king, standing on the floor of the House of Commons surrounded by armed gentlemen, looked in vain for his enemies among the seated parliamentarians. On the tenth of January Charles left for York in the north of England, intent upon raising a force to punish the parliamentary traitors.

Two final happenings completed the breach between king and Parliament: the Nineteen Propositions (1642) and Charles' attempt to take the arsenal at Hull. The propositions, desultorily rejected by the king, were a parliamentary ultimatum depriving Charles of all executive power and granting to itself control of the church, the ministry, the militia, membership in the Lords, and even the education of the king's children. Anti-Catholic laws were to be rigidly enforced.[3] Vast amounts of munitions had been stored for the projected war against the Scottish rebels at the town of Hull in the north. The king ordered that these be consigned to him. The governor of the garrison twice refused the royal command, and though Charles did not force the issue, this second incident can be viewed as the first act of hostility opening the war.

[3] It is interesting that though the Nineteen Propositions became the wartime program, throughout the war Parliament issued its orders in the king's name.

Chapter Three
THE GREAT REBELLION

Major Personages

Cromwell, Oliver, 1599–1658; commander of the Eastern Association cavalry; later lord protector of the Commonwealth

Essex, Robert Devereux, third earl of, 1591–1646; English parliamentary commanding general until 1645

Fairfax, Sir Thomas, third Baron Fairfax, 1612–71; commander of the New Model Army, 1645–50

Lilburne, John, 1614?–57; leader of the Levellers

Prynne, William, 1600–69; English Puritan writer and author of over two hundred books and pamphlets on theological and political subjects

Rupert, Prince, duke of Bavaria, 1619–82; Charles I's nephew, cavalry general in the Civil War

CHRONOLOGY

1642	Battle of Edgehill, the first major battle of the Civil War, October 23, (royalist victory)
	Battle of Turnham Green, London safeguarded from Charles I's advance
1643	Solemn League and Covenant (with Scotland)
1644	Battle of Marston Moor, a decisive victory for Parliament, July 2
1645	Self-Denying Ordinance reorganizing the parliamentary army
	Formation of the New Model Army
	Battle of Naseby, the final parliamentary victory, June 14
1646	Surrender of Charles I to the Scots in May
1646–7	Period of constitutional proposals including the Propositions of Newcastle (Parliament), the Heads of the Proposals (the army), and the Agreement of the People (Independents)
1648	Second Civil War, May to August, with Scotland fighting for Charles I
	Battle of Preston, the defeat of the Scots in August
	Pride's Purge: royalist sympathizers expelled from Parliament
1649	Charles I executed, January 30

I now have lived to see the day,
Wherein a fig-man [1] bears such sway,
 that knights dare scarce sit by him;
Yea, I have lived to see the hour,
In which a clothier hath such power,
 that lords are glad to buy him.

Thus do the froth of all the earth,
A spawn sprung from a dunghill birth,
 now prince it in our land:
A people come the Lord knows how,
Both fame and nameless till just now,
 must every one command.

Times Whirligig, 1647

The Caution of Dueling Rivals

  The manner in which the war was fought contrasts sharply with contemporary European practice. Massacres, plundering, and reprisals were the exception rather than the rule, likely because, as Manchester the parliamentary general sadly commented, "If we beat the king ninety and nine times, yet he is king still, . . . but if the king beat us once we shall all be hanged." On the reverse side of the coin, Charles' own standard bearer, Sir Edmund Verney, echoed royalist trepidation when he confessed, "I do not like the quarrel, and do heartily wish that the king would yield . . . to what [the parliamentarians] desire." The unorganized Clubmen, whose chief loyalty was to their property, frequently intervened to protect their fields from the ruins of battle by running both armies out of their districts. Many leaders had such difficulty defining their fidelities that it was not uncommon to find them exchanging sides in the midst of war. For instance, the young Anthony Ashley Cooper (who was to become leader of the Whig party) began as a royalist, deliberated joining the Clubmen, and gravitated finally to the forces of Parliament. As historian G. M. Trevelyan has noted, "Two minorities were fighting under critical inspection for the favor of all England, and when rivals duel they take care not to wound their mistress." [2] The conflict, pitting Englishman against Englishman, in all probability resulted from Parliament's need to retain the political laurels it had garnered from an unjust king in 1640–1. To Charles, obedience became the paramount test of kingship, with criticism bordering on treason.

[1] Probably grocer.
[2] Trevelyan, *England under the Stuarts* (London, 1949), p. 190.

The first Civil War raged intermittently between 1642 and 1646. It was regional inasmuch as the populous east and southeast declared for Parliament, as did the fleet, with the north and southwest siding with the king. Many pockets of resistance, however, lay in each area of influence. Although Parliament drew its strength from Puritans (including those Puritans who remained within the Anglican Church), Charles had the support of Anglicans and Catholics. As might be expected, the coastal towns were controlled by Puritan merchants. Noblemen's large estates were loyal to the monarch. Until the army reforms of 1645 tipped the odds in its favor, Parliament managed with its own small force under the earl of Essex and with the militias recruited from villages and towns. These latter units, the "train-bands," seldom fought outside their own home districts. Whereas Parliament was stronger in infantry, the royalist forces, as might be expected of an equestrian tradition, were superior in cavalry. In fact, when the war opened, the king had a top-heavy force of nearly three times as many horsemen as infantry.

The respective armies mustered between January and August of 1642 and clashed in October on the western road to London at the Battle of Edgehill. Charles' cavalry, under his nephew, Prince Rupert, squandered its energies pursuing the enemy's horsemen miles from the field. Had it wheeled around to deal with Parliament's infantry, there might have been a decisive victory for the king. Instead, Charles' opponents were allowed to retreat toward the monarch's ultimate objective, London, and he lost three additional weeks by casually occupying the Oxford district rather than spearheading through to his capital.

With the wealthy southeast in Parliament's hands, Charles' slender reserves necessitated a swift victory. When the king finally got down to business, his dilatory advance on London likely helped cost him the war. As it was, the city was more than ready for the onslaught. Its train-bands, the best in the kingdom joined the regrouped parliamentary units under Essex, becoming 24,000 strong. Londoners with Sunday dinner, in the mood for a day's outing, ringed the battle site at Turnham Green. The fighting consumed the day, at the end of which Charles followed the setting sun westward and London remained securely in the hands of Parliament.

Throughout 1643 and into the middle of 1644, the king frittered away his energy as well as his treasury by garrisoning market towns and besieging seaports. Desperately short of money, he ordered the Colleges of Oxford to melt down their silver plate for coinage so that he might pay his army.

Parliament, in full control of the government's tax gathering machinery, was multiplying its forces. Its Committee for Compounding later swelled the coffers by systematically fining Royalists, or confiscating their estates outright for resale.

In September 1643, Parliament greatly enlarged its military units with the Solemn League and Covenant, which extended Scotland's National Covenant of 1638 to include England. The league, completed three months before his death, was John Pym's final triumph over Charles I. It cemented the old rivals under the Committee of the Two Kingdoms by uniting their military efforts, committing the English and Irish churches to Presbyterianism "according to the word of God" (which later permitted England to evade the pledge with good conscience), and granting payment of £30,000 monthly, for which the Scots were to provide an army. Though the terms were obviously more favorable to Scotland, Parliament deemed it a great bargain when 21,000 of their new allies crossed into England in January 1644. In July, at Marston Moor, with odds against the Royalists of nearly two to one, and their dead, wounded, and captured totaling over 4,000, the entire north was won by the parliamentarians and their Scottish confederates.

Meanwhile, the Eastern Association (an amalgamation of eastern counties set up in 1642) was diligently producing a core of professionals, especially in its cavalry. Its horsemen succeeded in forcing the royalist general, Newcastle, to turn back in the east. Under the emerging leadership of Cromwell—"Ironsides," as Rupert respectfully dubbed him—this formidable force successfully challenged the high reputation of the prince's horsemen at Marston Moor.

In 1645 Parliament roused itself out of the world of medieval military organization with the Self-Denying Ordinance, which forced all officers to resign their commands. Only the capable were recommissioned. This act, together with the creation of the New Model army, styled after the more elite Eastern Association and made up largely of Independents (a polyglot, which, while generally Congregationalist and Baptist came to include members of various smaller sects), gave England its first professional fighting force and Parliament its decisive weapon. The 22,000 New Model troops, under Sir Thomas Fairfax, were trained to live indefinitely in the field, were inured to rigorous discipline, and were regularly paid (which was quite a novelty). Above all, as indomitable as they were in their conviction of God's support, they quickly trounced Charles' Cavaliers.

From the Battle of Marston Moor through June of 1645, the war took on the character of a chess match. Marching across the board of southwest England, parliamentary armies were busily engaged in countering Charles' and Rupert's deft maneuvers. Parliament had been winning the war but losing campaigns. The king had literally forced Essex's troops into the sea in remote Devon and had slipped out of Parliament's trap at Newbury.

The tragic turning point in Charles' fortunes came when his brasher courtiers opined that an encounter with the raw recruits of the New Model army would be quick sport. The city of Leicester had just fallen to Rupert, and the engagement would not only protect the king's flank but might also result in again opening the way to London, Though the New Model army out-numbered the Royalists, in June 1645, against Rupert's counsel, Charles chose what seemed a favorable risk. But the Battle of Naseby went badly for the monarch. Prince Rupert, having learned nothing from his identical tactical error at Edgehill, yielded once again to the enthusiasm of momentary triumph and pursued the parliamentary left wing far from the field. The parliamentary generals, Fairfax and Cromwell, charged the heart of Charles' forces, not only demolishing his infantry but also taking his baggage trains. In this one bold maneuver all the king's infantry and munitions were captured. The battle gave the midlands to Parliament, and Charles' cause was irrevocably lost.

For a year following Naseby, Charles and Rupert forlornly roamed the border hills of Wales desperately avoiding capture. The petty garrisons on which Charles had placed his hopes now proved insufficient for assembling new forces. Parliament besieged the garrisons at its convenience, hauling its artillery to each royal bastion until the last had capitulated. The first Civil War ended when Oxford was surrendered in June of 1646.

Many Royalists found the conditions of surrender uncommonly lenient. The tired and tattered men of Cornwall were even given twenty shillings each to pay their way home. Standard treatment for Catholics and their priests (especially if they were Irish) was less pleasant. Some of them found quick graves by firing squad. In those areas where Cavalier support had been strongest, the victorious armies were often welcomed as a lesser evil than the unpaid remnants of the king's forces, degenerated into bands of roving thieves. The army of Parliament not only paid for what it consumed but in most cases also gave peace with dignity. On May 6, 1646, anticipating more favorable treatment than he might receive from a tough-minded parliament and having received some assurances from the Scots, the king surrendered to them in hopes of winning over their army.

For the moment a peace of sorts existed, but it was far from tranquil. Parliament, with administrative fervor, had managed the war as if it would last forever. What now to do with the peace? On whose terms was the peace to be forged—the king's, Parliament's, the Scots', the army's? Could any of the victors be trusted with its management?

A Clash of Constitutions

The interlude from Charles' surrender to his execution in 1649 was one of the most harried times in the kingdom's history. This was a rare period when governmental policies had been forsworn, no rule bound the present, and the future was uncommitted. From every quarter treatises, pamphlets, manifestoes, and constitutions were ground out to fill the void. Thomas Hobbes, philosophical defender of monarchy's lost cause, belatedly tried to restore obedience to the king with his *Leviathan* (though not published until 1651, earlier versions had circulated since 1641), John Milton, who would turn to epic poetry after the Restoration, upheld Parliament in his writings and after 1649 served as an official of the Commonwealth. Hundreds of political tracts were produced, most notably by William Prynne and John Lilburne (who was to become leader of the army's extremist party, the Levellers); and while the great bulk of pamphlet literature was anonymous, mediocre, and written in haste, it does attest to the creative challenge stimulated in these years of reform.

The two allies, Scotland and Parliament, were particularly preoccupied with paper constitutions. Charles, in the Scots' custody, was given the Solemn League and Covenant of 1643 for his signature. His strong religious convictions caused him to procrastinate. He pleaded that he could admit Presbyterianism into the English church but for no more than three years. On his refusing the covenant, the Scots handed him over to Parliament in 1647. Parliament had proffered the Propositions of Newcastle to the king as early as July of 1646. This document contained much of the covenant, including the re-structuring of the Anglican Church into bishop-free Presbyterianism. Additionally, the army, as well as foreign policy, was to be under Parliament's control for twenty years, and the king, by punishing his supporters, was to admit his errors.

Though the chastened king was shunted about under house arrest, he was, after all, the only sovereign, and even after a Civil War, he was still deemed the one person entitled to solve the constitutional impasse. He was now in the unique position of having what his opponents had denied him in 1641. He had a choice of constitutions, and he had the time to consider them. While neither the covenant nor the propositions can have been to his liking, had he foreseen his fate, he may have happily embraced either. But he chose time in hopes that the animosity among the various factions would increase. By promising to pardon Irish rebels, remove all penal laws against Catholics, and appoint Catholics to high office, he even tried to lure the Irish into crossing the sea to invade England on his behalf. For the moment, however, his duplicity merely canceled potential support from all quarters.

Meanwhile the army, which Parliament had so carefully nurtured and was now planning to disband, watched these negotiations with the anxiety of the betrayed. Understandably, those who bore the actual wounds of the struggle now thought that they were witnessing a resurgence of Laudian

AN ALLEGORICAL REPRESENTATION OF THE COMMONWEALTH.
From the title page of Thomas Hobbes' Leviathan *(1651), a defense of the monarchy. Courtesy The Bettmann Archive.*

autocracy and divine right monarchy—those very evils they had so hotly opposed. They disagreed with both covenant and propositions, holding that while there ought to be state ties to religion, there should be no curbs whatever on congregational decisions. The Independents of the parliamentary army were in accord in rejecting Presbyterianism and episcopacy alike. They concurred on three cardinal points: that churches be directed by their congregations, that religious toleration be embraced as state policy, and that monarchy be rigidly curtailed or even totally abolished. The Presbyterians of Scotland and those of Parliament were opposed to these working class "enthusiasms," deeming them little more than the rantings of an undisciplined mob.

When orders arrived from Parliament in May 1647, disbanding segments of the New Model army and deploying other units to Ireland, the army recognized them as an attempt to drive a wedge into its solidarity. Inspired by the Independents in its midst, it pronounced itself the representative of the English people, the voice not yet heard in the councils of the king. Cromwell, impatient for a peaceful settlement and fearful that Charles would regain control, cast his lot with the Independents. In the first week of June 1647, a column of 500 troops removed the king from Parliament's custody at Holmby House to the Newmarket garrison. The army took Charles without opposition. The seizure of the king was Cromwell's Rubicon. Though he had himself been largely apolitical, his approval of the action rushed the army into politics.

In July, at Newmarket, yet another constitution was laid before the monarch, and with it, added hopes that his tormentors were dividing. The army's Heads of the Proposals, drawn up in large part by Cromwell's son-in-law, Henry Ireton, was far more comprehensive than either Scotland's covenant or Parliament's Newcastle propositions. It was no more acceptable to the king than the earlier documents, though he may have experienced some satisfaction from one clause, calling for the immediate dismissal of the present parliament. It also provided for future biennially elected parliaments that would have appointive powers over the king's ministers, religious toleration for all except papists, and parliamentary control over the army and navy for ten years.

With this document the Presbyterians, who had come to dominate Parliament, found reason to shudder at the military monster they had assembled. They would not yield to religious toleration and most certainly did not want their own dismissal. But when Cromwell's troops bloodlessly occupied London they had cause for fear. In August 1647, Cromwell "persuaded" eleven Presbyterian leaders to absent themselves from Parliament's sessions. In return, he withdrew the army, creating a momentary harmony.

But ridding Parliament of its leadership was insufficient for pacifying the troops, most of whom were Independents, and even nourished within the ranks a growing distrust of their officers. Why were these landed officers negotiating with the king through the Heads of the Proposals except to ingratiate themselves and throw their underlings back into the bondage from which they had escaped by their own blood? John Lilburne and the Levellers, in opposition to Cromwell as well as to the king, forcibly reorganized the army's council. This new group was largely responsible for framing the Agreement of the People, which they presented to the council of the New Model army in the Putney Debates of October and November 1647.

There had been protests for economic justice and religious reform as early as the Peasants' Revolt of 1381, but never had constitutional demands been made for granting power to all the people. Thus the Agreement is the first democratic constitution produced in England's long history of popular revolt. It demanded considerably more than the Heads of the Proposals, including that "the people [shall] choose themselves a parliament." Constituencies based on population, biennial parliaments, legal equality, and religious freedom were also demanded. One intriguing clause forbade compulsory military service. Throughout the autumn of 1647, a number of excited discussions concerning the Agreement occurred between the Levellers and the broader group of Independents. The most conclusive took place at Putney. The outcome was perhaps foregone, for obviously the proud landholding gentry, represented in the debates by the officers, would refuse to adopt any of the versions of the Agreement, however eloquently presented. In seeking the vote for all men, a Colonel Rainborough forcefully pleaded, "The poorest he that is in England hath a life to live as the greatest he. And therefore, truly, sir, I think it's clear that every man that is to live under a government ought first by his own consent to put himself under that government."[3] Cromwell and Ireton, with the other elected agents, continued in the conviction that only those who actually possessed land or a business enterprise were entitled to the vote. Ireton opposed republicanism and universal suffrage, while Cromwell held that they were simply not practical politics. The representatives were dismissed, and the Putney Debates produced a further rupture between soldier and officer. Shortly thereafter, distrust of Cromwell led to a short-lived army mutiny (November 1647).

The Defeat of the Royalists

That same month Charles eluded the army's grasp, escaped to the Isle of Wight, and plunged into the dangerous game of divide and conquer.

[3] "The Putney Debates, 28–29 October 1647," in *The Stuart Constitution, 1603–1688* ed. J.P. Kenyon (Cambridge, 1966), p. 313.

In December he concluded an agreement with the Scots that much resembled the terms traded while he was their prisoner. In return for an army he would establish Presbyterianism in England for three years and, while doing so, would suppress the Independents. He still, however, refused to take the covenant. Royalists in Wales, Kent, and Essex and in the navy came to his aid. Though many Scots continued to doubt his word, half who had fought against him now joined his new cause. The result was a second Civil War, which was put down with greater dispatch by Cromwell and the New Model army than was the first. It lasted only from May to August of 1648. To Cromwell's army of Independents, Charles had become the "man of blood," the betrayer of honest negotiations, a traitor to his English subjects, and their persecutor. Nothing less than his recapture would satisfy them.

The New Model's cavalry smashed the royalist pockets before they could consolidate. At Preston in August of 1648, in three days' action, Cromwell demolished the entire Scottish expedition, the only force to be reckoned with. From that summer he flailed relentlessly against his opponents under the mounting conviction that he was God's instrument to both purge and cure England. He banished the captured Scots to forced labor in Barbados. The Scottish sympathizers in Parliament were quelled in an act reminiscent of Charles' high-handed display of force in 1642, when he had attempted the arrest of Pym and company. Colonel Thomas Pride, with an armed guard that had been deployed to protect the House of Commons, jailed or expelled some hundred and fifty parliamentary Presbyterians in December 1648. "Pride's Purge" left a residue of about fifty members personally favored by the army. These few came to be called the Rump Parliament. Following up Pride's disposal of the conservative opposition, Cromwell called upon Fairfax to subdue his radical enemies, the remnant of the Levellers. A midnight raid on their camp at Burford in May, 1649 ended his last serious domestic threat. Next, Cromwell personally turned to Ireland and Scotland to engage and dispatch the Stuarts' following. Young Prince Charles, who was to become Charles II in 1660, fled from Scotland after the battle of Worcester in September 1651. From then until Cromwell's death no one seriously stood to his challenge.

In the midst of this cyclone of purges, the king was bound to topple. Charles bore the brunt of the storm in a trial conducted by a hand-picked commission in January 1649. He was condemned to death for having divided his subjects for his own aggrandizement. Even to this action Cromwell put his hand by ordering the justices, most of whom were reluctant, to sign the death warrant. With this resolved, he determined to "cut off [Charles'] head with the crown upon it," for the monarchy was to be abolished with the king's death.

A Continuation of Crisis: New Animosities

The nine years of perpetual crisis culminating in the king's execution began with a single issue contended between two nations (Scottish Presbyterianism vs. Laudian Anglicanism). Scotland's invasion of northern England prompted parliamentary participation in the name of purely English grievances (taxation, constitutional and religious reform). No sooner had these basic grievances been redressed than Ireland flew into rebellion, and Pym's party proceeded to new programs designed to curtail the crown's traditional powers. The king took a stand with his attempted arrest of Pym, and by the summer of 1642 three separate forces were in play (Scotland in alliance with Parliament against the king). Still, despite all animosities, the king was in power and was regarded by all as king. In the course of the Civil War, Parliament's army gradually evolved its own position (Independency), emerging in 1647 as a fourth factor, with the Levellers posing the threat of a further subdivision within the army. Even the staggering number of documents tended to cancel each other out. Scotland's National Covenant, enlarged upon to include England in the Solemn League and Covenant, was followed by Parliament's Propositions of Newcastle. With Parliament's attempt to disband the army, the army replied with the Heads of the Proposals, which demanded the dissolving of Parliament. The Agreement of the People was never agreed upon. Then, in 1648, the trend toward factionalism dramatically reversed itself as Oliver Cromwell assumed mastery. In one energetic year he imposed militant resolution by sweeping the Scots from the field, purging their Presbyterian sympathizers from Parliament, and subduing the Levellers within the army. The monarchy was doomed. What had begun in 1640 as a constitutional renovation finally resulted in a thinly veiled military autocracy.

But had England witnessed a revolution? The answer would depend on the observer. Cromwell and the Independents who won the day had seen themselves as betrayed by an ungodly king whose innovations were undermining the ancient liberties and reformed religion of a past stretching back to Saxon times. To them, it must have seemed a restoration rather than a revolutionary overthrow. To the Cavaliers, the king personified a national sovereignty that could not be wrested from him by vainglorious egoists such as Pym and Cromwell or curtailed by the petty jealousies of grubbing merchants unable to see beyond the gold of their counting houses. True, James I and his son, Charles I, had removed themselves from communion with their subjects, but to kill the king was an extremity that removed the one safeguard to a legitimate peace. To the Cavaliers, the years of war constituted rebellion.

For the mass of Englishmen, especially the thousands thronged around the scaffold outside Whitehall Palace on January 30, 1649, an inarticulate groan as the headsman's ax fell attested to their profound sense of loss. With the killing of the king, the panoply of majesty was ripped away, leaving nothing between man and God but the cold witness of the stars. Could men's baser acts be justifiable without the traditional excuse of having followed a "bad" king? The next ten years were to test whether the national conscience would stand the strain of self-justification for what it witnessed that raw winter day.

Chapter Four
THE PURITAN COMMONWEALTH

Major Personages

Monck, General George, first duke of Albemarle, 1608–70; fought in the Thirty
  Years' War and against the Scots in 1639; created duke by Charles II for having initiated the king's restoration

CHRONOLOGY

Cromwell, our chief of men, who, through a cloud
Not of war only, but detraction rude,
Guided by faith and matchless fortitude,
To peace and truth thy glorious way hast plough'd. . . .

JOHN MILTON

"To the Lord General Cromwell," 1652

Today the period between the death of Charles I in 1649 and the elevation of his son, Charles II, to the throne in 1660 is officially styled the Interregnum, the era between reigns. To some contemporaries, this span of years was the beginning of a new terrible-glorious age, the "rule of the saints," the "new Jerusalem"; to others, the time when fanatic king-killing pirates commandeered the ship of state. For those actively engaged, the revolution would "lay the cornerstone of the world's happiness" and the "reformation of the whole world."

Even as the coffin of the executed monarch was being constructed, parliamentarians—or the 10 percent left after two purges—were modifying the traditional constitution, which now declared "that the people are, under God, the original of all just power" and "that the Commons of England . . . have the supreme power in this nation." Within a day of Charles' beheading, the monarchy was struck down as "unnecessary, burdensome, and dangerous to the liberty, safety, and public interest." The House of Lords was abolished, as was episcopacy. A council of state, with a membership of forty-one under a year's tenure, replaced the Privy Council. The power of the people, which the Rump Parliament had voted itself on paper, was, of course, the power of the army, and in turn the power of Oliver Cromwell who totally controlled the army.

"God Did It": Cromwell's Rise

Born in 1599, Cromwell, the child of another century, was four years old when King James I succeeded Queen Elizabeth, seventeen when he entered Cambridge, and twenty-nine when elected to the parliament that secured the Petition of Right. By the time the Long Parliament convened, he was in his early forties and possessed a character at once severely practical and spiritually introspective. His years as a gentleman farmer in his native Huntington near Cambridge had trained his mind for careful management of land, horses, and men. A religious conversion to the puritan dedication of God's service involved him in a perpetual search for self-justification, for, like most Puritans, he was convinced that day-to-day occurrences were not mere chance, but the result of a cosmic plan. If one pursued a course in a Godly manner, if the course proved successful (as it eminently did in the example of his own career), assuredly God's hand must then be behind the venture. On the same testing ground, he was contemptuous of vacillation and failure. In all justice, he was not a plotter or schemer, and probably not an ambitious man. In fact he took pride in having premeditated nothing throughout his life, believing that "none climbs so high as he who knows not whither he is going"[1] but who allows and accepts the guidance of God.

In 1640 Cromwell knew little whither he was going, but it hardly then seemed to be in the direction of politics. After two years as a member of the Long Parliament, he had called scant attention to himself with a short speech supporting the Root and Branch Bill of 1641. His lack of personal political success and Parliament's flagging fortunes with the Grand Remonstrance caused him to consider emigration from England. However, the war put heart in him as he threw himself into the organization of a troop of horses from his own district, which through their victories came to be known after their leader as the Ironsides. Rising from captain to lieutenant general, the tangible battlefield successes gave his quest for spiritual certitude the necessary sense of achievement. He recorded after Naseby:

> When I saw the enemy draw up and march towards us, and we a company of poor, ignorant men . . . the General having commanded me to order all the horse, I could not, riding alone about my business, but smile out to God in praises, in assurance of victory, because God would, by things that are not, bring to naught things that are. Of which I had great assurance, and God did it.

It was this triumphant Cromwell who with equal severity attacked his own superior, Manchester, for his wavering loyalties, who judged the compromised scruples of the parliamentary Presbyterians and found them wanting, and who turned on the impractical Levellers in his own camp. Cromwell was possessed of a will indomitable enough for the task of bringing the king to trial. Now, in 1649, he was virtual commander of the army and a member of the Council of State; his God-given judgment would now descend on other untalented or wicked mortals who obstructed the designs of Heaven.

---

[1] See Christopher Hill, *God's Englishman: Oliver Cromwell and the English Revolution* (New York, 1970), pp. 217–250.

From Rump to Barebone's Parliament

The rule of the Rump Parliament and its Council of State lasted from January 1649 to April 1653. Until the last Royalist fell at the Battle of Worcester in September 1651, Cromwell remained distracted in the field, destroying the Irish and Scottish enemies of the Commonwealth (as the republic was called). Meanwhile, in London, the Commonwealth, possessed of no discernible sense of direction, embarked on a variety of disoriented policies. The Navigation Act of 1651 restricted imports into England primarily to ships of English or colonial ownership. Dutch importers were the target of the act. The enforcement of the law immediately involved England in the first (1651–54) of three trade wars with the Netherlands, yielding her little for their awesome expense but a vague sense of national pride. The recruiting of funds for the war drove taxes far higher than in Charles' reign. Under growing criticism a general pardon was extended to the Royalists in an attempt at keeping the domestic scene tranquil, but so many restrictions, exemptions, and land forfeitures were authorized that the healing intent was necessarily negated. With no existing national religion, there were efforts to reestablish the maimed Anglican Church, but under what form none could agree. With the Independents desiring total abolition of any national church and the Presbyterians still holding out for a strong Presbyterian establishment, nothing could be accomplished in the religious area beyond the granting of Sunday nonattendance privileges and the enacting of the death penalty for adultery. For fear of the Levellers, harsh printing regulations went into effect. Thus the toleration that was supposedly permitted could find no publishable outlet.

After three years the Commonwealth's record was held to be pedestrian, and some, including Cromwell, found it annoyingly petty. Perhaps the Rump members had gone stale after thirteen years of sustained activism. Cromwell, after a typically watchful assessment, again sprang into action by ordering the Rump to name a date for its dissolution. When it complied only by voting perpetual seating to its members, he strode into the House at the head of an armed column. Cromwell pointed to the pettifoggers man by man, in exasperation ordering them, "In the name of God—Go!" By the end of the day, pursuing his logic to conclusion, he had successfully "abolished" the Council of State.

Despite some disaffection among Cromwell's colleagues, many of whom joined the banished Lilburne's written outcries of tyranny against him, to Oliver the course was now defined. He would choose "persons fearing God, and of approved fidelity and honesty" for the membership of a new parliament. Congregational ministers throughout England were requested to submit the names of such men. An army committee sifted these and appointed 140 parliamentarians for their saintly attributes. This "nominated" parliament came to be known by its enemies by the name of the London representative, a religious fanatic and lay preacher called Praise-God Barebone (or Bardon), though his actual participation in the proceedings was insignificant. The Barebone's Parliament met from July to December 1653 and was Cromwell's final flirtation with consensus rule. Though its members were hand-picked and supposedly representative of the best of England's populace, by the end of the year, in a pattern now almost predictable, Cromwell was again to lose patience with fellow governors who lacked his own incisiveness.

The Barebone's parliamentarians, however remote and impracticable they appeared to their legalistic critics, were for all their sermonizing the only genuinely creative social reformers in the entire century. They abolished the overly complex Court of Chancery, which had ground many a family into poverty with crushing court costs and lawyers' fees under the cumbersome mechanics of due process. They embarked upon codifying the laws into the size of a manageable handbook, some members hoping to reduce them to the fundamental ten commandments. The debtor, who lacked any legal rights, was no longer to be kept incarcerated at the pleasure of his creditors or jailers; the insane were to be treated humanely and covered by legal protection; civil marriages were henceforth to be performed by justices of the peace; tithes were to be discontinued and church income to be equitably distributed. The Barebone's program, geared as it was to small rural landholders and tenant farmers, would have weakened the grasp of urban professional, clerical, and financial powers, not to mention large estate owners. Lawyers sneered and gentlemen farmers in Cromwell's council cringed, as much at the antiestablishment tendencies as at the interminable sermons that accompanied the deliberations. After a short six months the army engineered an early morning quorum of Cromwell's moderate adherents who, while the radicals were still at breakfast and morning prayer, passed a resolution transferring Parliament's powers to their leader.

The Lord Protector

The political distillation that had begun with Pride's Purge in 1648 culminated in a legislative coup against men who themselves had been nominated. As in the case of Colonel Pride's expulsion of opponents, this purge too was conducted without Cromwell's knowledge, though he never repudiated his colleagues' armed usurpations. It is little wonder that Oliver could indulge the figment that he was the pawn of destiny. So it was also in the drafting of the Instrument of Government (1654), England's only

OLIVERIVS CROMWELL EXERCITVVM ANGLIÆ DVX.

OLIVER CROMWELL.
After a contemporary copper engraving. Courtesy The Bettmann Archive.

written constitution ever adopted and put into effect. This product of an army council provided that "the supreme legislative authority of the Commonwealth of England . . . shall be and reside in one person and the people assembled in parliament; the style of which person shall be the lord protector." This dignitary was to be assigned military power and control over diplomatic decisions. Though a parliament would be summoned at least once every three years, its command of the nation's purse strings, so jealously guarded under the Stuarts, was loosened by a clause guaranteeing at least £200,000 in annual taxation for the maintenance of the protector's army. During intervals in parliamentary sessions, ordinances could be issued by the protector's council—though it was hardly clear whether these should supersede parliamentary statutes or not. The county electorate had their property qualifications broadened from the old forty-shilling freehold land base to a £200 valuation in either land or personal property. Clause 33 stipulated "that Oliver Cromwell shall be and is hereby declared to be lord protector . . . for his life."

The irony of the proposed protectorate further disillusioned many, even among the ranks of Cromwell's earliest supporters. While it was one thing to grant to the Commonwealth's greatest defender as much power as he might need to reduce its enemies, it reached beyond traditional bounds to allow him virtual immunity from Parliament's traditional holds over taxation, to present him with a standing army, and to endow him with a life office within the body of the constitution. King Oliver might replace King Charles. The forgotten Heads of the Proposals had been intended to curb any sovereign, and now Cromwell had garnered more power than Charles had ever owned.

In September 1654 the lord protector opened the first of his two parliaments by imperiously informing the delegates that he regarded the fundamentals of the Instrument of Government as undebatable and that they must sign a pledge committing them to one-man rule before they could take their seats in the House. Even without the thirty members who refused to sign the document, Cromwell's relationship with his parliaments was tempestuous. With the House remonstrating that the protector's council must be appointed by the parliament, and that the size of the army was not to be increased or to be in the hands of the protector without parliament's guidance, Cromwell, in a torment of frustration, waited the five months prescribed as the minimum in the Instrument of Government. Then, blaming the parliamentarians for fostering national discontent, he sent them home.

After 1655 the protectorate's domestic policy dwindled to mere retrenchment. Its ordinances were purgative and administrative, not creative or regenerative. Roads were improved, mail delivery (first inaugurated by Charles I) was regularized, taxi coaches in London were licensed, legal fees were reduced, and a host of blue laws were prescribed to reduce the number of sensual outlets for the ungodly and to remove unsightly conduct from the eyes of their better brothers. Cockfighting and bearbaiting were abolished, horse racing curtailed, theaters closed, and any moment's pleasure, if it condoned or abetted sin, was purged. The statuary and stained glass of many a parish church and cathedral were pulled down by zealots who believed they executed God's commandment against idolatry. There was a proposed act, in the hope of keeping the Lord's day holy, that would even have forbidden sitting, leaning, or standing in doorways on the Sabbath. Little wonder that each year saw increased dissatisfaction with the government. Penruddock's rebellion of the Royalists in 1655 and Sindercombe's assassination plot in 1657 were but two of many insurrectionary schemes that sometimes saw Royalists and republicans working together against Oliver's absolutism.

The lord protector's response to the growing wave of resentment came in June 1655, when he carved England into eleven military districts, each of which was commanded by a major general with supervisory powers exceeding those of local authorities. As the effectiveness of these martial rulers increased, however, so did opposition to them, especially when their added expense required the summoning of a new parliament to yield supporting taxes. The major generals at the local level and the government in Westminster bent every effort to exclude their critics. If the members survived scrutiny at the election polls, they still had to receive certificates of admission to take seats. Some hundred were barred. Over sixty others joined them outside Parliament in protest. Nearly a third of the House was removed, including a few members who had sat on Cromwell's earlier Council of State. The remnant were allowed to deliberate, but they too refused to sanction taxes for the major generals' rule, urging that it be abandoned. Wiser and sadder, Cromwell acquiesced. Martial law was ended, and the major generals were withdrawn from the countryside.

The protector was increasingly troubled by his inability to solve the executive's dilemma: thanks to his army comrades, his rule was absolute, but while England was generally pacified, could order be maintained without sacrificing Christian toleration and civil justice? Two alternatives momentarily seemed to provide a constitutional answer; and throughout 1657, the parliment debated two propositions designed to provide security, which, considering the events of the near past, could seem startling to all but politicians. Both were embodied in The Humble Petition and Advice of 1657, a proposed amendment to the Instrument of Government. First, should Cromwell be made king? Second, should a renewed House of Lords be established? As monarch, Oliver could graft his revolutionary sword to the traditional scepter. Though this might not be totally acceptable to all Englishmen, it would, at least, be a familiar pattern. A new House of Lords would serve a double purpose: it would provide a means of rewarding the able corps of officers who had stood like a bastion around Cromwell since Naseby, and it would provide a balance to his growing number of critics in Commons.

From March to May the debate revealed the general disenchantment with the proposed monarchy. Most of the army deplored the idea but would have yielded had their commander seen it as the only way of avoiding the frequent revisions that had unsettled the government. A hard core of counselors and relatives advised that the assumption of monarchy would be too close to betrayal, so Cromwell, though he agreed to nominate his successor, contented himself with the revised title of address "Your Highness" and let the regal issue lapse.

A House of Lords, or "other house" as it was euphemistically named, he would have, however. Seven lords were drawn from his own family, and what with seventeen personal adherents recruited from the army, over half the membership of the other house was comprised of sympathetic appointees. Nevertheless, by the end of 1657 Cromwell's continuing search for governmental stability resulted in an even smaller base of personal support. The ranks of the faithful were again depleted when the most dedicated of the republicans within the parliament attempted to restore the Long Parliament as the only solution to counteract the lord protector's high designs. In January 1658 Cromwell sent his second, and last, parliament home, robbing the malcontents of an arena for their attacks. He later executed some and imprisoned others for their part in the plot.

Mercantile War: New Bids for Conquest

If England's domestic tranquility was held together by constitutional makeshifts and major generals, her foreign policy during the decade of the Interregnum was proudly expansionist. Equipped with a better fleet than any king had, England's republican masters fully realized her destiny as a naval power. The captains produced in this period, such as Blake and Penn, were as able as Elizabeth's Sea Dogs and far better disciplined to carry out the Commonwealth's designs, which invariably considered mercantile interests above all others. Though there was much talk in Cromwell's councils concerning protection of fellow Protestants throughout Europe (especially the French Protestants, the Huguenots), and at one point even consideration of a great Protestant alliance including political union with the Dutch, at every diplomatic juncture it was mercantile advantage that took precedence. Even the religious fellowship of the Dutch Protestants did not preclude the trade wars against the Netherlands for economic reasons.

Spain, however, proved to be the most attractive enemy. Cromwell at first considered a military alliance with Spain against France, which had given sanctuary to Charles I's widow and children and sanctioned attacks by her ships on England's merchantmen. But by 1654 Spain, spurning Cromwell's overtures by refusing England trading rights in her Caribbean empire, proved the more likely target. Besides, as Cromwell reminded Parliament, she was England's old enemy in religion as well as in trade. In 1655 Admiral Penn cruised into the heart of the Spanish Main with General Venables' 2,500 badly trained men, mostly conscripts, intent on seizing Hispaniola (now the Dominican Republic). The expedition was repulsed. Nothing daunted, it set sail for Jamaica, a lightly defended island in the midst of Spain's larger Caribbean holdings, and easily routed the few Spanish defenders. Jamaica was to form the basis for England's Caribbean wealth until the collapse of her sugar-based economy in the nineteenth century. The Jamaica expedition was the only fruit of Cromwell's Western Design, a somewhat pretentious plan to infiltrate the Spanish empire by military landings supplemented with colonizers. Finding fault with the expedition's leaders because they fell far short of the Western Design, the lord protector slapped both Admiral Penn and General Venables in the Tower for cowardice and for failing to leave an adequate holding force on the island of Jamaica. An advertising campaign to attract New Englanders to England's new holding lured no one, and of the few left behind in the initial expedition, over half died of a variety of tropical maladies.

The Western Design was abandoned in favor of striking Spain in her home waters. In September 1656 a Captain Stayner realized the old Elizabethan dream of capturing a plate fleet. These annual flotillas transported Spain's yearly collection of silver (grossed largely from Peruvian mines) in heavily guarded convoys across the Atlantic, usually to the southern port of Cadiz. Stayner brought thirty-eight wagons of silver home to the Tower while Admiral Blake maintained a blockade of the Spanish port over the winter. But this quickly gained wealth was soon dissipated as Cromwell made an even more ambitious bid for conquest by uniting with France in a joint campaign against the Spanish Netherlands (presently northern France). Prince Charles (the future Charles II), now enjoying the protection of the king of Spain, had been proffered a Spanish army to enforce his claim to an English throne, for which he offered the return of Jamaica. Cromwell, now anxious to display his New Model tactics on the grander stage of European power politics, deployed 6,000 troops to France, and the combined French and English armies marched on Dunkirk. There the Battle of the Dunes (June 1658) proved the English mettle, and even the beaten Charles had to salute the bravery of his countrymen as he fled from the defeated Spanish garrison. Dunkirk was ceded to England, and for the first time since 1559 an English flag flew over a Continental port.

The Cromwellian regime interjected itself into European diplomacy in an arc encompassing the Baltic Sea and the Mediterranean. Treaties assured England's growing fleets the right to trade for requisite goods—hemp, pitch, tar, cordage, and masts—in the northern sea. The navy now regularly convoyed merchantmen to guarantee safe voyage uninterrupted by piratical plunderers. Portugal saw her only port, Lisbon, blockaded and in 1654 conceded to England the right of trade with Portuguese colonies. In 1655 Blake subdued the Barbary pirates, opening the Mediterranean to English shipping. Though many of these gains were forfeited after Cromwell's death, the proud display of English might on the world's seas was to be revived forty years later in King William's reign.

Whatever the value of the glory achieved on the seas, at Cadiz, and on the beaches of Dunkirk, the cost at home was nearly insurmountable. Just fifty years before, the government had struggled with an income of £250,000 per year. Now the protectorate's revenues topped two million, and yet the national indebtedness had passed the million mark. New taxes made supporting the regime of the Godly too exacting, and when a tax on the construction of new housing within a ten-mile radius of London was imposed, there was talk of a taxpayers' revolt. Arrears in pay and supplies to the army and navy by themselves came to over £800,000 by 1658.

The man whose gargantuan efforts had forestalled worse cries, was, however, slowly losing his grasp. Weakened by gout and totally disabled (possibly by malaria), in August 1658 he was too ill even to attend his daughter's funeral. He died on September 3, 1658.

After Cromwell

On his deathbed the lord protector, as provided in the Humble Petition, named his son, Richard, to succeed him. With "Tumbledown Dick's" inability to hold the army's personal loyalty or the parliament's political allegiance, the English republic entered a tragic twilight.[2] The bands of soldiers and politicians—Levellers, fanatical sectarian preachers, the ejected Rump and Barebone's parliamentarians, the Presbyterians—who had been kept at bay only by Cromwell's indomitable will, now threatened to engulf the state's fabric. English politics had not as yet produced a system whereby factions could work cooperatively on joint enterprises.

None knew this better than General George Monck. The opportunity is given to few men to play a singularly decisive role in history, and few powerful men remain content with only momentary greatness. Monck came from relative obscurity, accomplished the monarchy's restoration, and returned to his

[2] Richard Cromwell retired to a country estate. Other relatives were not politically ambitious.

private domain when the act was achieved. Until his capture in 1644, he had fought for Charles I. After three years as a prisoner, Parliament granted him a commission in Ireland and then in Scotland, the position he held until Cromwell's death. Purging his ranks of overly ambitious power seekers and instructing his men in his own belief in a thoroughly obedient military, he was one of the very few commanders who held aloof from the political scramble that followed the demise of the lord protector. A fresh parliament must finally be elected, he urged, but told few of his conviction that only a restored monarchy could save the country from chaos. In the first days of the new year, 1660, he moved his army across the Scottish border. With Cromwell's former commanding officer, Fairfax, whom he had roused from retirement to seize the city of York, he proceeded to London. Once in the capital Monck dispersed the other regiments from the London area and quietly issued invitations for the return of the parliamentary members who had been excluded since Pride's Purge in 1648. With a prearrangement that would have awed Cromwell, Monck secured pledges from this reassembled parliament that it would dissolve itself and summon a new parliament, and from the army that it would abide by whatever Parliament proposed. In mid-March he opened negotiations with Charles concerning the conditions under which the prince ought to return to his kingdom.

Astonishment and joy were the twin emotions governing the nation that spring of 1660. Charles had acceded to Monck's advice, embodying it in his Declaration of Breda, whereby he promised full and free pardon

> to the end that the fear of punishment may not engage any conscious to themselves of what is past to a perseverance in guilt for the future . . . who . . . return to the loyalty and obedience of good subjects. . . . No crime whatsoever, committed against us or our royal father before the publication of this shall ever rise in judgment or be brought in question against any of them to the least endamagement of them, either in their lives, liberties or estates. . . .

He also recognized land sales transacted since 1642, agreed to prompt payment of military arrears, to freedom from persecution, and "to consent to any act or acts of parliament to the purposes aforesaid." The declaration was speedily accepted by the newly elected and preponderantly royalist Convention Parliament. On May 25 Charles landed at Dover to the cheers of the parliamentary deputation sent to greet him, echoing the general relief from twenty years of perpetual crisis. Charles' restoration would spell the end of a tortuously conscience-stricken era, and England's exhaustion made her ready for the reign of the "Merrie Monarch."

Chapter Five
FROM THE HAPPY RESTORATION TO THE GLORIOUS REVOLUTION

Major Personages

Charles II, 1630–85; king of England, 1660–85, known as the Merry Monarch; presided over England's Restoration era

Clarendon, Edward Hyde, first earl of, 1609–1674; Charles II's first lord chancellor, retired to France to become the first major historian of the Civil Wars

Danby, Thomas Osborne, earl of, 1631–1712; Charles II's lord treasurer, traditionally regarded as the founder of the Tory party

James II, 1633–1701, duke of York until he succeeded his brother as king, 1685–8; died in exile in France

Jeffreys of Wem, George Jeffreys, first baron, 1648–89; infamous for heading the Bloody Assizes after the Monmouth Rebellion in 1685

Monmouth, James Scott, duke of, 1649–85; illegitimate son of Charles II, led the Monmouth Rebellion against his uncle, James II; executed in 1685

Oates, Titus, 1649–1705; fabricator of the Popish Plot

Shaftesbury, Anthony Ashley Cooper, first earl of, 1621–83; traditionally regarded as the founder of the Whig party, organizer of opposition to Charles II

Sunderland, Robert Spencer, 1640–1702; president of the Council under James II, supporter of James II's autocratic policies

CHRONOLOGY

1660	Restoration of Charles II, May
	Abolition of Feudal Tenures Act
1660–5	Clarendon Code
1665	Great Plague of London
1665–7	Second Dutch War, concluded by the Treaty of Breda
1666	Great Fire of London
1667–73	Period of the Cabal
1670	Treaty of Dover (with France)
1672	First Declaration of Indulgence
1672–4	Third Dutch War, concluded by the Treaty of Westminster
1673	Test Act
1678–80	The Popish Plot
1679	Habeas Corpus Act
1679–81	The Exclusion crisis
1685	Death of Charles II
1688	Trial of the Seven Bishops
	Birth of the Prince of Wales
	Invasion of England by William of Orange, October and November
	Flight of James II to France, December

In good King Charles's golden days,
  When loyalty no harm meant,
A zealous High Churchman was I,
  And so I got preferment;
To teach my flock I never miss'd
  Kings were by God appointed;
And damn'd are those who do resist,
  Or touch the Lord's anointed.

And this is law, that I'll maintain,
  Until my dying day, sir,
That whatsoever King shall reign,
  I'll be the Vicar of Bray, sir.

When royal James obtained the crown,
  And Pop'ry came in fashion,
The penal laws I hooted down,
  And read the Declaration;
The Church of Rome I found would fit
  Full well my constitution;
And had become a Jesuit,
  But for the Revolution.

And this is law, that I'll maintain,
  Until my dying day, sir,
That whatsoever King shall reign,
  I'll be the Vicar of Bray, sir.[1]

Individuals sometimes have the opportunity to make new beginnings; nations rarely have. Seventeenth-century England was blessed with four such occasions. Back in 1603 many of Queen Elizabeth's subjects could scarcely conceal their relief when the aged and infirm matriarch died, bequeathing to England a new king, a new dynasty, and new hope. Then in 1640, the ensuing disillusionment over the first two Stuarts, James I and Charles I, was dispelled by reborn faith in the newly appointed Long Parliament. During the succeeding twenty years the Puritans were to consume their spiritual fuel in the Civil Wars, and Englishmen became impatient for the jollier times promised by the restoration of the third Stuart king, Charles II, in 1660. He and his brother, James II, brought the country to still another

[1] For additional verses to this anonymous ballad, see the epigraphs for Chapters Six and Seven.

impasse through their autocracy, causing the English again to set out afresh under the banner of William of Orange after the Revolution of 1688.

Charles' Return: Promising Beginnings

At the beginning of each era—1603, 1640, 1660, 1688—preachers and pamphleteers optimistically extolled a promising future. This sense of perpetual renewal probably accounts for the stimulation behind the brilliant men and movements that were a part of the Restoration era. England's greatest scientist, Sir Isaac Newton, was born in 1642, the year the Civil Wars broke out; John Locke, the philosopher, was eight years old when the Long Parliament first met, twenty-eight at the Restoration, and fifty-seven when his famous *Treatise of Government* was published after the Glorious Revolution of 1688; Sir Christopher Wren, the most renowned of the island's architects, born the same year as Locke (1632), achieved eminence as the man who rebuilt London after the fire of 1666; Henry Purcell, possibly England's greatest native composer, who first saw life the year of Cromwell's death in 1658, created his earliest music for the lyrics of the esteemed poet John Dryden; John Milton wrote his masterpiece, *Paradise Lost*, during the Restoration era; Jonathan Swift was twenty-one when the Glorious Revolution began and rose to fame as the nation's greatest satirist during the squabbles that followed that event. The Royal Society, incorporated in 1662, serves as the patron for scientific research to this day. The roots of modern rationalist philosophy can be found among the Cambridge Platonists, whose dictum "The understanding of man is the candle of the Lord" inspired them toward toleration, bold and free religious thought, and scientific inquiry. Their light illuminated the way to the eighteenth century's Age of Reason. In many respects the Restoration era constituted a renaissance of larger magnitude than did the age of Shakespeare a hundred years earlier.

Traditionally the Restoration begins with the entrance of King Charles II into London on May 29, 1660. Twenty years of repression, rectitude, and restraint were merrily swept away in the gala welcome accorded him. As described by an eyewitness, Sir John Evelyn:

> This was also [the king's thirtieth] birthday, and with a triumph of above 20,000 horse and foot brandishing their swords and shouting with inexpressible joy; the ways [were] strewed with flowers, the bells ringing, the streets hung with tapestry, fountains running with wine; the mayor, aldermen, and all the companies, in their liveries, chains of gold, and banners; lords and nobles clad in cloth of silver, gold, and velvet; the windows and balconies all set with ladies; trumpets, music, and myriads of people flocking even so far as from Rochester, so as they were seven hours in passing the city, even from two in the afternoon till nine at night.[2]

[2] *The Diary of John Evelyn,* ed. William Bray (London, 1952), I, 241.

Charles II seemed admirably suited to preside over the restoration of monarchy. Personable, open, charming, witty, he greeted the deputations from all parts of his recovered realm with such cordiality that he scarcely found time to eat during his first week as king. He stated openly that he would not go again on his "travels" (by which he meant a return into exile) and that he would do virtually anything to retain the serenity that had, after the hard years, returned to England with its traditional government.

The Privy Council chosen by Charles reflected the new monarch's desire to achieve broad support among his subjects. Edward Hyde, who had remained loyal to Charles I and the young exiled Prince of Wales, was of an earlier world, having been born in 1609 in the reign of the monarch's grandfather, James I. Unlike most courtiers of the day in that he was an expert lawyer, the new lord chancellor possessed a dour mien and an utter sobriety that should have balanced Charles II's love of the flamboyant, With his new title, earl of Clarendon, Hyde carried the burden of state until his dismissal in 1667. Another member of the Council was General Monck, now the duke of Albemarle, who retained the respect of the old army commanders of Cromwell's time. Anthony Ashley Cooper, though he had fought against the crown, had also been Cromwell's leading detractor. He too became a member of the king's Council, though Charles might well have heeded the lord protector's complaint that no one was more unmanageable than the little man with three names. Within twenty years Ashley Cooper was to prod England to the brink of another civil war.

The Nonconformists

Charles II's first decade, however, consisted largely of placation and compromise. He had granted Parliament a full pardon for its transgressions against monarchy and had promised to be bound by its determinations. Out of the sense of trust placed in it—or out of duty—or out of revenge—that body exempted from pardon fifty-seven men who had sat at Charles I's trial. Many of the regicides managed to escape; some were expressly pardoned by the beheaded monarch's son; and only a dozen made the acquaintance of the executioner. Cromwell's remains were disinterred, ignominiously hung, and buried at the base of the gallows. But despite the demands of some embittered courtiers, there was no systematic hunt for rebels. So long as they were not troublesome to the restored regime, the Nonconformists— the new name for the Puritans of the Civil Wars—were left largely in peace. Interference in their Congregational or Baptist chapels was rare, though their right to public worship was declared illegal. The Clarendon Code, falsely and maliciously named for Charles' chief minister with all intents to make that gentleman unpopular, contained the Corporation Act of 1661, which deprived Nonconformists of the right to hold office in municipal governments (corporations). In 1662 the revised Act of Uniformity forced out all incumbent clergy who would not rigidly adhere to Anglican doctrines. Nearly a thousand Presbyterian-minded clerics who had received appointments under the puritanical Commonwealth were deprived of their ministries. The Quakers, or Friends, the most detached from Anglican doctrine and generally regarded as antisocial rebels, were hobbled by the Quaker Act of 1662, which authorized imprisonment for merely being a member of the sect. Other fringe denominations were not treated in kind. The Conventicle Act (conventicles being Nonconformist services) forbade any but Anglican worship. The Five-Mile Act of 1665 fettered Nonconformist clergy by prohibiting them from coming within five miles of a corporate town.

Though the Clarendon Code reflected royalist revenge, it was, oddly, a product of false enlightenment. A popular lampoon of the day, Samuel Butler's poetic *Hudibras*, mirrored the common prejudice that Puritans/Nonconformists were theological bigots willing to revolt against neighbor as well as king. It was widely circulated that these zealots, claiming to be the executors of God's will, had perpetrated the Civil Wars on a generally unwilling populace. With peace and order dictating that religion never again become the cause of division, the answer seemed to lie in curtailing Nonconformist activities.

This public disavowal of the Nonconformists completed their demoralization, which had begun with the collapse of Cromwell's "New Jerusalem." It was as though they had fumbled their one God-given chance for national regeneration. Many of their sons abandoned the sectarian beliefs for the opportunities and safety proffered by the Anglican Church and conventional society. Of those who stayed with their brethren, some went into scholarly seclusion. Others, clasping their Bibles, combated the devil in the everyday business world, giving birth to the social phenomenon today called middle class morality. A gifted few converted their millennial visions into moral literary masterpieces—Milton's *Paradise Lost*, Bunyan's *Pilgrim's Progress*, Defoe's *Robinson Crusoe*, Richardson's *Clarissa* were such outpourings. Then too, despite the volley of laws enacted against them, many Nonconformists, harking back to the Biblical adage, "Render unto Caesar the things that are Caesar's," were more than willing to render unto Charles the things that were Charles'. A surprisingly large number found their way back into all governmental levels, inventing a new device, "occasional conformity," in the face of Anglican and royalist oaths required of all officeholders. Though the Puritans had failed to govern England in the seventeenth century, by the nineteenth their Nonconformist descendants were to succeed in gradually capturing her public life under the banner of Victorian morality.

In May 1660 some sixty Nonconformists, mostly Presbyterians, managed to find seats in the king's first and long-lived Cavalier Parliament. Together with their sympathizers, they were probably responsible for the political and constitutional curbs imposed on the monarch. It was made unmistakably clear to Charles that there would be no wholesale return of Royalists' lands. Certainly the crown lands would be restored, as would the church's, but of the over 700 royalist estates sold by the government between 1640 and 1660, only those confiscated outright would be immediately returned to their previous owners. Well over a million pounds had exchanged hands during the Interregnum, and those transactions had to be guaranteed or the government would court economic chaos. Charles, by his disinterest, seemed content enough with these decisions.

In order to further remove monarchical temptations of land confiscation, the Abolition of Feudal Tenures Act was passed in the parliament's first year. Kings could never again exercise escheat, wardship, or any control whatever over private lands, ending that particular aspect of English feudalism. Ownership of land would, in the future, be determined in law courts and would be subject to the laws of private property. Now farmers could improve their holdings without the ancient fear of losing them through royal recovery. To compensate for the resultant loss of income, Charles received the yield from a variety of tax sources, customs, and postal revenues, which were expected to produce over a million pounds annually—an expectation never realized.

The king's right to summon Parliament at his pleasure was curtailed in a Triennial Act of 1664, compelling him to call that body every three years. Unlike its forerunner of 1641, however, this version gave the king discretion in its implementation. Charles manipulated the law under the loosest possible construction, holding the first of his four parliaments, the Cavalier Parliament, for eighteen years and dispensing with a parliament altogether for the final four years of his twenty-five year reign. While the Restoration Settlement included two measures making it treasonous to plot against the monarch or to raise arms against him (reemphasizing the divine right of kings theory), Parliament abolished standing armies. The militia, raised and captained by the country gentry, would be hereafter the monarch's only military support.

The Case Against Clarendon

On the one hand, the Royalists realized their vengeance against the Puritans by restoring Anglicanism as the national faith and by driving them into underground worship. On the other hand, the resilient

Nonconformists retained the minimal economic and political restraints on the crown, restraints they had originally imposed on Charles' father. No one, as a result, was thoroughly content. Though the compromise kept the political pendulum near dead center, both sides jealously guarded against efforts to push it again to an extreme. The king and his brother, James, duke of York, detached from party haggling, indulged themselves in the luxuries of life—the theater, masques, and a seemingly endless succession of mistresses. This left Charles' ministers, particularly Clarendon, whose tiresome sobriety had come to annoy both king and court, to take the brunt of political criticism.

Ambitious or distrustful political figures cultivated the practice of directing barbs at the defenseless chief minister, hoping to topple, and perhaps succeed, him. A period of robust and sometimes vicious political skirmishing had begun, from which would eventually emerge a sophisticated party system for formulating national policies and laws. But in this early age of partisanship, "loyal opposition" was a thing of the future. It was simply not safe for individuals or groups to object from the floor of Parliament to policies favored by the monarch. With opposition to the king bordering on treason and royal favor dominating appointment to high office, factions could react prudently only against those policies proposed by the ministry. Nonetheless, a judicious chief minister needed not only to court royal patronage but also to maintain a parliamentary following. In time, the latter was to become more necessary to his survival than the former, but in this day, if he possessed neither, his fall was rapid and inevitable. So it was for the earl of Clarendon, perhaps the last English minister to place his trust wholly in the crown. His private preachments against the king's excesses lost him the royal favor, making him vulnerable.

As it was, Clarendon's multitude of enmities and ineptitudes brought about his final banishment from England. The Royalists condemned him for his failure to recover their lost lands. The Nonconformists gradually saw in him a recrudescence of Laud. Although he had not sponsored the infamous code that bore his name, would it have passed without his tacit approval? His daughter, Anne, had been first the mistress, then the wife, of the duke of York. Didn't marriage into the royal family constitute the grossest way to curry royal favor? Dunkirk, the foothold won by Cromwell from the Spanish in bloody battle, was sold under Clarendon's auspices to France for £400,000, and while it had required an upkeep of £100,000 per year, it could have remained England's bastion on the Continent. Rumor had it that the earl had profited from the negotiation, building his London residence, Dunkirk House, with the graft. He was further reproached for having married off Charles to the frail Portuguese queen, Catherine of Braganza, merely for her dowry of £800,000, which equaled nearly a year's royal income. While

Portugal had also conferred on England the ports of Tangier and Bombay, Englishmen understood their worth no better than their locations. Bombay was conveyed to the East India Company in 1668; Tangier was unceremoniously abandoned altogether in 1683 for want of funds to maintain its garrison. Clarendon's standing deteriorated further, as if he were personally responsible, as Catherine failed, year after year, to provide the kingdom with an heir.

The last three years of the earl's administration witnessed two natural disasters and one national humiliation. The plague, or Black Death, had become a resident of the island in the fourteenth century. It remained essentially dormant from the time of its inception, reasserting itself only in small outbreaks. But in 1665 its final rage equaled its earliest incursion. Its fury was concentrated on London. From April to October, those financially able to do so fled to the doubtful sanctuary of their country estates. Of the tragic remnant of Londoners, nearly 100,000 in a population of 460,000 died, sometimes at the rate of 5,000 a week, the corpses accumulating more quickly than sanitary facilities could dispose of them. The virulence exhausted itself in one terrible year, for with the frost the plague departed from England as dramatically as it had arrived three hundred years earlier.

Scarcely had the bedeviled city's populace put its affairs into some semblance of order than it was again overwhelmed. On September 2 of the following year the Great Fire of London leveled over half the city within the walls, as well as portions of the suburbs. For five days an east wind fanned the blaze, blowing showers of sparks over the heads of the fire fighters, who sometimes found escape cut off by new infernos behind them. Days after the holocaust, sightseers and refugees returning to the city could not walk on the superheated ground. The remains of parts of medieval London were melted bottles and door handles, suitable as souvenirs and museum pieces. Thirteen thousand homes and eighty-nine churches were gone. Though public funds were set aside to rebuild the city, with Sir Christopher Wren receiving the king's commission, the allotted money was scarcely sufficient to erect a new St. Paul's Cathedral, refurbish the Tower of London, and reconstruct a few of the public buildings. Out of the tragic death of the city came a small recompense. By the stricter building codes requiring stone, brick, and tile, the proliferation of plague-carrying rats was slowed. But with the retention of its hodgepodge of streets, London lost an opportunity to become a model of rational design.

These calamities placed extraordinary burdens on the country during the second of its three wars with the Netherlands. The first Dutch War (1651–4) had been fought largely over European coastal trade. The second was expanded to include competition in colonizing the African Gold Coast and North America. England did not officially declare war on her adversary until 1665, though Dutch and English admirals had been actively seizing ships and forts.

Etiam periere Ruinæ

ST. PAUL'S IN FLAMES.

This cathedral, destroyed by the Great Fire of 1666, was redesigned by Sir Christopher Wren. Courtesy The Bettmann Archive.

Parliament, in expectation of plundering the world's most prosperous commercial empire, voted nearly £4 million for the effort. But within a month of the official declaration, the plague took its first victims, and a year later London's business district disappeared in flames. The navies, so evenly matched that neither could gain an advantage, exhausted their supplies. First France and then Denmark joined the Netherlands, and within two years England was compelled to sue for peace. In the midst of the ensuing negotiations, the Dutch forcibly demonstrated their ability to drive a hard bargain by sailing up the Thames estuary, burning four English vessels and towing away the very *Royal Charles* in which the king had returned from France at the Restoration. The English sailors, whose salaries were in arrears for months, refused to defend the fleet until they received due compensation. Alarmed Londoners fully expected the city to be sacked. Such sobering humiliations hastened the signing of the Treaty of Breda in July of 1667. The Netherlands won the right to trade certain commodities directly with England, effectively neutralizing the Navigation Act of 1651. By the treaty, England was forbidden East Indian trade, but in return the Dutch magnanimously ceded New Amsterdam. While the value of this concession was held lightly at the time, the holding added New York, New Jersey, and Delaware to England's central block of colonies, giving her control of the North American coastline from Virginia to Massachusetts.

Each disaster took its toll on Clarendon. The credulous public held him responsible for them all, but it was his mismanagement of naval funds that finally undermined him completely. When Parliament demanded an account of all moneys it had voted for the war, Charles found pleasure in seeing the man who had preached against his excesses humbled for his own malfeasance. Edward Hyde, earl of Clarendon, was proved incompetent and, amid a rising clamor, was forced to resign in August 1667. He was impeached but, wisely recalling Lord Strafford's fate, fled overseas. Until his death in 1674, he remained in self-imposed exile, completing his mammoth history of the civil war years, the first comprehensive study of England's revolution (*History of the Great Rebellion*).

The Cabal and the Pursuit of Loyalty

The aftermath of Clarendon's fall produced a hardening of positions. An investigation of the earl's mismanagement of military funds disclosed that half a million pounds had been sidetracked into private pockets. Its faith in the king's Court shaken, Parliament required Charles to reorganize his naval board before voting additional grants. The indignant king resolved to find an income independent of legislative control. Yet he understood the need to establish a ministry capable of placating Parliament or at least capable of bringing him greater personal support than he had been able to summon in Clarendon's rule. The king sought to increase his personal following among the people by reviving a scheme he had shelved in 1662 for lack of his chief minister's backing—toleration for Nonconformists and Catholics. In 1667 he courted parliamentary loyalty with the unique device of replacing a single minister with a ministerial committee.

This Cabal, so named for the last initials of its members, had the apparent virtue of giving voice to the leading parliamentary camps. Of its members, Sir Thomas Clifford favored Catholic toleration, as did Lord Arlington, secretary of state since 1662; the duke of Buckingham, a mere court fixture, was friendly to the Nonconformists; Anthony Ashley Cooper (Ashley Cooper being his unhyphenated last name), was the only one to take his position seriously. The earl of Lauderdale, secretary for Scottish affairs, completed the alphabetical game. It was Ashley Cooper who would reawaken parliamentary opposition to the king, precisely what the monarch had hoped to avoid by appointing a council of five. Though Charles might find one of his cabinet members antagonistic to his programs, this would be offset by a presumed support of the others.

The Cabal's effectiveness was soon tested by the 1670 Treaty of Dover negotiations with France. For her part, England was to join France in yet another Dutch War, a vengeful prospect relished by most Englishmen. However, the treaty was actually part of a larger French plan by which Louis XIV hoped to purchase England's aid in extending his country's borders to the Rhine River, or at least to buy the island's neutrality. Charles, seeing an opportunity to free himself from parliamentary control of his purse strings, was quite willing to be bought off. But the secret clauses in the treaty, not brought to light until 1682, would have frightened his subjects. The king was to declare himself a Roman Catholic and to work for the reestablishment of Catholicism in England, with £166,000 from Louis and, if necessary, 6,000 French troops to aid in convincing Charles' subjects. Only the pro-Catholic ministers of the Cabal, Clifford and Arlington, were aware of the secret clauses. The public agreement was accepted by the other members, and England entered the third Dutch War in March 1672.

Charles' motives in this agreement have long been queried. The facts that he never did announce his conversion, that he refused to bind himself irrevocably to Louis, that he continually exacted ever more French money without substantial return indicate that he deliberately played his ally for a fool. On the other hand, by his actions he perilously courted civil war, since Englishmen, almost to a man, were confirmed in their hostility to Catholicism.

Within three years of negotiating the Treaty of Dover, its secret provisions were rumored throughout London. The king's next move convinced his subjects that he was heading down his father's autocratic path. In January 1672, just prior to the war declaration against the Dutch, the king stopped payment on most of his debts, purportedly to reserve funds for the campaign. Numbers of bankers and merchants quickly toppled into bankruptcy. Furthermore, Charles issued a Declaration of Indulgence granting religious toleration to Catholics and Nonconformists alike, promulgating it by his own seal as a royal decree, rather than by proper parliamentary statute. Parliament had not been in session for over a year, and when it met, tempers were short. Tough old parliamentary Royalists had not fought in Charles I's cause only to have his son betray the Church of England. Even Nonconformists, though they had received the right to public worship along with Catholics, were indignant that "papists" should be considered as worthy as reformed Christians. Parliament would be amenable to voting over a million pounds for the war effort, Charles was presumptuously informed, but not until he rescinded his extralegal device for granting toleration.

The monarch abandoned his pro-Catholic policy in the face of intensifying opposition. In 1673 he was politically bludgeoned into accepting the Test Act, which gave Catholic officeholders the unpleasant choice of surrendering their posts or taking an annual test composed of the Anglican sacrament of the Lord's supper plus signing a declaration against transubstantiation (the Catholic belief that the bread and wine served in the mass are in fact the body and blood of Christ). The test swiftly depleted the ranks of Charles' Catholic courtiers. Even the Cabal collapsed when Clifford refused to comply; and when the king's brother resigned from the Admiralty, the rumors of James' conversion to Rome were authenticated.

While the country was engrossed with anti-Catholicism, the third and final Dutch War languished. England became increasingly aware that she was a pawn in France's drive to absorb the Netherlands. In February 1674 she pulled out of the engagement altogether, signing an unusually innocuous peace with the Dutch, in which she agreed to abstain from aiding their enemies. Even during the negotiations for this Treaty of Westminster, public feeling turned—Catholic France, not the fellow-Protestant Netherlands, was the nation's true enemy. By the end of the year, all that Charles could safely promise Louis was that, despite the changing mood of Parliament, England would not return to the war on the side of her former adversary.

Tories and Whigs

The five years following the Test Act on the surface resemble the decade preceding the Civil Wars. Increased hostility to the crown, combined with growing religious suspicions, marked both eras. It may be that only the recent memory of bloody civil turmoil saved England from a similar divisive disruption. The antagonists, court and country, wisely refrained from issuing nonnegotiable demands, and both sought to keep debate within the confines of constitutional settlement. Charles avoided risking political rupture over the intransigent notion of royal honor that had felled his father, and the "country party," as the opposition was now known, went to great lengths to escape the derogatory name "rebel." Within these self-imposed confinements, a two-party tradition took shape, with the floor of Parliament as the testing ground for the opposing factions. This tendency toward factiousness was not welcomed with any pride. The word "party," coined during these last decades of the seventeenth century, connoted to contemporaries groupings that represented only fractions of the whole. To the end of the next century, nearly all writers contended that political parties were symptomatic of a divided society, legacies of the Reformation or the Civil Wars. It was thought that only when a beneficent monarch comparable to Good Queen Bess again ruled, would these divisions cease, all voices and all special interests finding accommodation in that wise counsel.

The phenomenon of parties was there to stay, however. The old nomenclatures, Royalist/Cavalier, Puritan/Roundhead, gave way to "Tory" and "Whig"—both holding equally unsavory associations, the former being an Irish Catholic bandit and the latter a Scottish Presbyterian rebel. These originally derisive names stuck fast, and not until the nineteenth century were they to symbolize proudly their respective philosophies. When coined in Charles II's reign, a Tory was presumedly an advocate of strong royal prerogative and total conformity to the Church of England, which meant that he was hostile to toleration for both Nonconformists and Catholics; conversely, a Whig was an adherent of prescribed monarchy, a believer in parliamentary supremacy, toleration for Nonconformists (but most definitely not for Catholics), and liberal interpretation of Anglican theology and worship. The Tories naturally enough thought that their position qualified them for the king's preferment; but both parties, disorganized and quarrelsome as they were, were as suspicious of Charles as of each other. The Tories viewed the king's pro-Catholic sentiments as disloyal to the Anglican Church's divine right preachments. Neither the Tories nor the Whigs favored his reliance on France, and the latter had special reason to suspect that the monarch would hardly hesitate to use French troops to destroy his domestic opponents. Thus neither party trusted Charles, and when James (who became king in 1685) went even further than his brother's departure from conventional Protestant and parliamentary norms, this lack of trust was to undo the House of Stuart.

The two men traditionally credited as founders of the English party system are the Whig leader Anthony Ashley Cooper, given the title earl of Shaftesbury in 1672 for his services in supporting the anti-Dutch war clauses in the

Treaty of Dover, and the Tories' Thomas Osborne, created earl of Danby in 1674. Shaftesbury's motives for organizing an opposition party are clouded with the speculations of later commentators. His enemies accused him of an unscrupulous ambition and self-gratification. And yet his disregard for his own safety displayed an overabundance of heroism. In 1673, on being relieved by Charles of his lordship of the chancery because he supported the Test Act, Shaftesbury threatened that if he were to resign, it would be to take up his sword. Though he never made good the threat, the statement itself could well have landed him in prison then and there. As opposition to Charles grew, the king tried to buy Shaftesbury off with enormous grants and high positions. Despite miseries of feeble health, he continued his attacks on the crown, though they ultimately brought him two visits to the Tower and then exile, in which he died in 1683. He might have been a Machiavellian, but his spirit courageously founded a permanent tradition of opposition in English politics.

Danby's one great accomplishment was the cementing of an alliance with the Dutch by marrying Mary, James' older daughter, to William III of the House of Orange, Stadholder of the Netherlands. Appointed lord treasurer in 1673, the Tory leader contributed by his attempts to bring the crown into closer accord with Parliament—doomed efforts, since the forces he sought to reconcile were totally ungovernable. In order to gain even a modicum of cooperation, he resorted to the clumsiest expedients. Lavish bribes to members of Parliament brought only cynical, half-hearted support. He was less than successful in dissuading Charles from his pursuit of Catholic toleration, and though he disapproved of the French bribes the king had been pocketing since 1670, he was unable to exact additional moneys from Commons to loosen France's hold on the monarch. Since Parliament's grant to the king came to barely a tenth of his £2 million indebtedness, the chief minister was forced to acquiesce when Charles accepted £500,000 from Louis in return for English neutrality. Perhaps Danby's real blunder, considering the era's unrelenting factiousness, was that he had the ill luck to be caught. Shaftesbury had been attempting to impeach the chief minister for the larger part of a year. He was quite delighted when a bitterly jealous enemy of Danby's, who had been stationed in Paris, exposed before the House of Commons the secret negotiations relating to the bribes. This exposure and charges connected to Danby's financial derelictions resulted in a five-year sojourn in the Tower of London, despite the king's express pardon, which Commons rejected.

The Popish Plot

Coincidental with these events came outlandish revelations from one of the most improbable political cheats ever entrusted to high office—Titus Oates, chief fabricator of the infamous Popish Plot. This incredible man stumbled onto the political stage in 1678 just as Parliament tightened the Test Act to debar all Catholics from both houses. It had successfully coerced the king into excluding his brother from the Privy Council, had switched the nation's support from France to the Netherlands, had diverted much of the revenue from the royal treasury to the City of London's treasury, and had threatened additional ministers with impeachment. The Popish Plot thus came at a most opportune time for the budding Whig party, elevating its role from that of political schismatic to defender of national honor.

The tall, sinister Oates, survivor of imprisonment on a charge of perjury, expelled from school, from a naval chaplaincy, and from a Jesuit college in France for scandalous behavior, made a threadbare career out of ruining reputations and causes. In late 1678, having convinced a pious, if short-sighted, county justice of the peace, Sir Edmund Berry Godfrey, of the veracity of his charges, Oates gained access to the Privy Council. He laid before it the outline of an enormous plot he claimed to have unearthed while sojourning in Spain and France. He asserted that Charles was to be assassinated (as related by D. L. Farmer, "to be poisoned by the Queen's doctor, shot by Jesuits, and stabbed by Irishmen for good measure"[3]), James raised to the throne, and Protestant leaders throughout the realm hunted down and slaughtered. Initially the king scoffed at these allegations, but when the justice in whose hands Oates had placed the original deposition was found in a ditch, stabbed and strangled, even sane heads questioned if they might not contain some truth. Oates proclaimed Godfrey's murder as the signal for the uprising of the underground Jesuit fiends.

Shaftesbury, who was very likely aware that Oates was a charlatan, nonetheless supported him. His sparring with the court had put him in danger of following Danby to the Tower, and the plot provided camouflage behind which he could take refuge. A Whiggish parliament and a panicked nation forced the government to confer on Oates, summary judicial power to name those he supposedly knew to be implicated. A two-year reign of terror followed. Swollen with haughtiness, the accuser sent hundreds to prison, had thirty-five innocents executed, and was tragically esteemed a heroic Protestant crusader by humble folk who proudly displayed the "Doctor's" picture on their cottage walls (Oates was a self-styled doctor of divinity via the University of Salamanca in Spain, though he had never entered that city).

Finally, in January 1679, a vexed Charles saw fit to dissolve his Cavalier Parliament, which had eighteen years before declared unending loyalty. He acted now to save the earl of Danby's life and also to forestall an embarrassing

---

[3] D. L. Farmer, *Britain and the Stuarts* (New York, 1966), p. 231.

demand from Parliament that Queen Catherine, accused by Oates of Jesuitical treason, be removed from his presence.

Shaftesbury used the plot's spectacular diversion to engineer the boldest challenge to the crown ever contemplated within parliamentary confines. His agents and followers, united in the Green Ribbon Club, the first political association, kept up the frenzy of Oates' dangerous sideshow by creating slogans, marshaling demonstrations, and organizing vigilante groups. Charles' calculations told him that the Whigs were overplaying their vicious game and exhausting the country's patience. However, in February 1679, when he issued election writs for a fresh—and Tory—parliament, his miscalculation was monumental. The Tory presence in the new parliament was less than a third of its strength in the former. In another misjudgment, the hamstrung king offered Shaftesbury the presidency of the Council, hoping to thus placate his overabundant ambition. But, though he accepted the position, the man who had challenged Cromwell refused to be bought with his new eminence. He drafted the Habeas Corpus Act, whereby any arrested person became entitled to know on what charge he was held and to have his case speedily brought before a court of law. No longer could king or Parliament arbitrarily hold a suspect under indefinite confinement, using technical delays to circumvent the old writ of habeas corpus. In structuring this lasting monument to civil liberty, Shaftesbury is perhaps redeemed from his callous disregard of rights associated with the exploitation of the Popish Plot.

In May 1679 Parliament, which had not been consulted on the succession to the throne since Henry VIII's day and then only by royal command, introduced the Exclusion Bill. This bold effort to remove James, duke of York, from the royal succession was vital inasmuch as Charles refused to consider legitimizing his mistresses' children, intending that his brother should succeed him. The effrontery to the royal family caused the king to follow the bill more assiduously than any other deliberation of his reign. As it passed the House by a solid majority of seventy-nine, Charles, dispelling his usual languor, dissolved Parliament within three months of its first meeting and dismissed Shaftesbury from the Council.

Two parliaments came and went in rapid succession, the king always in hopes that a popular reaction might break the Whigs' grasp. In the first, which met throughout 1680, Shaftesbury was again active. He succeeded in ramming through Commons a strengthened Exclusion Bill, hinting that he favored setting aside James in favor of the duke of Monmouth, Charles' illegitimate son. The duke, though heartily loved by his father and the people, possessed only the virtue of being Protestant. He was inept as a statesman and foolhardy as a soldier. But as a liberal Anglican and an admirer of Shaftesbury, he suited the exclusionists admirably as the man to succeed the king. Despite Charles' pointed renunciation of Monmouth's claim, the Exclusion Bill was sent from Commons to Lords, meeting defeat by a large margin. Nothing daunted, Shaftesbury then tried bringing James to trial under the Test Act. When this failed, he desperately sought to embarrass the court by indicting the king's current mistress, the duchess of Portsmouth, as a common nuisance. Blocked again, the Whigs pumped new life into the flagging Popish Plot, bringing to trial and execution an aged Catholic peer, Lord Stafford. Charles' mild annoyance now turned to raging anger over the intensifying hysteria, and he sent this, his third parliament, home in January 1681.

From January to April Charles moved with unaccustomed action and convinced Louis XIV that England's neutrality, should a new anti-French coalition be formed, was worth another grant. Not only was the fate of English Catholicism in the balance, but France could also find herself in a war declared by the Whigs, he argued. This time £400,000 was exchanged, a sum sufficient to allow the king freedom from parliamentary control and from the need to tolerate Whig impertinence. Charles rapidly surrounded himself with loyal and Catholic peers, the most notable of whom was Robert Spencer, earl of Sunderland, successor to Danby. Whigs and Whig sympathizers were excluded from court. When at last the king felt strong enough to take on the exclusionists, he convened his fourth parliament at the end of March 1681. Its summons to Oxford, far from the rantings of London's Whig demonstrators, was a mark of Charles' new-found confidence.

The Whig contingent, headed once again by Shaftesbury, came warily to that old royalist stronghold. It had no knowledge of the French gift but was all too aware that the victims of the Popish Plot had finally gained the nation's sympathy. Every day Charles was seeming more a wronged monarch. April in Oxford could become a time of reckoning for the exclusionists. The king held the session for one week, proposing to the assembly that his brother hold the throne under a regency. The Whigs might have thus negotiated a compromise but, out of fear or exasperation, risked all on total exclusion. Charles withdrew this final concession and dissolved the Oxford Parliament within forty-eight hours of its taking up the Exclusion Bill.

The Whigs, with no alternative plan, scattered to their constituencies, leaving a resurgent Tory ministry to hunt them down separately. Danby, still in the Tower, might have softened the blow that was to fall on the Whigs— he at least was staunchly Anglican—but Sunderland, soon to become a militant Catholic convert, began a systematic search for the exclusionists. Shaftesbury was arrested for treason in July 1681, and though committed to the Tower, he ultimately escaped trial through judicial technicalities and fled to the Netherlands. London and the key Whig urban centers were purged of their exclusionist leaders by the simple expedient of revoking the municipal charters, giving the king power over local and national elections. When a group of Whig extremists, including Lord William Russell and the republican philosopher, Algernon Sydney, became remotely involved in a plot to kill Charles and James (the Rye House Plot), they paid with their lives along with other victims equal in number to those who had fallen during the Popish Plot. Titus Oates escaped death with a fine of £100,000, for default of which he spent the next seven years in chains. From 1681 to his death in February 1685, Charles was allowed to spend his declining years in almost total peace. Shaftesbury had died in exile, leaving no political heir, nor was there a parliament in which Whig opposition could be renewed.

Popery and Power: The Reign of James II

King James II, last male heir of the House of Stuart, came to the throne under the most propitious conditions. His severest opponents were dead, languishing in prison, or safely in exile. His own hands were clean of the purge, since his brother had ordered him from the capital during most of the years of the exclusion crisis. At fifty-three he had forsaken the licentiousness of his youth and now lived a stable and continent private life. A good man and a conscientious monarch, he could have become, as a critic admitted years later, one of England's better rulers but for the flaw of his utter devotion to the Catholic faith. It drove him to the hasty and immoderate measures that ultimately alienated his subjects, driving them into the camps of the militants.

But during James' first half-year everything went well. In May 1685 the first parliament since the Oxford convened, and its solid Tory majority yielded bountiful tax grants of £2 million. When in the same month the duke of Monmouth denounced the new monarch as a usurping murderer and crossed over from the Netherlands with the intention of seizing the crown, the people rallied for the king. The Monmouth Rebellion was easily broken at the Battle of Sedgemoor on July 5, and the duke was hauled off to London and beheaded as a traitor. James was hailed by Parliament as the nation's defender.

Within weeks of Monmouth's death, however, the good people of the western counties, the locale of the rebellion, were given reason to venerate his name. That summer of 1685 James dispatched the vicious Judge George Jeffreys to bring quiet to the shires. Jeffreys more than exceeded his warrant. In the shabbiest of due process, he executed somewhere between 150 to 320 persons, transported about 800 to servitude in the West Indies, and actually gave some prisoners to courtiers to sell into virtual slavery. Though Charles had disliked Jeffreys, the "Bloody Assizes" (sessions) earned from James the post of lord chancellor for Jeffreys. With such brutal conduct gaining rewards, many observers' affections were alienated by the king's blatant disregard of the rights of Englishmen. Another object of suspicion was James' personal army of 16,000. It had been rapidly equipped for the rebellion and had not disbanded after Sedgemoor. Its garrison outside of London was an ominous threat to the legal prohibition against standing armies. Nor did its increasing number of Catholic officers seem consistent with the Test Act. By the autumn of 1685, James had dissolved his obviously disgruntled parliament and called no more until the end of his short reign. Catholics received high appointments in the Privy Council and universities, and the king heard mass openly. He assumed the right to dispense with lawful procedure by publishing a Declaration of Indulgence granting to Catholics religious toleration, with the Nonconformists receiving some freedom as well. The Church of England had reason to feel itself as threatened by its monarch as it had been by the lord protector. The dispensing power might one day be exercised against its fundamental laws. As it was, James had created the Commission for Ecclesiastical Causes—which too much resembled the old Court of High Commission, abolished in 1640. He used this vehicle as a bridle on tough-minded churchmen like Henry Compton, the bishop of London, who was removed for resisting the new pro-Catholic policies. No wonder that when the hour for revolution arrived in 1688, Anglicans took the forefront in precipitating the conflict.

Throughout 1687 James tightened his grasp over the municipal corporations (most of whose charters had been revoked by his brother), thus keeping the city governments passive. Regulating the shires, however, was a more delicate matter. When James made a simple inquiry of the country gentry as to how many might favor repeal of the Test Act in a new parliament, the overwhelming response was negative and occasionally hostile.

By 1688 the king's standing among his subjects had plummeted. While few actually regarded him as a tyrant, none would have taken up his cause. Nonconformists were especially divided, for they now possessed not only the pleasure of public worship but also that of seeing their high-and-mighty Anglican persecutors rudely handled. The archbishop of Canterbury, William Sancroft, suggested that Anglicans would gladly support Nonconformist toleration—for unless Anglicans and Nonconformists united to form a Protestant front, the body of the church risked being consumed by its Catholic head. Nonconformists, after all, needed only to look at France to guess where Catholic toleration might lead, for Louis XIV had recently revoked the right of Protestant public worship in his kingdom. Yet, understandably, it was difficult to bring about such an alliance, since even Quakers had found freedom under James' policy.

On May 7, 1688, James promulgated a second Declaration of Indulgence. With the provision that it be read from the pulpits of every Anglican church in the kingdom, all the ill will that had mounted since the Bloody Assizes spilled into outright hostility. Sancroft, who by frequent pleadings of illness had avoided collaboration with the pro-Catholic agents James had insinuated into the church, in a sudden surge of good health became the anti-Catholic leader. He and six episcopal colleagues published a petition gently suggesting that the king reconsider his command. They hinted that his claimed dispensing power might be unconstitutional. The nation was thunderstruck when James counter-moved by charging the seven with seditious libel. Sancroft was generally con-sidered the most loyal of men, with the most patient of tempers. Should his voice be stifled, what of those less moderately critical? The sensational Trial of the Seven Bishops was concluded on June 30, 1688, when a harried jury, resisting pressure from the king, brought in a verdict of not guilty, bringing also, by implication, a charge of false accusation against the crown.

Surreptitiously published pamphlets, often written by Whig exiles in the Netherlands and smuggled into England, began making the rounds. Some were denunciatory; all were critical of James' latest blunder. They clamored for governmental reforms, particularly for freely elected parliaments. Public cynicism had already heightened when on June 10, without the usual formali-ties, it was announced that the queen had given birth to a son. This seemed particularly odd since James' second marriage had, in fifteen years, produced no surviving children. The country's mood was such that it welcomed the malicious warming-pan tale—the supposed heir was not the queen's child but one smuggled into the waiting chamber in a container, which, under more ordinary circumstances, held hot coals to warm the bed. Considering that the prospect of an endless Catholic Stuart dynasty had become too gloomy for most Englishmen to swallow, it is understandable that the ridiculous story was then wholly believed.

June 1688 also saw the consummation of an elaborate design with the announced aim of saving England's religion and liberties from popery and arbitrary power. The Prince of Orange, William III, who had assumed leader-ship of the United Netherlands in 1672, was invoked in a lengthy letter to conduct a crusading invasion. Signed by Danby (who had been released from the Tower by James in 1685), by the deprived bishop of London, Henry Compton, and by five other notables, it urged that the domestic scene had degenerated to such an intolerable extent that only William's intervention could possibly save the nation. The prince had long considered that Louis XIV's march through the Low Countries might be halted by a combined English and Dutch force. In fact, an attempt at creating such an alliance had resulted in a visit to the island in 1681, with hopes of having the exclusionist Whigs name him their alternative to the then duke of York. But the exclu-sionists had recklessly placed their faith in Monmouth. Now, after seven years of cultivating English leaders, William again proposed himself as the solution to James' autocracy. In April of 1688 he apprised Admiral Russell that his only requisite to launching an invasion was some assurance from England's great men that it was by their wish. That letter of commitment was carried by the disguised Russell the very night the seven bishops were acquitted.

The Challenge from William of Orange

During the autumn of 1688 a fantastic gamble for an entire kingdom was risked by the frail, asthmatic Prince of Orange. Through an indomitable sense of duty, a Calvinist faith in Providence, and an uncanny ability to gauge men and to time his moves, he became the master of an extremely problematic situation. Would the English, he questioned, relish the invasion of their soil by the foe of three past wars? Supposing he were successful in the field—might not taking on his father-in-law (who was also his uncle) turn the island against him? Establishing a proper diplomatic atmosphere among his European allies was a Herculean task. In his own country William found his adherents questioning the wisdom of reducing the number of Dutch troops along the French frontier for a possibly protracted war on English soil, which might sap the Netherlands' energies. Even James, who had wind of the plan, was persuaded by the French ambassador that to cross the English Channel late in the year was a fool's venture—surely William would not make the attempt until spring. Yet despite these obstacles, a Dutch flotilla of 15,000 troops crossed the autumn Channel in 250 ships sailing smoothly on a propitious east wind, bypassed the English fleet, and landed on the beaches of far-west England at Torbay on November 5, 1688.

The polyglot army of Dutch, English, Scots, Germans, Swiss, and Swedes moved by easy stages, the west country of Judge Jeffreys' wrath welcoming William's advance. James, beset by indecision and rightfully suspicious of every counsel, first decided to attack, then declined, then issued writs for a new parliament, then recalled them. He abolished the Ecclesiastical Commission, restored the charters to the towns and universities, dismissed Sunderland, and reinstated Compton. These conciliatory measures were viewed as symptoms of weakness. Through November and December, defections to William's banner multiplied. When James' younger daughter, Anne, fled from London and John Churchill, commander of the king's horse, took his contingent into the prince's camp, the king felt obliged to dispatch his wife and infant son to France. Then, finding himself totally deserted, he withdrew forever from England. William was now master of the island.

Chapter Six

THE DEFENSE OF THE REVOLUTION SETTLEMENT

Major Personages

Anne, 1665–1714, queen of England, 1702–14; younger daughter of James II

Bolingbroke, Henry St. John, Viscount, 1678–1751; leader in the brief Tory resurgence in Queen Anne's reign, also noted as a significant cultural leader in the Enlightenment

Godolphin, Sidney, first earl of, 1645–1712; holder of office in the treasury from Charles II's reign; served as Anne's lord treasurer

Marlborough, John Churchill, first duke of, 1650–1722; perhaps England's greatest general, leader of the allied armies in the War of the Spanish Succession

Mary II, 1662–94, queen of England, 1689–94; elder daughter of James II, wife of William III and able royal partner during their brief reign as England's only joint rulers, noted for her piety and support of the church

Oxford, Robert Harley, first earl of, 1661–1724; began the Tory reaction to Whig policies; secretary of state under Anne

Sacheverell, Henry, 1674?–1724; focal point of the Sacheverell Affair of 1709–10

Somers, John, Baron, 1651–1716; Whig leader who facilitated passage of the Bill of Rights and the Act of Union

William of Orange, Stadholder of the United Netherlands, 1650–1702, King William III of England, 1689–1702; central figure behind the Revolution of 1688, commander of the allied armies in the War of the League of Augsburg

CHRONOLOGY

1689	The Convention Parliament
	Bill of Rights
	Toleration Act
	Mutiny Act
1689–97	War of the League of Augsburg, concluded by the Treaty of Ryswick
1690	Battle of the Boyne (defeat of James II in Ireland)
1694	Triennial Act
	Bank of England established
	Death of Mary II
1701	Act of Settlement
1702	Death of William III
1702–13	War of the Spanish Succession, concluded by the Treaty of Utrecht
1707	Act of Union with Scotland
1709–10	Sacheverell Affair and Tory resurgence
1714	Death of Queen Anne

When William was our King declared,
*   To ease the nation's grievance,*
With this new wind about I steered,
*   And swore to him allegiance;*
Old principles I did revoke,
*   Set conscience at a distance;*
Passive obedience was a joke,
*   A jest was non-resistance.*

And this is law, that I'll maintain,
*   Until my dying day, sir,*
That whatsoever King shall reign,
*   I'll be the Vicar of Bray, sir.*

When gracious Anne became our Queen,
*   The Church of England's glory,*
Another face of things was seen,
*   And I became a Tory;*
Occasional Conformists base,
*   I damn'd their moderation,*
And thought the Church in danger was,
*   By such prevarication.*

And this is law, that I'll maintain,
*   Until my dying day, sir,*
That whatsoever King shall reign,
*   I'll be the Vicar of Bray, sir.*

One perplexed gentleman who had endured the political cyclones of 1688 "injoined his relations to bury him with his face downward, saying, that in a short time the world would be turned upside down, and then he should be the only person who lay decently in his grave. . . . there has been a considerable revolution."[1] But since no blood was spilled, and because the preponderance of opinion was favorable to the Prince of Orange, the Revolution of 1688 has been hailed as the Bloodless, the Respectable, the Great, the Happy, and most commonly, the Glorious, Revolution. The gains achieved fifty years earlier under rebellion's bloody banner were augmented peacefully

[1] "A Dialogue Between Two Friends," *Complete Collection of Papers Relating to the Great Revolutions in England* (London, 1689), ninth collection, p. 1.

after 1689 by the most extensive constitutional overhaul since Magna Carta. This·remarkably permanent revolution also brought England out of a self-imposed isolation dating from the early sixteenth century. The ensuing seven wars with France during the late seventeenth, eighteenth, and early nineteenth centuries have been alluded to as the second Hundred Years' War. England's victories were to yield her an unparalleled age of imperial and commercial prosperity. But during the grim months after the Prince of Orange's entrance into England, there was considerable fear for the future.

A Dual Monarchy

The legal king had disbanded his army, had thrown the great seal into the Thames, and in taking flight to France on December 23, 1688, had left the country without an executive authority. Virtually no government document was binding without the royal signature. The Prince of Orange summoned the members of Charles II's final parliament, and the day after Christmas it was decided that a new parliament was eminently necessary to the continuity of government. The Convention Parliament that resulted convened on January 22, 1689. It was composed of a unique diversity of Tories (Danby), Whigs (John Somers), Anglicans, and Nonconformists—and even a few republicans from pre-Restoration days. Upon one thing the entire body agreed—James should not be returned to the throne without constitutional restraints. The largest single group initially pushed for some form of regency over the ousted king, if and when he could be induced to return, most favoring his elder daughter, Mary, William's wife. Some saw Mary as queen in her own right. But the royal couple forced the issue by declaring that the prince would not accept consort status, and on February 13 the crown was jointly conferred on William III and Mary II, the only dual monarchy in England's history.

Parliament's decision by no means gladdened all factions. A regency, though it would have made a figurehead of James, would have avoided disrupting the legal succession. When this plan was decisively abandoned, James' adherents, many of whom ironically had taken the lead in halting his absolutism, gradually withdrew themselves from Parliament's tangled deliberations. They became the nucleus of the amorphous group known as the Jacobites (after *Jacobus*, Latin for James), a frustrated band of snobbish malcontents who offered little opposition to ˙William's rule beyond simple toasts "to the king" over bowls of water (representing the English Channel) and mutterings over growing taxes. A few of his more dedicated following left their homeland to share James' French exile, though he increasingly discouraged the loyalty of all but Catholics. The Scottish Jacobites, whose allegiance to the House of Stuart was a championing of their native dynastic head against the traditional English foe, gave James his most prolonged and hearty support. Even the Anglican Church split its loyalties. Some four hundred nonjuring ministers, headed by Sancroft, archbishop of Canterbury, refused to take the oaths of allegiance to William and Mary or to recite the traditional prayers for any but the former monarch. However, their rigid retention of passive obedience made them an innocuous opposition, though these nonjurors did make an attempt to erect a separate Anglican worship. To more active Jacobites and passive nonjurors alike, William's regime was no better than the piracy of a crown.

Those more readily transferring their loyalties to the new monarchs were confronted with the initial task of justifying their actions to a quiescent but skeptical populace. In presenting a Bill of Rights to Parliament, Lord John Somers sponsored the most Whiggish explanation—that James had broken a basic contract with his people when he set aside the law of the land to suit his policy. By the king's severing of the social contract, were not the people of England at liberty to select a new sovereign who would conform to the legal use of power? This interpretation was gradually embraced by republican writers and was to feed arguments for rebellion a century later during the American and French revolutions. Yet the revolutionary tactics of 1688, at all times under aristocratic management, scarcely constituted a people's revolt. Nor was the House of Lords about to encourage that concept, and the clause that embodied the social contract was voted down. A more conservative interpretation fostered by the church leaned on history. With consummate flattery it compared William's invasion with Henry VII's attack on Richard III in 1485. But the attempt at comparison was soon dropped, for the Tudor dynasty, though rich with the lore of Henry VIII's and Elizabeth's brilliant courts, had nonetheless been founded by the first Tudor's freebooting insurrection. On second thought it seemed unwise to compare William III to a usurper.

The Revolution Settlement

At last, on February 12, 1689, the Bill of Rights, containing a clause so noncommittal in wording as to offend hardly anyone, was presented to Parliament: "King James having abdicated the government, and the throne being thereby vacant, . . . the Lords spiritual and temporal and Commons assembled at Westminster do resolve that William and Mary, Prince and Princess of Orange . . . be declared King and Queen of England." Few critics outside the Jacobite camp cared to delve carefully into whatever was meant by "abdicated," though most could agree that the throne was in fact vacant. William and Mary were simply declared to be the new rulers, which nicely avoided these highly debatable propositions. Nevertheless, that their legitimate right to the throne was embodied in a parliamentary statute has caused constitutionalists since 1689 to assume that Parliament thereby received a peremptory right to name, if not to create, new monarchs.

The Bill of Rights' more radical clauses narrowed monarchical authority. The privileged dispensing and suspending powers claimed by James II, who high-handedly dispensed with the law in some instances or occasionally suspended laws altogether, were abolished. In a repetition of abortive earlier attempts, Parliament gained the sole right to levy taxes, standing armies were again outlawed except under parliamentary authorization, elections were freed from royal interference, and civil liberties and due process were to be rigidly observed. Additionally, no future English monarch could deviate from Protestantism or marry a Catholic, and should he convert after his succession, he was to be considered deceased, his heir succeeding him immediately. To assure his Protestantism, the king must subscribe to the Test Act at his coronation. With this final requirement Parliament sought to subject England's future monarchs to the laws they swore to uphold.

The Convention Parliament completed its work by passing two other basic statutes: the Toleration and the Mutiny acts. Throughout the final months of James' reign, harried Anglicans had made vague promises of early toleration to Nonconformists if they would support resistance to James' Catholic infiltration of the Anglican Church. Now the time for reckoning had come. Two measures were initially introduced: the first, a Comprehension Bill; the second, granting toleration. Comprehension could have "comprehended" about two-thirds of the Nonconformist minority into the fold through a liberalization of Anglican ritual and organization. This generous offer was the last effort of the Anglican Church to widen its membership so that it might more truthfully be called a national church rather than a government-sponsored denomination. But the "high-flying" churchmen, as the conservative Anglicans were called, would not cater to the Presbyterian belief in congregational policy making if it meant undermining the traditional supremacy of Anglican bishops. Comprehension therefore was unacceptable.

The Toleration Act immediately became the alternative, passing handily in 1689. Nonconformist ministers, if they declared belief in the trinity, swore fidelity to the crown, and kept their church doors unlocked, could be licensed to hold services by the local Anglican bishop. As demeaning as this now appears, it did present a more liberal approach to freedom of thought and the right to express that thought. There was even an abortive attempt to grant to Nonconformists the right to hold office despite the Test Act. Though this measure was unsuccessful, the Convention Parliament evinced a magnanimity not displayed by an English legislature again for a hundred years.

The Mutiny Act of 1689 decisively settled the persistent problem of standing armies in a most direct and imaginative way. Though Parliament could not take from the king the ancient feudal power of levying troops, it could make military discipline by courts martial subject to statute law. After the act's passage in March of 1689, it was theoretically possible for the king to issue a command that the soldiers might disobey if the Mutiny Act regulating soldierly obedience had run out—and Parliament's enactment was initially effective for only six months. To this day, the law is rarely extended beyond a year at a time. Thus an ambitious monarch, prompted to dispense with Parliament or to overawe his subjects with a display of military force, might well find himself with an unruly mob for an army, if any army at all. He must risk convening Parliament for the sake of reinstating the Mutiny Act. True, no monarch was ever lured into matching wits with his legislature over the statute, and there were times when Parliament allowed it to lapse without incident. Nonetheless, the act is regarded as one of the surest dissuasions to depriving the nation of a parliament for any length of time.

Throughout this period of rigorous law enactment, there was still no regularization of parliamentary elections, despite the passage of two Triennial Acts since 1640 ordering that Commons be freshly chosen every third year. There was reason for concern. Charles II had kept his Cavalier Parliament for eighteen years; James II had called only one parliament, and that he had rendered powerless. Now there were misgivings that even good King William, obviously agitated with pettifogging English politicians, might make do with as few sessions as possible. He had vetoed a Triennial Bill in 1693. In 1694, however, forced by the need to finance his mounting expenses for the French War, he was compelled to indulge Parliament and assent to what became the third Triennial Act of the century. Its simple requirement, that writs calling for elections every three years be sent automatically to election officials, placed the matter finally beyond royal equivocation.

The four major pieces of legislation—the Bill of Rights and the Toleration, Mutiny, and Triennial acts—which comprised the Revolution Settlement, were rounded out with a fifth statute, the Act of Settlement of 1701. By that date it seemed clear that William would not produce an heir. Twelve years before, the Bill of Rights had covered this exigency by transmitting the succession to Mary II's sister and her children. But by 1701 Anne had reached her forties, and her son, the duke of Gloucester, had died. When the exiled James II died that year, his son, the "Old Pretender" (James Edward Stuart of the warming-pan tale), was hailed by the Jacobites as James III. But he was hardly acceptable to the nation. Though the Bill of Rights had eliminated any Catholic monarch, James III or otherwise, the Protestant succession was doubly assured by naming Sophia of Hanover as Anne's successor in the Act of Settlement. The German granddaughter of James I, a Stuart by blood, she was suitably Protestant and desperately wished to be queen of England. The act also forbade monarchs succeeding Anne to leave the country without Parliament's consent, decreed that they must embrace the Anglican Church, excluded foreigners from state positions, and prohibited the dismissal of judges at royal pleasure. Even now, this freeing of judges from the pressures of returning verdicts favorable to the crown is the only element of separation of power to be found in the English governmental system. Since 1714, when the act was finally put into practice, English judges have enjoyed tenurial independence based solely on personal performance.

The War of the League of Augsburg

Safeguarding this monumental Revolution Settlement was an uneasy task in William's reign. Not only had the French given succor to James II by turning the palace of St. Germain over to him, but they also disavowed William and Mary's government. In retaliation for these slights England declared war in May 1689. Actually, the new king of England's greater objective was to maneuver his recently acquired subjects into the larger War of the League of Augsburg, which had preceded England's declaration against France by half a year (November 1688). The league, of which he had been the leading architect, consisted of the German emperor, Brandenburg, Saxony, Bavaria, Spain, and the Netherlands. The prospect of attacking French merchant shipping in concert with the mighty Dutch fleet lured England into signing the alliance papers in September of 1689.

This war with France lasted eight years. In the first four years James II's efforts to achieve his restoration were decisively thwarted. The former monarch made his first move in March 1689, landing in Ireland with 8,000 troops. His army, swelled by thousands of Irish Catholics, was barely contained for over a year by a garrison of only 10,000 English. William's arrival in June 1690, with an additional 35,000 soldiers, ended the Jacobite threat. On July 1, James' hold on Ireland was shattered at the Battle of the Boyne River. Though William magnanimously extended amnesty to the rebels in the resulting Treaty of Limerick, the haughty English officials remaining after his departure in September of 1690 felt no compulsion to keep faith with the "barbaric" Irish. The following twenty years of anti-Catholic acts divested Ireland's majority of the right to hold office, buy land, or educate their children, while the Protestant minority enveloped the country's wealth and power. The Protestant "Orange" to this day celebrate the battle, while Irish Catholics mourn it as a calamity.

The Boyne was James' cue to flee the British Isles forever. His real defeat was his despair, for the preceding day the French had won control of the English Channel in the Battle of Beachy Head, the only time in modern history that England was to suffer this indignity. When at last Louis mustered sufficient troops, England, braced for an invasion, had recovered from the debacle. Parliament had poured over half a million pounds into the outfitting of an additional twenty-seven ships. In May 1692 a combined Anglo-Dutch flotilla of nearly one hundred vessels scattered the forty-four ship French fleet at La Hogue, ending France's two-year control of the Channel. James, who was to have sailed with the invasion army, watched from the shore as his hopes sank with the shattered transports.

The victor of the Irish campaign and the redeemer of the Channel found stiffer going in the next phase of the war. Despite a striking arm of over 90,000 troops, the offensive that William mounted in Flanders effected little more than a holding action. A third of his forces were killed or captured at the Battle of Neerwinden in 1693. In 1695, at Namur, his only gain was the retaking of a fortress lost three years earlier. Both sides, nearing exhaustion, were now ready to parley. Negotiations at one of William's country homes in Ryswick, Netherlands, resulted in the Treaty of Ryswick (1697), concluding England's most ambitious foreign enterprise in 250 years. Though favoring the Netherlands more than William's adopted country, the treaty at least forced Louis' recognition of the king of England's legitimate rule. The conflict had proved the country's ability not only to withstand, but also to contain, the mighty French empire—a feat comparable to David's encounter with Goliath.

A Growing Debt Made Public

Of equal astonishment was the government's capacity to enlarge its taxable wealth while creaking and groaning under eight years of wartime's financial outlays. Besides the loss in men and munitions, £3 million of merchant shipping had been sunk in France's efforts to destroy England's trade. Yet the nation's surplus yielded nearly £5 million annually, totaling £40 million spent throughout the war, an amount that would have run Charles II's less complex kingdom for almost forty years. Formerly untapped sources of taxation accounted for much of this amount. The new poll tax (forerunner of the income tax) and land tax brought in a third more than had been gleaned by past customs and excises.

This monetary success was offset by a debt of more than £2 million, inherited from James' reign and carried on the books until as late as 1704. To compound the fiscal problem, regularly anticipated taxes failed to find their way into the treasury the same year they were levied by Parliament; they customarily trickled in in bits at the collectors' convenience. The government had no means to determine whether its full assessment had been met, for with the exception of customs and excises, which had been assigned to crown agents in Charles II's reign, most taxes were farmed out to licensed tax gatherers. These officers withdrew their fees from the moneys they collected. Needless to say, their withholdings were exorbitant. Some even made short-term loans, sending the public proceeds on to Westminster only after interest had yielded a fat profit.

The desperate monetary needs during the gargantuan war with France could hardly be met by funds that might not be in government coffers until hostilities ended. Therefore the government took loans for ready cash in the amount of anticipated tax returns, sometimes having to surrender as much as 14 percent interest to the hard-to-find lenders. In 1694 the government resorted to a lottery to induce more investors to loosen their purse strings. The lending public, considering the irresponsible fiscal record of previous reigns, was understandably loath to make loans to the crown. After all, in 1642 Charles I had seized the mint, and in 1672 Charles II had arbitrarily stopped all payments from the exchequer. Aggravating the problem facing William's government was a suspicion, shared even by a few leaders, that the revolutionary regime might not endure. Obviously a solid guarantee for repayment of borrowed funds had to be offered. In 1694 a band of London financiers supplied the confidence in the king's policies by establishing, under royal charter, the Bank of England, which raised £1.2 million by selling annuities to some 1,300 shareholders. The money, loaned to the government at 8 percent interest, was guaranteed by nothing less than a statute, the Tonnage Act of 1694. This earmarked import duties solely for repayment to shareholders and explicitly prohibited their use for any other purpose. The scheme was an immediate success and, together with an improved coinage, quickly convinced William's subjects that their sovereign intended to honor his financial obligations. They read the monarch correctly—in one of his final pronouncements he urged that the House of Commons "take care of the public credit." The government's sound fiscal priorities created a happy alliance between merchants, shop-keepers, bankers, and crown; and the allurement of assured returns caused the middle class to take a more positive concern for the success of the revolutionary government.

The Revolution Settlement, the War of the League of Augsburg, and the involvement of the public in the government's indebtedness were gigantic enterprises bound to hold political consequences. The numbers of those in court politics alone more than doubled. Policies were no longer monopolized by supereminent individuals—a Strafford, a Clarendon, or a Danby—for William's multitudinous needs forced him into communication with all quarters. Nor were politicians now simply court figures. They were men whose business acumen made them useful in advisory and administrative capacities, men whose professional approach to public life easily eclipsed the older courtly dilettantism.

Early in his reign, William, striving to rule with as broad a base as circumstances allowed, included both parties in his cabinets. Consequently, the Tory Danby was installed as president of the Council, and in 1693 even the architect of James II's absolutism, Robert Spencer, earl of Sunderland, was pressed into service. It was hoped that he might bring his conservative friends into the fold. Sunderland, more professional than partisan, concurred with a common view that William should drop the Tories because "whenever the government has leaned to the Whigs, it has been strong; whenever the other has prevailed, it has been despised."[2] Among the Whig appointees were the lawyer Lord Chancellor John Somers, the defender of the Seven Bishops and shaper of the Revolution Settlement, and Charles Montagu, the financial wizard whose genius engineered the founding of the Bank of England. With such diverse representation the king's magnanimous aim to conciliate everyone was unrealistic.

The Tories, powerful under Charles and James, increasingly found their strength diluted, especially after 1693, when William ended his three-year experiment in placation and resolved to place his confidence in the Whigs. It is ironic that the preeminently royalist Tories, holding the opposition to be rank republicans, were pushed into an antiroyal position. When in 1694, with the death of Mary, the Tories found their support at court ebbing, they began to oppose the crown's policies. Many Tories suspected that the burdensome land taxes were filling Dutch pockets now that the threat of invasion was past. They sponsored a bill, aimed at William's Dutch appointees, to limit the king's admiralty assignments. To cut his patronage, another bill tried to exclude "placemen," those hundred-odd officials who by virtue of office sat in Parliament. The loyal Danby was again impeached, ostensibly for bribery, but more truly because his Tory colleagues felt he was selling them out. From 1695 through 1698 the resulting enmity encouraged royal cultivation of commercially connected Whigs. Tirades were printed against the charter of the new Bank of England, but the rival Tory-sponsored Land Bank failed in its challenge. Though animosity temporarily diminished in 1696 with the exposure of the Turnham Green Plot (William was to be assassinated on his way home from a hunting party), the Tories had difficulty containing their delight when the leader of the plot, Sir John Fenwick, falsely implicated highly placed court Whigs.

William's most serious contest with the Tories occurred during the tenuous

[2] Clayton Roberts, *The Growth of Responsible Government in Stuart England* (Cambridge, 1966), p. 269.

peace following the Treaty of Ryswick in 1697. Reasoning that hostilities with the recent enemy were not forever concluded, he urged that the army be kept at wartime strength. But Commons reduced the ranks from 87,000 to a paltry 8,000, allowed the Mutiny Act to lapse, and insultingly ordered the king's favorite Dutch guards disbanded. The "impertinences" imposed upon him caused William to contemplate moving from England altogether, and in 1698 he spent five months sulking in his native Netherlands.

The War of the Spanish Succession

The impasse was resolved by 1702, when a new European crisis, prompted by France's renewed ambitions, again galvanized the fragmented English. At issue was France's breach of the Partition Treaty of 1700, in which she had agreed to cooperate with Austria in dividing the sprawling Spanish empire on the death of its ruling monarch, Charles II. The treaty was meant to prevent France or Austria from eclipsing all of Europe by apportioning the Spanish holdings (in the Netherlands, Milan, Naples, Sardinia, the New World) between them. Spain's moribund monarch (who held the dubious distinction of having become senile at the age of thirty-nine), was without direct heirs. Both the Bourbons of France and the Hapsburgs of Austria possessed excellent blood claims through collateral family branches. For two years William held Louis XIV to the agreed compromise by threat. Before Charles II died in October 1700, he attempted to preserve the Spanish empire intact by bequeathing the whole of it to Louis' grandson, Philip. The expectations of trade and the possible unification of Spain and France were far more tempting to Louis than the meager Italian portion he would have gained under the terms of the Partition Treaty. Within a month Philip became Philip V of Spain, and Europe edged into the War of the Spanish Succession.

As in 1689, William had to convince his subjects that the Continental conflagration was an English concern. The Tories, again resisting war, talked of impeaching the ministers who had supported the Partition Treaty. The Whigs, once more favoring William's stand, cheered on a group of Kentish petitioners who marched on London to urge Parliament to back the king unstintingly. Then, in September 1701, the exiled James II died and Louis presumptuously recognized James' son as true king of England. The elections held that November reflected a momentary loyalty, stirred by the French attempt to determine the English succession, and a solid Whig majority was returned to Parliament.

Throughout the autumn of 1701 England made rapid arrangements to join the Grand Alliance (the Netherlands and the Holy Roman Empire's congeries of German states) in its efforts against France and Spain. An army of 80,000 was hurriedly pulled together. But while the administrative mechanisms that had so successfully managed the War of the League of Augsburg were being dusted off, the man largely responsible for pushing England into its international role was losing strength. William, who had nearly been killed off by smallpox, who had been wounded twice in battle, and who had survived numerous plots against his life, broke his collarbone when his horse stumbled in a molehill. Medical complications caused his death two weeks later, on March 8, 1702.

The Jacobites now had a new toast—to "the little gentleman in black velvet," the assassin mole. But England was not to be undone by this trifling toast either. Jacobite hopes for confusion necessitating the recall of the Stuarts never materialized, and the Bill of Rights' provisions for James II's younger daughter, Anne, to become queen of England were peacefully executed. The army William had commanded with consummate skill had already been turned over to a new commander-in-chief, John Churchill, duke of Marlborough; the treasury was in the capable hands of Sidney Godolphin; and the House of Commons was under the speakership of the wily Robert Harley. With Queen Anne's blessing, these three outstanding leaders were to form a powerful triumvirate.

So long as victory followed victory, as happened from the time of England's entrance in the war in 1702 to 1710, few questioned the wisdom of the War of the Spanish Succession. Those who did criticize did so on the basis of tactics and taxes, wanting the war to pay for itself through the plundering of the Spanish Main, a war which would be confined consequently to the seas and in which the navy would seldom stray from protecting England's coastal trade. But the new commander-in-chief's sweeping vision of the European scene gave him a grasp of strategy that entitles him to his reputation as England's greatest general. First Marlborough placed both the military and the diplomatic offices under his personal direction; then he authoritatively demanded (and most often received) recognition as supreme commander over the various contingents from the Netherlands and Germany; finally, he revised the customarily narrow tactical approach—desultory dismembering of remote garrisons—by pushing for an ultimate invasion of the enemy's heartland. These brilliant innovations, united command and unlimited offensives, brought England victory upon victory. Oddly, they were not again utilized by English commanders until World War I and not fully employed until World War II.

During the first two years of the war, the Great Alliance was engaged in encircling France. Sir George Rooke sailed south in July 1702, intending to take the famed Spanish target that Drake and Essex had assaulted so effectively in Elizabeth's reign, the city of Cadiz near the mouth of the Mediterranean.

Though he failed in this, he did seize a gold fleet that October at Vigo Bay (which also yielded so much snuff that it became a universal habit in England). However unsuccessful, the expedition pointed up the need to complete the encirclement of France by control of not only the Strait of Gibraltar, but the western Mediterranean as well. The great Rock of Gibraltar was taken by Sir Cloudesley Shovell in 1704, and four years later the second objective was realized when the fleet captured the Spanish island of Minorca.

In 1703 the diplomatic front profited by the defection from France of two of her prominent allies, Savoy and Portugal. With the first she lost her chance to hold Italy, while the second gave the Grand Alliance a base for the invasion of Spain itself. The Portuguese–English entente was bolstered by a trade agreement, the Methuen Treaty, whereby each country gave favored treatment to the other's exports, the English clothing the Portuguese with their wool, the Portuguese warming English stomachs with their port wine. Future application of this "most favored nation" principle was profoundly effective in luring countries into a friendly association with England. English drinking habits were changed by the treaty, for the cheap port replaced banned French wines, even native English beers, as the domestic beverage. Tories registered their disapproval of this wartime commercialism by smuggling in French claret, much of it through Scotland, which had passed a special wine act to emphasize its independence from English control. Thus a guest could discern a household as Whig or Tory by the wine served.

England and Scotland: Unification

The Wine Act was only one defiance in a continuing rift between Scots and English. While Scotland was England's unwilling ally in the war, their only common bond, dating from 1603, was the sharing of a single monarch. Administratively the two kingdoms had forever been separate. Underscoring the national rancor, Scotland's parliament passed a bill preventing future monarchs from involving the country in hostilities unless its legislative body acquiesced. In 1704 the Security Act—declaring that with the demise of Queen Anne, Scotland's Parliament would thereafter exercise the right to choose its own sovereign—was passed into law. The Scottish militia was called to arms; three English seamen were executed on minor charges in Edinburgh. Yet amid this violence English Whigs reached the high point of their domestic policy when the rival governments quietly and effectively formed a commission to formulate a treaty, from which came the Act of Union uniting the kingdoms.

There is no doubt that the discordant neighbors rushed into unification in order to further special interests: Scottish merchants relished free trade with

England and her colonies and the English ministry could not afford a northern war while her armies were engaged on the Continent. Whatever the cause, the Act of Union was a rare international consolidation, achieved without bloodshed. Considering that the English had subdued Wales by literally chopping down the forest cover protecting its rebels and then erecting a line of castle strongholds to hold them in check, and had shackled the Irish with puppet governments, absentee landlords, and occasional annihilations, this union displayed an extraordinarily civilized approach to absorption. The Scottish parliament was even granted a priority to debate the recommendations of the joint commission. It passed its version of the Act of Union in January of 1707, and the English legislature liberally accepted virtually all its requirements for confederation. From that first of May the Scots sent forty-five members to the English Commons and sixteen peers to the House of Lords. Additionally, they retained their ancient laws and courts (to the present English barristers must be familiar with two sets of laws if they are to plead north of the border). Presbyterianism remained Scotland's national religion; her merchants gained free trade within the English system; she was exempt from the war taxes currently burdening Englishmen. The union abolished the ancient names, "England" and "Scotland," (which are now properly only geographical), substituting "the United Kingdom of Great Britain," the official designation to this day.

During these events the war on the Continent was proceeding favorably for the allies. Marlborough had busied himself consolidating the fortresses along the entire defensive line of Flanders on the Dutch–French border. Suddenly, in 1704, France had opened her major offensive, a direct assault on the Hapsburg capital of Vienna. By a series of swift and secret dispatches, the duke managed to convince the Dutch war commissioner and the head of the English treasury, Sidney Godolphin, that the defense of their countries began at Vienna's gates. But because even the war's most ardent advocates at home could not back such a notion, Marlborough was directed by the vaguest of orders that on departing from his Dutch base, he confine his advance to the Moselle River in eastern France. He ignored these directives, marching to the Danube with an Anglo-Dutch expedition of 19,000. There his forces joined with the beleaguered German-Austrian army under Prince Eugene of Savoy; and the mastery of Europe was decided during the first two weeks of August 1704, in a series of engagements culminating in the Battle of Blenheim. There Marlborough hurled his cavalry against the village. By nightfall of the thirteenth there were three French generals occupying his coach, well treated, but prisoners nonetheless. Of the 54,000 French troops, 13,000 were captured and 23,000 were casualties. Not until a hundred years later, under Napoleon, would the French again muster the strength to strike beyond their Rhine

frontiers. The results at Blenheim exonerated Marlborough's obvious dis-
obedience—a country does not chastise its heroes. Even the Tories bit their
tongues.

But after this victory it was the duke's fate to be harnessed by timid policies,
by those who feared less gratifying results the next time he exceeded his orders.
Despite his skillful victories at Ramillies in 1706, Oudenarde in 1708, and
Malplaquet in 1709 in "the cockpit of Europe" (the frontier between the
Netherlands and France noted for the scores of decisive battles it witnessed
over a thousand years), Marlborough was forced into older tactics, fighting
a war of attrition instead of invasion, a war of limited goals and offenses. He
was never allowed to march on Paris. By 1710 his enemies at home were
demanding termination of the war on the reasonable grounds that Louis XIV
was begging terms. But the duke's policy of attrition had indeed worked—
the French had been forced out of Italy and the Low Countries and by 1706
had lost half of Spain, including Madrid. In addition to these debilitating military defeats, by 1709 France was internally racked by starvation and economic collapse. She would have sued for peace, but the allies foolishly insisted on
crushing terms, requiring Louis not only to disavow his grandson, Philip V's,
claim to the Spanish throne, but also to use his own forces to dislodge him if
necessary. The exhausted monarch refused to betray his family, and the war
lumbered on, with the apparent objective of the utter destruction of the Sun
King's empire.

The Resurgence of the Tories

Yet in a series of startling events, by 1713 England left the war,
deserting her allies, and Marlborough had been dismissed. Her hard-earned
gains in Spain were retaken by the French, and the Dutch and Austrians under
Prince Eugene were defeated at the Battle of Denain in July 1712. These
reversals vie with a no less remarkable political counterrevolution in England,
for it was largely the resurgence of the Tories that caused the country to pull
out of a war it was winning.

The Tory party had never accepted the war. Nottingham, secretary of state
from 1702 to 1704, maintained that it was fought purely to protect Dutch
interests. Anne's uncle the earl of Rochester despised William, as did most
Tory members in the cabinet and Parliament, and held the king responsible
for both the wars of Augsburg and the Spanish Succession. Although Robert
Harley, the moderate member of the triumvirate, saw as speaker of the House
that sufficient money was voted for the hostilities, he could not prevent his
party from earmarking twice as much for the navy as for Marlborough's
army. This Tory move championing Admiral George Rooke at the expense

of Marlborough was an attempt to dim the duke's Blenheim victory because of his defection from the party.

During the early years of the war, the personal friendship of Marlborough's influential wife Sarah and of the duke himself with Queen Anne was largely responsible for enabling Whigs to maintain key positions despite Tory opposition. In 1708, however, the Whig–Tory balance was toppled by a rift in the triumvirate. Its two Whig members, Marlborough and Godolphin, were contending that their party, dominated as it was by commercial interests, could best provide the steady support and financial power needed for the war. It followed that the Whigs stood to benefit most from war contracts and from the trade concessions that might be wrung from the dismantled French and Spanish trade empires. Harley, resenting these engrossments, with the queen's support moved to take Godolphin's place in the treasury. Marlborough and Godolphin blocked him with a threat that they would both resign and take most of the cabinet with them. Hamstrung by these political turns, there was nothing for Anne to do but to accept Harley's gentlemanly resignation. The Marlborough–Godolphin junto returned to office with a Whig-packed ministry dedicated to the war. But their victory at the polls in May 1708 drove the thoroughly disillusioned queen irrevocably into the Tory camp. The Whigs further offended Anne by asking her ailing husband to resign from the admiralty. Though for the moment she could vent her spleen by doing little beyond excluding Lady Marlborough from her household and surrounding herself with Harley's friends, the Whigs' final reckoning was only months away.

The reconstituted palace brought to the queen's ears all the Tory rumors and mutterings: that she was a political and financial prisoner of the Whigs; that the war for the preservation of the Glorious Revolution and the Protestant succession had degenerated into "Marlborough's war," through which he was pilfering a private fortune from public funds. How else to explain why the struggle was going into its eighth year without an end in sight? Why else had the Whigs rejected Louis XIV's peace overtures? Why, while merchants were paying trivial nuisance taxes on malt, windows, and coal, were land taxes the highest of wartime assessments? By this juncture a vast number of Englishmen, not necessarily in the opposition party, were questioning whether the revolution had not precipitated endless war. The Stuarts had, after all, kept England in relative peace, even in plenty—but now the doorways of London were filled with maimed veterans with tin cups. The gloom was heightened by the bitter damp seasons of 1708–9, which ruined harvests, driving grain prices to one of the highest peaks of the century.

Just as at the end of Charles II's reign when the accumulation of resentments burst into mass recriminations through acceptance of the rabble-rousing Titus

Oates' malicious Popish Plot, so now dissatisfaction with Whig policy found voice in the denunciatory sermons of the conservative Dr. Henry Sacheverell. Like Oates, Sacheverell was a powerful and eloquent speaker (though he possessed a high-mindedness not found in the former); and as the Whigs had used the Popish Plot, so now the Tories advanced against their political adversaries behind the popularity of Sacheverell's incitements.

On November 5, 1709, the anniversary of William of Orange's landing in England, Dr. Sacheverell preached in a sermon before the lord mayor of London that the Glorious Revolution was little better than a usurpation, that Nonconformists were irreverently dismantling the Church of England, and that Whigs were no more than thinly disguised republicans. Ordinarily such utterances would have been ignored as typical high-church grouchings. But the Marlborough–Godolphin junto foolishly overreacted, accusing the learned doctor of seditious libel. In the furor raised by the arrest of the popular hero, frenzied mobs burned Nonconformist homes and chapels.

Harley suggested to Anne that the propitious moment for freeing herself from the Whig ministry had at last arrived. Throughout 1710 she gradually exchanged one after another of her Whig cabinet members for Tories; Godolphin was finally removed in August and replaced by Harley, who was quickly elevated to an earldom (Oxford). The Whigs in Parliament, though they found Sacheverell guilty of libel, in the face of public demand prudently meted out a light sentence, a three-year suspension from his religious duties. Even this slap on the wrist was swiftly rescinded by the queen. When a new parliament was summoned, a swelling pro-Tory wave swept the Whigs from Commons. The session of 1710–11 witnessed recriminatory acts designed to deny Whigs parliamentary seats, to break the Bank of England's monopoly by setting up a rival structure to manage the debt (the South Sea Company), even to imprison the former Whig war secretary, Robert Walpole (England's future prime minister), on charges of corruption.

The genius behind this Tory resurgence was not Harley's, however, for his continuing connections with Whigs, his honest desire to reestablish a broad coalition, his failing health, and his hard drinking dissatisfied the militants' expectations of leadership. It was Henry St. John, made Viscount Bolingbroke in 1712, who assumed that role by his earnest plea "to break the body of the Whigs, to render their supports useless to them, to fill the employments of the kingdom down to the meanest with Tories."[3] A member of the notorious October Club (which worked closely with the Jacobites and was dedicated to ending the war and to bridling the Nonconformists), the imperious Bolingbroke, with Queen Anne's good wishes, as secretary of state conducted a series of negotiations with the French. An accusation of embezzlement made it

[3] Quoted in Derek Jarrett, *Britain, 1688–1815* (New York, 1965), p. 144.

possible to replace Marlborough with a Tory general who was ordered not to engage the enemy. Peace terms were submitted to Commons and immediately approved. To push these terms through the upper house, which was still Whig-dominated, Anne stacked the deck by creating twelve new Tory lords. With this strong domestic backing, Bolingbroke rapidly concluded the Treaty of Utrecht in 1713, gaining the gratitude of the war-weary English as well as of the exhausted French, who were still battling the Dutch and the Austrians.

By the treaty England was ceded Gibraltar, Minorca, Nova Scotia, and Newfoundland. A clause, the *asiento* contract, bestowed on England the sole right to sell slaves to the Spanish colonies and to send one ship annually to trade in the West Indies. Louis XIV recognized Queen Anne and the Act of Settlement guaranteeing the Protestant succession. The cause of the war, Philip's inheritance of the Spanish throne, was resolved by an allowance that he remain king of Spain but that the French and Spanish nations never unite under a single monarch. Although its terms were generous to England, the Treaty of Utrecht had been achieved by royal interference with standard parliamentary procedure, which reeked of the Stuart high-handedness of the previous century. The country's desertion of her allies with Marlborough's withdrawal from the Continent in 1712 merited the name "Perfidious Albion" in diplomatic circles. More than a hundred years elapsed before England, the treacherous country that dishonored obligations, lived down the demeaning nickname.

The Hanoverian Succession

Nonconformists fared badly under Bolingbroke. His assiduous assaults on them resulted in the Occasional Conformity Act of 1711. Despite compliance with the Test Act by the taking of the Anglican sacrament once a year, they were deprived of office if they then continued to worship in their own chapels. Three years after the Occasional Conformity Act, Nonconformist schools were assailed by the Schism Act, which forced their teachers to worship in the Anglican Church. This last absurd requirement was aimed at wiping out the burgeoning Nonconformist educational complex.

Until 1713 the aristocratic Bolingbroke had things much his way. But his success depended on the queen's favor, and when Anne fell desperately ill in the autumn of that year the specter of the Hanoverian succession loomed like a personal judgment. The elector of Hanover, George, who had become Anne's successor in the Act of Settlement when Sophia of Hanover died, naturally despised the Tories for pulling England out of the alliance against France during the War of the Spanish Succession. Should he become king, charges of treason against both Harley and Bolingbroke could be expected.

Frantically the doomed pair attempted to swing England behind an improbable Stuart restoration. In February 1714 the Old Pretender, James Edward Stuart, James III to the Jacobites, was assured that if he renounced Catholicism and entered the Church of England, both Anne and Parliament would favor him over Germany's George. The twenty-four-year-old pretender's curt refusal chilled the ebullient Tories. Bolingbroke, in an excess of immoderation, pursued a self-seeking course. The queen's health declined markedly in July 1714, and he easily imposed upon the ailing monarch a promise to dismiss Harley as lord of the treasury. He saw himself in that premier cabinet post issuing orders acclaiming James king of England on Anne's death. But before the queen expired in August, she entrusted the treasury, not to Bolingbroke, but to the little-known and little-understood duke of Shrewsbury. Shrewsbury threw the weight of his office completely on the side of the Hanoverian succession.

The outfoxed Bolingbroke, who complained to his illustrious friend Jonathan Swift that "fortune turned rotten at the very moment it grew ripe,"[4] had no choice but to declare for the first Hanoverian king, George I, with the majority of the Privy Council. The elector of Hanover, arriving in England in September of 1714, on consideration of Bolingbroke's past performance, issued orders for the confiscation of his papers. As writs for his trial appeared, the jinxed Tory judiciously fled to Paris. There he publicly avowed his allegiance to James III. For Harley the bitter medicine of dismissal and a two-year residence in the Tower followed; Marlborough was reinstated as commander of the army, but at sixty-four was too worn to reenter the political arena; Godolphin was denied the pleasure of the Whig triumph by his death in 1712. With all the leading actors, Whig and Tory, of the Stuart era gone from the stage, the Hanoverian dynasty was to require a fresh cast for the nation's new royal director.

[4] Quoted in G. M. Trevelyan, *England Under the Stuarts* (London, 1949), p. 428.

Part Two

THE EPOCH OF THE MERCHANT PRINCE AND THE INDUSTRIAL PIONEER

Chapter Seven
THE DAWN OF INDUSTRIAL ENGLAND

Soon shall thy arm, unconquer'd steam! afar
Drag the slow barge, or drive the rapid car;
Or on wide-waving wings expanded bear
The flying-chariot through the fields of air.
Fair crews triumphant, leaning from above,
Shall wave their fluttering kerchiefs as they move;
Or warrior-bands alarm the gaping crowd,
And armies shrink beneath the shadowy cloud.

ERASMUS DARWIN
The Botanic Garden, 1792

It used to be said that the Industrial Revolution arrived in England in 1760 as certainly as Columbus came to America in 1492. Just as the Spanish hordes after Columbus toppled the mystic Aztec shrines, bled the native Incas of gold and silver and enslaved their people, so supposedly did inventors, technicians, and capitalists convert pastoral England into shabby, soot-smirched slums. Current historians view the arrival of industrialization more broadly and less grimly. Some revise the inaugural date backward to 1740, 1660, and 1540; others, forward to 1780 and 1850. Most scholars now agree, however, that the factory system evolved slowly over all these decades. At some point midway between the extremes of 1540 and 1850, perhaps around 1700, the preconditions of industrial organization had emerged.

From Market Town to Mill Town

The human ecological changes within the market town may best explain how industrial transformation overtook agrarian England after 1700. The market town, immemorial redistribution center of the district's rural foodstuffs and crafts, might suddenly find that its proximity to a water-fall was especially attractive to a local mill owner. Perhaps this mill owner had purchased or invented a new mechanized process for making his product, which had been turned out for years by local domestic pieceworkers. Now his mill, using water power, employed these same pieceworkers and produced the identical product under totally supervised conditions.

It was at this point that the market town evolved into a mill town. At first the change was barely noticeable, for the townsmen continued to depend on the rural environs for their food and livelihood. Only a few hands worked regularly at the mill, and then in tasks they had formerly performed in their homes. The old congeniality still persisted. Other domestic workers saw no threat, and the mill owner, as before, drew his raw materials from the country-side.

After 1780, if the town had proximity to improved roads or canals or if some particular mineral such as coal or iron abounded, the small mill might suddenly convert to a factory. It might take nothing more than increased sales to turn the mill town into a factory town. The purchase of a steam engine, allowing the plant to expand anywhere across the countryside, might spark a rapid trans-formation of the area and life style. At some point the mill adopted the trap-pings of the factory system—an impersonal management, an imported labor force, raw materials and sales outlets located far beyond the area, capital drawn from London or even the Continent—and the mutual reliance between market town and mill died forever. In fact, the eighteenth-century factory became insensitive to the needs of both town and adjacent country.

The number and types of buildings that sprang up in the old market towns are descriptive of the factory system itself. By 1800 a son returning to his market-town home after a thirty-year absence would have been amazed at the changes. The trip itself would have differed in that he would probably have arrived on one of the new coach systems traversing the improved turnpikes. The center of town would have abandoned its rural character. There would now be a bank, likely in the neoclassic style of a Roman temple. This stolid reposi-tory of the factory owner's capital stood in mute testimony of the town's new monetary god. The high street, once lined with the open shops, shambles, and pentices frequented during market days by farmhands and rural craftsmen, would now feature fashionable shops, a theater, a library, and clubs catering to the factory managers' families, whose tastes were imported from London, possibly even from Paris. Once off the high street, some of the old town would be seen to have fallen to slums and warehouses, with a few workers' clubs and a union hall. Outside the walls that had once jealously guarded the boundaries of the incorporated town, layer on layer of workers' housing would have enveloped the area in a sea of roofs and chimney pots. On a secluded and picturesque hillside, the factory owner's mansion, surrounded by the sump-tuous homes of his managers, would now dominate the landscape. The most obvious departure from the rural character would be the great gray-block structure of the factory itself. Less easy for the eye to discern, the market town's homogeneity would have disappeared as a result of the specialized needs of its industry and the class barriers the industry erected.

The market town transformation was most noticeable in a band stretching from central west to northeastern England, from southern Wales into York-shire. The south, except for the ever continuing growth of the London area, became static or depopulated (and to this day retains much of the character it possessed at the end of the eighteenth century). But a county like the once wild Lancashire in the northwest attracted industry initially to the streams that tumbled down from the Pennine Mountains. Its coal deposits later fired the new forges at Salford, and by 1800 the area had eighty-four steam engines consuming ever more coal. Lancashire's cotton industries, sprouting in the middle of the century, quickly absorbed England's surplus population— workers trekked or were shipped from as far away as London at the rate of 15,000 a year. Little more than a thriving market center of 17,000 in 1757, Manchester, in Lancashire, grew in population to 84,000 by the year of England's first official census, 1801. Within a mere fifty years one of the greatest population shifts in history transpired, and by 1851 nearly half the population was urban and lived in London or the northern shires.

The Ingredients for Industrialization

These surface alterations hardly explain the most difficult question of economic history: Why did industrialization come to England before it touched the rest of Europe or, for that matter, the world? There is as yet no sure answer, though at least one or more of the conditional ingredients were present in England: extensive mineral deposits, skilled labor possessing craft traditions, inventive genius, mobile surplus capital and a capitalistic outlook, business and managerial talent, transport facilities and expanding trade outlets. No historian is sure which factor was dominant in England or if the presence of any single one was vital, but many feel that when at the end of the eighteenth century each factor had reached a certain maturity and was interlocked with the others, there occurred an economic takeoff that has since made the growth of the industrial system automatic and self-perpetuating.

One key industry, the mining of iron, had existed since at least the Saxon era. Small foundries flourished in scattered locations in Tudor and Stuart times. They produced "a particular blessing of God given only to England," according to one enthusiast in 1601, "for albeit most countries have their iron, yet none of them all have iron of that toughness and validity to make . . . ordnance of."[1] During the Civil Wars one foundry employed a hundred men making stirrups and cavalry equipment. But until the eighteenth century iron was a marginal industry because of its dependence on forest fuel; whenever one woodland was exhausted, the foundry moved on to another. The English iron industry was actually threatened with extinction before 1709, when a new smelting process using coke instead of charcoal was developed by Abraham Darby. When Darby's process was popularized decades later, iron foundries naturally gravitated to the coal fields of the midlands, especially around Coalbrookdale, Sheffield, and Birmingham. The marriage between iron and coal was strengthened by Henry Cort's invention of the puddling process (stirring

[1] Quoted in G. M. Trevelyan, *English Social History* (London, 1942), p. 187.

the molten iron until most of the fuel's impurities burn off), which used common coal rather than coke for fuel and yielded a malleable wrought iron. This allowed everything from mining to the finished product to be accomplished at one site and encouraged unified ownership and efficient use of capital.

The incentive that iron smelting gave to coal production is a prime example of how industrial techniques interlock. Coal for London's hearths had been mined at Newcastle for centuries but had limited industrial uses until joined with iron. Early mining had been a casual rural occupation, the miners working at open seams not far from the pastures and fields where they lived as part-time farmers. Around 1700 the diggers began to follow the coal seams into the earth, two hundred feet or more, through tunnels supported by columns of coal. The deepening shafts were difficult to drain and called for the first extensive industrial use of the steam engine—the pumping of water. In 1777 cast-iron rails for the pony carts that hauled coal were installed in the Sheffield mines; and iron shorings, braces, and tools allowed the shafts to sink ever deeper below the surface.

The steam engine, the ideal symbol of the coal–iron age, began its career of power and speed as a humble drudge. In 1708 Thomas Newcomen developed an early model for pumping water from the mines. As ungainly, clumsy, and dangerously explosive as it was, over a hundred were in use at the middle of the century. The versatility of steam was unsuspected, though an engine was used by Darby's ingenious son to pump the water driving the bellows of his blast furnace. In 1760 John Smeaton invented an engine solely for that purpose. The contrivance was as yet confined to an up-and-down motion, and its action was periodic rather than continual because most of the force was lost as the steam cooled and condensed in the cylinder. The inventor of the modern steam engine, James Watt, identified both problems and in 1765 came up with a machine that had a separate condensing chamber, making it four times as efficient as Newcomen's earlier engine. In 1782 Watt solved the problem of pump-handle motion by inventing a flywheel, which, by converting the piston's thrust into a circular motion, made the steam engine capable, as many came to realize, of being attached to any revolving mechanism from the spinning wheel to the coach wheel.

Watt's work furthered the expansive nature of industrialism and involved a variety of skills. Because his initial discoveries were made while repairing a Newcomen engine provided by the University of Glasgow, he involved the scientific community in his studies of steam and heat properties; his capital came from industrialists, notably a hardware manufacturer, Matthew Boulton of Birmingham; he enlisted scores of engineers to develop fine-parts technology, precision cutting and boring, and metallurgy.

By the end of the century some five hundred steam engines were at work, not only pumping but also driving hammers in foundries, turning textile equipment, and milling flour. As the idea of the steam-driven flywheel caught on, its number of uses expanded. In 1811 steam was harnessed to the printing press, and by 1814 the London *Times* could print a thousand sheets an hour. The most dramatic use of steam came in 1790 in transportation when an American, John Fitch, operated a steam ferry across the Delaware River. It was not until a second American, Robert Fulton, influenced by Watt and employing one of his engines, began regular Hudson River runs with his paddle-wheel steamer, the *Clermont*, that steamships became feasible. Land transport owes its beginnings to designer Richard Trevithick, whose experimental steam coach chugged through London in 1803. In 1809 he ran his engine, the *Catch Me Who Can*, on a circular track in London's Euston Square for the price of admission. He was to die penniless, however; and not until George Stephenson built his *Rocket* in 1829 for the Liverpool–Manchester Railway did locomotive power come into its own.

However successful these innovations in coal, iron, and steam were, the first large fortunes and notoriety came with inventions in textiles. At the start of the eighteenth century, wool still dominated domestic dress, though the colorful imported cottons of India, exciting to the eye and softer to the skin, made an immediate impact. Their imitation by Manchester weavers brought on riots and parliamentary laws restricting cottons for seventy-five years. But demand could not be stifled, and by the end of the century cotton displaced wool as the chief export.

The successive inventions that converted textiles from handicraft to mechanized production began with John Kay's flying shuttle in 1733. The device allowed a weaver to operate his shuttle remotely by pulling strings attached to hammers that drove the shuttle back and forth. Heretofore one weaver could absorb the daily output of five or six thread spinners; now he could double this output and make a broader bolt of cloth as well. The increased demand for thread prompted the Royal Society to offer a prize for a spinning machine, but there was no breakthrough until 1764, and then it came by chance. One day a spinner, James Hargreaves, startled his wife, and she overturned her spinning wheel. The wheel continued to revolve on its side even though the spindle stayed upright. To Hargreaves there came a vision of a set of spindles all driven by one wheel, and with a mechanic's aid he fashioned a "spinning Jenny" (named for his wife) that could spin eight threads at a time. Unlike Kay, Hargreaves exploited his invention, gave up spinning to manufacture the Jennys, and became one of England's first industrial entrepreneurs.

The pace of invention quickened, and in 1768 Richard Arkwright, a barber, added a system of rollers to the spinner so that the thread was drawn finer and tighter. Arkwright assimilated the work and capital of others, plowed his profits back into the concern, and by his death in 1792 owned ten spinning mills. Of even greater significance is the fact that his "water frame" was too large to be housed at home. It was also too expensive for a domestic operator to buy and needed water power (which was soon replaced by steam) in its operation. The ex-barber's startling success brought him a knighthood in 1786; he was perhaps the first industrialist to be so honored.

When spinning departed from the cottage for the factory, weaving was left behind as a domestic occupation. Raw cotton was flooding England in an avalanche; 3 million pounds in 1760 became 32 million in 1789. The bottleneck in weaving before the power loom, together with the clamor for cotton goods, brought on a golden age for weavers. Looms were installed in every back room and shed, even in barns, to take advantage of the high remuneration. With the invention of the power loom by Edmund Cartwright in 1784, the demand for domestic weavers gradually subsided, though some were retained to produce the superior grades of cloth. By 1800 hundreds of water- and steam-powered looms appeared throughout Scotland and the northern shires. Cartwright was lionized as an industrial pioneer. He was voted a gift of £10,000 by Parliament in 1809.

The remarkable increase in productivity—coal output went from 2.5 million tons in 1700 to 16 million in 1815, iron from 20,000 tons in 1720 to 250,000 in 1806—could never have come about with old England's muddy, rutted, narrow roads. Before the middle of the eighteenth century it was far cheaper, if longer, to trundle goods to the nearest river or sail them around the coast, since many interior towns were isolated in winter. Then a persistent cry for improved travel brought thousands of miles under turnpike trusts (small local corporations maintaining toll roads) by 1815. The railroad would one day obviate the highway for mass transportation, but for seventy years after 1759 the canal, even more than the improved turnpike, was the wonder of commerce. In that year the duke of Bridgewater's brilliant servant, James Brindley (who was functionally illiterate), conceived a unique waterway that would flow from the depths of the duke's coal mine to Manchester, crossing an intervening river by way of an aqueduct. When the waterway was completed, the cost of shipping his master's coal was halved. With proof of such dramatic savings, canal companies were soon chopping through every shire in central England.

A Redistribution of Capital

The technical interconnections between resources, manufacturing, and transport might have been negligible but for an earlier revolution (sometime after 1640) in capital. Investments for the new industries were amassed from a dozen sources: wartime contracts, increased land speculation, commercial farming, successful trade wars and new trade routes, the growth of imperial holdings throughout the world, the introduction of new tastes (coffee, chocolate, cotton, tea), the cultivation of old pleasures (tobacco, sugar, silk, wines), the centralization of international trade in London. After 1688 and the formal establishment of the standing debt, the English government was forever wedded to private enterprise, the largest source of its loans. It has been estimated that between 1700 and 1780 surplus capital rose from 5 to 6 percent. As small as the gain now seems, it was fluid and in the hands of men willing to gamble. Initially the most spectacular fortunes came from the trading boom that overtook England after 1660. These were the surpluses that in 1694 founded England's first great repository for capital, the Bank of England. But whereas it had been customary for rich merchants and craftsmen to conclude their hectic careers by pouring their fortunes into expansive land holdings, the wealth of the eighteenth century was actively reinvested in industry. From the few studies that have recently appeared, the flow of money into new mining and textile operations can be discerned as originating largely from tea and tobacco interests. In some cases (as was true of the duke of Bridgewater), even landed wealth was converted into industrial capital. In any case, by the early nineteenth century industrial production was generating its own capital.

Of equal importance is that wealth became easily convertible and transferable—the mightiest fortune is useless to a country if it cannot be transmitted. The goldsmiths of seventeenth-century London developed an international reputation for a willingness to hold other people's money, even to make interest payments, in a manner similar to the functions of a modern bank. But this service applied only to London and the international trading community. In the provinces a form of banking aiding local farmers and shippers appeared late in the seventeenth century; whenever cattle, crops, or textiles were transported, even a distance of a few miles, it became increasingly common for the shipper to issue a "bill of exchange" in a sum promised by the distant purchaser. The bill was then paid by a local man of means who first "discounted" a fee for assuming the risk that he might not receive a return. Before long in much of England (particularly where industrial capital financed mining and textile plant operations), bills of exchange became a type of true paper currency. The men who took the financial risks—wealthy farmers, merchants, even parsons—frequently dropped their own professions in favor of full-time banking, as did a former draper, James Wood of Bristol, in 1716. He appears to have been England's first provincial banker. The banking idea seems to have advanced slowly: in 1750 there were only twelve banks outside London; in 1793 they numbered nearly four hundred; by 1815 about nine hundred. Perhaps nothing signalized the arrival of industrial capitalism more surely than that some renowned manufacturers (Arkwright, Boulton, and Watt) established their own banking houses.

The new industrialism affected the consumers' market in only a few notable ways: cheap cotton goods rapidly replaced the formerly popular linen and wool; the superior highway networks brought a richer variety of food to the table. The spectacular signs of industry were seen in the more massive productions: by 1797 there were three iron bridges; a metal plate ship was built in 1787. John Wilkinson, the owner of the Wilkinson iron works, widely advertised his products. He constructed iron chairs and pipes and vats for breweries and even speculated about houses made of iron. He suitably, and with confidence, had his coffin constructed of iron.

During the years when Trevithick was unveiling his steam carriage, a new coal by-product became the rage:

> What can occasion such a ferment in every house, in every street, in every shop, in every garret about London? It is the Light and Heat Company. It is Mr. Winsor [the financier] and his lecture, and his gas, and his patent, and his shares—those famous shares which are to make the fortune of all who hold them.[2]

The 1807 coal gas lighting of one of London's major thoroughfares, Pall Mall, was at first a curiosity. Eight years later there were fifteen miles of illuminated streets in the London area. This led to the inevitable conclusion that:

We thankful are that sun and moon
  Were placed so very high
That no tempestuous hand might reach
  To tear them from the sky.
Were it not so, we soon should find
  That some reforming ass
Would straight propose to snuff them out,
  And light the world with gas.[3]

The Industrial Worker: A New Life Style

A change in temper to match the pace of the Industrial Revolution appeared. As early as 1758 a correspondent in the north wrote of her neighbors,

> The great gain made by several branches of the coal trade has turned all attention that way. Every gentleman in the country, from the least to the greatest, is as solicitous in the pursuit of gain as a tradesman. The conversation always turns upon

[2] Quoted in M. Dorothy George, *England in Transition* (London, 1953), p. 112.
[3] Quoted in Henry Hamilton, *England: A History of the Homeland* (New York, 1948), p. 182.

money; the moment you name a man, you are told what he is worth, the losses he has had, or the profit he has made by coal mines.[4]

By 1767 an increased tempo was obvious. "Everything wears the face of dispatch," said one commentator, noting the coaches rattling about, the businessmen scurrying from one part of England to another. Time was essential. The duke of Bridgewater, furious with his workers for taking too long for lunch on the excuse that they had not heard the clock strike one, had the clock reset to strike thirteen instead.

The problem of retraining rural workers to match the expeditious machine was frustrating to the owner who despised seeing his plant sit idle. The English worker now had to come to work at an appointed hour and to stay on the job when the fish in the nearest brook beckoned in spring or the autumn's harvest festivals called. Factory owners summoned their employees with bells or whistles that sounded across the land at five or six o'clock. Thereafter the workers' time was separated by the same sound for breaks, lunch, and dinner, until they were dismissed by a final bell at eight or nine. Time cards were issued to keep track of workers; incentive was rewarded, tardiness or drunkenness was fined. Above all, the laborers were exhorted to be obedient and tractable. The new industrial organization required rigid division of labor, perpetual (often deadening) attention to detail if a mass-produced uniform product was to result. The old life style of the domestic worker was forsaken in a rebirth of labor habits.

The worker did not accept the change gracefully or quietly. Almost every industrial innovation was greeted with derision or outright rebellion: no sooner had word spread of Hargreaves' spinning Jenny than neighbors broke into his home to destroy the prototype; turnpike riots attended the new road systems; in 1765, when time cards were issued to the miners of the Tyne, cables were cut, engines smashed, and the mines were fired; in 1789 hand weavers destroyed Cartwright's Manchester power loom factory. The best known saboteurs were the Luddites, an organization that spread from Nottingham throughout the country in 1811. Though they were as much a reaction to the economic depression at the end of the Napoleonic Wars as to the growth of mechanization in textiles, every industrial shire, particularly Yorkshire, had to post guards around its factories against the systematic breakage of "King Ludd's" followers (named for Ned Ludd, perhaps Ludlow, who thirty years before had destroyed stocking frames). In 1813 the Luddite riots were broken by hangings and deportations, but the memory of their organization was to carry on into the decades of the nineteenth century's labor strife.

[4] Quoted in Emily J. Climenson, *Elizabeth Montague . . . Her Correspondence from 1720 to 1761* (London, 1906), p. 149.

The general lot of workers in the early stages of industrialization is difficult to characterize. An industry-by-industry study would probably reveal that overall wages increased considerably during the late wars with France (but then, so did prices) and that the extreme hardships came with the ending of wartime contracts in 1813. There were three areas in which a loss in freedom could be registered: the use of time was certainly curtailed by the factory bell's demands; the wild oscillations in many industries made the laborer the victim of depressions due to overproduction; the quality of workers' housing—airless, lightless, and cramped—in the new factory cities made the one-room country cottage of his past idyllic.

For all its importance it must be remembered that as late as 1800 industry accounted for no more than a quarter of the national wealth. There were still many aspects of production that were not then, and would not be, mechanized for decades. Furthermore, wage slavery, supposedly introduced by the factory system, had been a part of the domestic workers' lot as well; it has been estimated that as early as 1688 a third of the national income was paid in the form of wages. Mass employment, depersonalized and coldly contractual, was also a feature of pre-factory labor; in 1713 a sailmaker reported that he employed about six thousand people in three shires. Older records indicate that industries employing one hundred to two hundred men were not uncommon in James I's day. It seems, then, that the Industrial Revolution only attained fruition under George III. Its demands committed England to a form of production, a capitalistic temper, and an organization of labor which she had been nurturing perhaps since Cromwell's day. The greatest problems, those that face a totally industrialized society, still lay in England's, and the world's, future.

Chapter Eight
THE ERA OF ROBERT WALPOLE

Major Personages

Frederick Louis, Prince of Wales, 1705–51; oldest son of George II; leader of the Leicester House party and father of George III

George I, elector of Hanover, 1660–1727; king of England, 1714–27; great grandson of James I; the first Hanoverian monarch

George II, 1683–1760; king of England, 1727–60; frequently unable to control his ministries; the last warrior king in English history

Newcastle, Thomas Pelham-Holles, duke of, 1693–1768; eccentric but highly effective political patron behind Walpole

Pulteney, William, 1684–1764; opponent of Walpole and founder of the first opposition newspaper (the *Craftsman*); later earl of Bath (referred to here as Pulteney)

Stanhope, James, first earl, 1673–1721; first major minister of George I and an extraordinary talent in foreign affairs.

Walpole, Robert, 1676–1745; traditionally regarded as the first prime minister in English history, a financial genius (earl of Oxford upon retirement but called here Walpole)

CHRONOLOGY

1714–27	Reign of George I
1715	Jacobite rising (the Fifteen)
	Riot Act
1716	Septennial Act
1718	Repeal of Schism and Occasional Conformity acts
1719	Peerage Bill crisis; rise of Walpole
1720	South Sea Bubble
1721–42	Walpole's great ministry
1727	Death of George I
1733	Excise Bill crisis
1739	War of Jenkins' Ear (against Spain)
1744–8	War of the Austrian Succession, concluded by the Treaty of Aix-la-Chapelle
1745	Jacobite rising (the Forty-five)

When George in pudding-time came o'er,
*   And moderate men looked big, sir,*
I turned a cat-in-pan once more,
*   And so became a Whig, sir;*
And thus preferment I procured,
*   From our new faith's defender,*
And almost every day abjured
*   The Pope and the Pretender.*

And this is law, that I'll maintain,
*   Until my dying day, sir,*
That whatsoever King shall reign,
*   I'll be the Vicar of Bray, sir.*

The illustrious house of Hanover,
*   And Protestant succession,*
To these I do allegiance swear,
*   While they can keep possession;*
For in my faith and loyalty
*   I never more will falter,*
And George my lawful King shall be,
*   Until the times do alter.*

And this is law, that I'll maintain,
*   Until my dying day, sir,*
That whatsoever King shall reign,
*   I'll be the Vicar of Bray, sir.*

The House of Hanover

As the year 1714 ebbed, a Tory commentator, reflecting on Anne's death and St. John, Viscount Bolingbroke's flight to France, resignedly penned this epigram:

Farewell, old year, old monarch, and old Tory,
Farewell, old England, thou hast lost thy glory.

While one could anticipate Tory lamentations, the words were somehow prophetic.

The quality of Hanoverian politics would seem highly disreputable when compared to the Stuarts' if the lost "glory" meant the high-mindedness of a Clarendon, James II, or William III. In 1728 a newspaper upheld a score of officials suspended for nefarious dealings, contending that they were "only taking care of their families and making the most of their places."[1] The English government came to resemble a questionable business enterprise. Cynicism was cultivated, ideals were suspect, quick expedients were attractive, and power was lustily enjoyed. Though it may be difficult to name one individual singularly devoted to these crass pursuits, the powerful Sir Robert Walpole might well have been singled out by his enemies. Actually, the durable prime minister's career was no more tainted than that of others in this era, but he indulged his corruption while most others hypocritically made excuses for their unwholesome politics. His lustiness was easily identified with venality. He swore, drank, and partied to excess. Yet he was decidedly effective, and many who followed him in high office availed themselves of his questionable methods while struggling to avoid his unsavory reputation.

The early eighteenth century lacked monumental issues. The Civil Wars were history; the Glorious Revolution was a memory. With little more at issue than regulatory tariffs or enclosure petitions, attendance in Parliament noticeably diminished. As public morality changed, party politics declined. By the 1720s Daniel Defoe perceived that "no one . . . has really been either Whig or Tory, or governed in the least by the principles of such according to the common acceptation of them." Although party banners were unfurled on all the customary occasions and toasts were drunk to such political heroes of old as Dr. Oates or Dr. Sacheverell, the earlier organizations that had dominated elections and rammed bills through Parliament were no longer evident. On the surface the deterioration of party activity is explained by the collapse of the Tories after 1714. With their leaders linked to Jacobitism and with the court partial to the Whigs, two-party contests could be expected to vanish. However, the ousted Tories were never outlawed as a group, and individual party members continued their vigorous activities, especially after Bolingbroke bribed his way back into England in 1725.

The Growth of Patronage Politics

Politics became a professional's game based largely on the power to control votes. The players were the wealthy patrons who financed rising young politicians or bought seats in Commons for themselves or for relatives, so that on an average 17 percent of the lower house was comprised of the sons of peers. A lord could also ensure both the nomination and election

[1] See Derek Jarrett, *Britain, 1688–1815* (New York, 1965), pp. 38–44; Robert Smith, *Eighteenth-Century English Politics* (New York, 1972), pp. 76–92.

of the county's two representatives; voting was still done by voice or an open show of hands and neighbors dared not risk the disfavor of the shire's most powerful landholder. Friends and relatives in nearby market towns helped swing the vote of the local enfranchised boroughs (Commons consisted of a preponderance of borough members—409 to 80 county members) to the lord's preference. At the very least he could name a few of the five thousand customs officials of the realm. As a patron, he might be assigned a placeman by the government, perhaps the groom of the stole or gentleman of the ewery (two of the many high-salaried posts conferred by the king). These "places" might be directly obtained through a favorably situated patron's wife; for instance, Lady Sundon of the queen's household received a pair of diamond earrings from the earl of Pomfret for the "place" of master of the horse.

There had never been an attempt to redistrict the seating in Commons. Controlling an urban representation could therefore be childishly easy if the patron was so fortunate as to have on his estate a rotten borough (boroughs in which the population had declined, or disappeared altogether, perhaps having been wiped out by plague but still holding two seats in Parliament). At one time the town of Rye claimed only six voters and numerous other towns scarcely a dozen, whereas Bristol listed six thousand and London twelve thousand. All but London, which had four members, sent two representatives to Commons. The town of Haslemere, settled largely by tenants of Lord Lonsdale, dutifully voted for his nominees. The earl of Radnor had Downton "in his pocket" through ownership of nine-tenths of its franchised tenures, making it a pocket borough as well as a rotten borough. The duke of Newcastle outclassed all patrons by manipulating the vote in seven boroughs and four shires, thus directly controlling twenty-two seats in Parliament.

The expense of election rigging was enormous. Wholesale bribery included great ale parties for the town electorate and extravagant baubles in return for political favors. On an average it cost £70 to swing an election in 1690. The price rose to £700 in 1717 and upwards of £30,000 by the end of the century.

Despite the precautions by which a ministry garnered votes, an unpredictable fluidity in public affairs sometimes undid its artful designs. The mercurial electorate would occasionally ignore bribed blandishments if it was reached by patriotic pleas. There were also powerfully charismatic leaders who attracted followers by their extreme independence. One of these, William Pitt the Elder, the earl of Chatham, eventually succeeded in thrusting his policies on an unsympathetic court. His son, evincing the same magic, became chief minister at the age of twenty-three. There were also attempts to establish a broad-bottomed ministry to call upon the talents of all factions.

Even at the local level a patron's well-laid plans could be undone by the fickleness of a town electorate succumbing to the blandishments of a second borough monger. With inns being hired by competing politicians, election years often became seasons for feasting and drinking. Charles Dickens' *Pickwick Papers*, though written much later, gives a notable example in his imaginary town of Eatanswill that could have been set in the eighteenth century, where Sam Weller, Mr. Pickwick's servant, is paid to see that the pampered electorate vote for its benefactor: "Every man slept where he fell down; we dragged 'em out, one by one this mornin' and put 'em under the pump, and they're in reg'lar fine order now. Shillin' a head the committee paid for that 'ere job." After the Triennial Act of 1694 the two-hundred-odd parliamentary towns quickly adapted to the regular business of politics, and despite the stretching of elections to every seven years in 1716 there was no loss of lusty venality.

About a quarter of the boroughs had retained a virtually democratic franchise from the time of their incorporation in the Middle Ages. In these any "potwalloper" (a man having a hearth upon which he could boil, or "wallop," his kettle) or anyone who paid the "scot and lot" (borough taxes) was entitled to vote. In these types of boroughs the sheer numbers involved made election managing more difficult than in others. Corporation boroughs allowed the vote to none but legal founders of the town or their heirs, and usually these families had to belong to the ancient guilds as well; burgage (for "burgher," or townsman) boroughs enfranchised home-owners; freeman boroughs ironically had the most restricted franchise since only families inscribed as freemen in the original charter could vote. At times, in order to build a majority, a patron would find it necessary to furnish travel expenses for those hereditary freemen who no longer lived in their ancestral towns.

Another stumbling block in patronage politics was the decisive role played by the court. Though the monarchs of the age usually stayed aloof from the dirty games played beneath their thrones, William, Anne, and the first two Georges allowed the patronage system to exist because it worked smoothly in the hands of its adept managers. George III rebelled against it and brought upon himself a serious charge of royal interference when he became a patron of sorts with his own cultivated clique, the "king's friends." He had intended no tyranny but wished only to exert royal pressure to lift English politics from its unsavory level.

An untouchable faction, variously called the reversionary interest, the Leicester House reversion, and the Leicester House gang (defined by Derek Jarrett as "that group of politicians who preferred to support the person to whom the crown would revert rather than the person who was actually wearing it"[2]), formed a minor and alternative court until 1760. Leicester House, purchased in 1718 by George I's son, the Prince of Wales, became a

[2] Jarrett, *op. cit.*, p. 127.

center for those currently out of favor with the ruling monarch. It was no secret that king and prince hated each other (at one point in their strained relations, George had even considered having his son pirated off to the colonies). But however strong their animosity, the prince was of the royal family, and as such, though they might be his father's enemics, the prince's friends were safeguarded by his protection. This counteraction to the monarch was tolerated as a form of loyal opposition inasmuch as participation in the prince's miniature court constituted a form of royal service. The reversionary factor can be traced as far back as Charles II's breach with the duke of Monmouth, through the rift between King William and his sister-in-law, Anne, onward to George I and his son, and to George II and his reversionary antagonists, both his son and his grandson.

George I's heir was not the first Hanoverian's only problem. The fifty-four-year-old monarch, who succeeded Anne in August of 1714 through the Act of Settlement, also experienced difficulties owing to his German birth and background. Fat, uncouth, and unable to speak a word of English, he declared his desires in poor Latin through his ministers. An era of Whig supremacy accompanied the coronation but quickly dissolved into patronage politics pitting Whig against Whig. The Jacobites again sought power by holding out the prospect of a native English dynasty under the warming-pan baby of 1688, the relatively attractive twenty-six-year-old James III. They contended that just as the Dutch King William had drenched Europe with English blood, so now would German George do the same— an argument strong enough to persuade country conservatives in remote parts of England as well as in Scotland to join the Rebellion of 1715. Under their countryman, the earl of Mar, the Highland Scots to the number of 15,000 were again the backbone of the Stuart cause. The well-drilled veterans of the duke of Marlborough, however, drove a wedge between the Scottish forces and their English allies, and the two armies were prevented from combining. Robbed of victory, the Jacobites disbanded and surrendered; they were hanged or deported. By the time James II's son arrived in Scotland, his army had been depleted to 3,000 by defections. He left for France early in 1716, never to return to the land of his birth.

Recriminations against the Jacobites were predictable. In 1715 a Riot Act was passed to suppress mass demonstrations for the Old Pretender. By the reading of the act, any gathering of twelve or more people could be ordered to disperse or suffer penalty of death. Because the elections of 1715 had been so tumultuous, the following year the Whig majority terminated the Triennial in favor of a Septennial Act requiring elections every seven years. This conferred an additional four years of life on the existing parliament. Other tokens of Hanoverian loyalty were hastily passed by the Whig ministry. The position of lord treasurer, so powerful an instrument in Godolphin's and Harley's hands, was regarded as too critical a post considering how a Bolingbroke might use it. It was therefore abolished and the treasury placed under a commission ruled by a first lord of the treasury. Next, the clause in the Act of Settlement forbidding monarchs from leaving the kingdom without Parliament's consent (originally intended by the Tories as an insult to William of Orange) was annulled. Finally, in 1718, the Schism and Occasional Conformity acts passed by Bolingbroke were revoked, lifting the heavy restrictions from the Nonconformists.

Beyond these obvious punitive measures aimed at their old Tory foes, the Whigs lacked any semblance of unity. Between 1718 and 1720 the borough mongers slowly gravitated to one of two camps—the court under the leadership of soldier-statesman James Stanhope or the self-styled country faction under Robert Walpole. Where personality clashes left off and ideological conflicts began was difficult to determine. On the surface, at least, the issue lay in Stanhope's support of a strong involvement in Europe versus Walpole's policy of peace and retrenchment. Initially Stanhope, a vigorous diplomat and militant anti-Tory, suited George I perfectly. He negotiated a Quadruple Alliance with France, the Dutch, and the Emperor of the German states that forced peace terms on the two most belligerent powers of that moment, the Swedes and the Spaniards. For over ten years these arrangements were to keep the peace, but only at a cost to England of arms, money, and ships for a variety of nations from the Baltic to the Mediterranean. Walpole argued that the country could not stand this incessant drain, especially since the policy protected Hanover's, not England's, borders. Sir Robert's was then the voice of an unemployed politician, for in 1717 he had been relieved of his initial term as first lord of the treasury, a post in which he had served from October of 1715.

Two issues again rallied the patrons to Walpole's banner: the Peerage Bill of 1719 and the financial failure of the South Sea Company in 1720. Both were domestic crises, and Stanhope knew as little of these matters as did Walpole of foreign affairs. Stanhope persuaded the king that a forceful Whig policy would give the House of Hanover a less foreign flavor. The monarch's speech opening the parliamentary session of 1719 accordingly called for the end of the Septennial Act by the indefinite prolongation of the present parliament, the crushing of Tory influence over the two universities, and an alliance between the crown and the London plutocracy for the control of finances. Most devastating of all would be the Peerage Bill, intended to place a statutory limitation on the number of peers who might be seated in the House of Lords.

This last item was meant to outlaw the crude Tory contrivance that had licensed Queen Anne's creation of twelve peers for the sake of gaining a Tory advantage over the Whigs. George also had been privately assured that his loathed son's power of creating favorites would be curtailed by the act, so he championed it all the more. Throughout the year the bill was quietly debated in both houses. Then, with a dramatic flare, Walpole questioned, "how can the Lords expect the Commons to give their concurrence to a bill by which they and their posterity are to be forever excluded from the peerage?" Though the measure was sponsored by the court, Sir Robert demanded its defeat on the grounds that the king's power to create lords at will, a major means of rewarding loyal service, should not be stinted. The bill was beaten 269 to 177. Walpole's first collision with the court manifested a knack for manipulating the House of Commons, one the king was to note. Stanhope, not wishing to risk further embarrassment, withdrew his other plans for purging the Tories.

Walpole's Rise to Power

The following year Walpole rescued the nation from the "South Sea Bubble," England's first stock market crash. The South Sea Company had been chartered in 1711 to carry a large portion of the government's deficit. Rumors of its staggering resources circulated, and, indeed, in return for a monopoly over Central American trade, in 1720 the company obligated itself to pay off £7 million of the national debt. Expectations were high that in quick course riches pouring in from Spanish America would swell the coffers of the exchequer and the pockets of the company's investors; after all, was not the king himself on the governing board? Stock shares soared to a thousand times their par value between April and August. Imitative ventures blossomed, though the schemes they advanced— for extracting silver from lead or fresh water from the sea and one company's prospectus for "an undertaking which shall in due time be revealed"—were dubious. The investment mania was a glorious insanity of eternal wealth and freedom from taxation.

At the end of August 1720 public confidence evaporated. First the smaller companies, then the mighty South Sea Company found capital vanishing as investors redeemed their depreciating certificates. There was, of course, not nearly enough cash to repay creditors. The South Sea Company, having yielded to the temptation to use its millions for finance instead of trade, had in reality in twelve years outfitted only two ships for the Caribbean venture. Stanhope's ministry tumbled amid the outcries of ruined thousands, and during a vindictive attack on him in Lords, the guiltless chief minister suffered a stroke from which he died. In 1721 Walpole, accepting the invitation to become again first lord of the treasury, halted all the company's transactions and pooled the remaining assets for a token repayment to its investors. By refusing to prosecute, he spared all but the most culpable from prolonged

ROBERT WALPOLE IN PARLIAMENT.
Engraving by William Hogarth. Courtesy The Bettmann Archive.

legal process. He feared, as did the court, that continued exposures might undermine the entire Hanoverian succession, encouraging another Jacobite bid for reinstatement. His dictum "Let sleeping dogs lie" became the rule over issues that seemed better left ignored and unreformed.

From 1721 to 1742 Sir Robert enjoyed unparalleled power. He was the first chief minister to whom the nomenclature "prime minister" stuck. While the designation had been used before, it was an insult implying subservience to the court. The title was not formal or official until the twentieth century. The equivalent of the post, however, did exist long before Walpole held it, usually in the person of the lord treasurer, later the first lord of the treasury.

The trust placed in Walpole by the two Georges under whom he served and his partnership with Thomas Pelham, duke of Newcastle, the most powerful patron of the age, accorded him parliamentary strength when even he expected defeat. Newcastle ("Hubble-bubble" to his colleagues) disarmed his enemies by an inveterate absent-mindedness, beneath which lay an astute organizational talent. Public occasions flustered him. His understanding of issues was minimal. Yet when it came to managing votes, he could predict to a man what the majorities would be. Without his machinery Walpole's tenure might have been halved; and when Newcastle eventually abandoned him for a new protégé, there was nothing for the prime minister but resignation.

Steps to Financial Reconstruction

Walpole embodied the trend toward encouraging private business, a trend started in William III's day. Though he cannot be given full credit for the era's commercial success, he did strive to remove impediments from trade. The land tax, which had furnished funds for a large part of wartime expenditures, was reduced, and military spending was cut to the bone by his assiduous avoidance of foreign commitments. In 1717 he established a sinking fund, a general emergency repository to be used for repaying old debts. It worked beautifully from 1717, when the national deficit stood at £54 million, to 1727, by which time the amount had been reduced to £8.5 million. The average interest charged to the government dropped impressively from 9 to 4 percent. Without the recurring wars the sinking fund might possibly have paid off the entire indebtedness, though extraordinary demands in other parts of the budget often tempted ministers to plunder the fund to cover miscellaneous liabilities even in peacetime.

Walpole also established bonded warehouses where international shippers could store goods until reshipment overseas. The lack of duty on goods in transit attracted traders from all of Europe. On those commodities that found buyers in England, he reduced or abolished many customs and consolidated the five or six petty duties that were frequently imposed on a single item. He tightened the efficiency of collecting internal excises, making smuggling less profitable. He ensured the quality of key exports so that foreign buyers came to expect uniformity in such items as bricks, tiles, sailcloth, serge, and linen. The results were astonishing. What the government lost in reduced export revenue it more than made up in increased volume. Not only did London become the world's mightiest shipping center, but also many foreign traders, particularly the Dutch, were willing to pour millions into English ventures. Export business rose from £7 million to £10 million between 1720 and 1738.

Three crucial political episodes punctuated Sir Robert's career: the death of his most stalwart supporter, George I; the excise scheme of 1733; and the War of Jenkins' Ear, which began in 1739 and merged into the War of the Austrian Succession. Walpole had scarcely begun his financial reconstruction when the first of these tests, the death of the king, occurred in June of 1727. When the new monarch, George II, ordered him to take his directions from Sir Spencer Compton, Sir Robert packed his papers. Compton was the king's closest personal adviser at Leicester House and the most likely to succeed as first lord of the treasury. But Compton, who was devoid of any alternative to Walpole's vigorous policies, beseeched him to write the royal speech outlining the ministerial program. For Compton the task was simply too overwhelming. The old master drafted an address so impressive that George II forgave his departure from Leicester House seven years earlier. With the hope of renewed preferment now shining, Walpole and Newcastle put their parliamentary machinery into full gear and pushed through Commons an augmented civil list elevating the king's personal income from £700,000 to £800,000 and granting £100,000 each for the queen and the young Prince of Wales. This demonstration of parliamentary prowess was more than shallow financial flattery; it proved the power of the Walpole–Newcastle connections, a power that could, it was strongly implied to the king, be of enormous assistance. Within two years Sir Robert sat as firmly in the regard of George II as he had in George I's.

The Burgeoning Opposition

As the entrenched prime minister weathered this threat from above, so, in 1733, he withstood an even greater challenge from below, brought on by an inborn penchant for stirring up opposition through his dislike of competition. Newcastle was never a threat since he was content to run Walpole's show as a silent partner. But year after year Sir Robert sent many highly competent but competing officeholders into political exile: in

1724 John Carteret was replaced by Newcastle as secretary of state; in 1725 William Pulteney was dumped for criticizing the prime minister on the floor of the House; Lord "Turnip" Townshend retired to his estate after an altercation with Walpole over foreign policy.

Pulteney put an edge to his bitterness and took revenge by organizing the first elements of a true opposition party since Harley's attack on the Whigs in Queen Anne's day. In 1726 he founded the *Craftsman*, perhaps England's first opposition newspaper, which announced, "The mystery of statecraft abounds with . . . innumerable frauds, prostitutions, and enormities of all shapes." The old Tory leader Viscount Bolingbroke joined his talented pen with Pulteney's, as did most of the literary luminaries of the day. For shelter from Walpole's wrath his antagonists could turn to the new tenant of Leicester House, Prince Frederick Louis, who, like his father before him, was a spiteful and resentful offspring. Rounding out the spectrum of mounting opposition were Cobham's Cubs, the protégés of Richard Temple, Viscount Cobham. They were more than a generation younger than Walpole (who was born in 1676) and voiced the discontent of English youth. To these younger politicians—William Pitt, George Grenville, and others of their persuasion—the slogans of the Glorious Revolution were Walpolean cant designed to gull the people into a belief that only this one man could save them from the illusory threat of a Jacobite restoration.

It was this new generation of idealistic leaders, not for sale to borough mongers or places, who formed the Patriots. They hoped and planned (once the dragon Walpole was slain) to rule England above factions for the benefit of all. As their supreme test, the opposition chose the stopping of the prime minister's proposed excise reform of 1733. In his master plan to bring the government into total solvency, Walpole had miscalculated the yield of a salt tax of 1732. His solution lay in a slight extension of the excise to cover wine and tobacco, as well as tea, coffee, cocoa, and chocolate, which were already under the bonded warehouse system. He was heading in the direction of placing minimal duties on a variety of items not previously taxed. When the word "excise" was applied to the scheme, especially to the bill for wine and tobacco, it raised unsavory memories of brutal excise officers. Their relentless search for contraband had plagued many a shopkeeper since Cromwell's day. The excise man had become a symbol of tyranny that the editors of the *Craftsman* knew well how to exploit. They predicted that Walpole would try for a general excise, and when he introduced the extension in 1733 they informed the world that the prime minister had begun the totalitarian campaign.

The streets swelled with demonstrators chanting, "No slavery, no excise, no wooden shoes" (such as those worn by French peasants) as they burned mock excise bills and effigies of Sir Robert. Throughout April, Walpole and

Newcastle scavenged for a parliamentary majority to resist motions to have the bill thrown out. With each reading, the ranks of the faithful dwindled until Walpole resignedly removed further consideration until June 12, 1733, well after the adjournment for the year. He thus spared himself the embarrassment of open defeat.

He next repaired his defenses and the following year destroyed the opposition at the polls. The outstripped and beaten Bolingbroke went back into voluntary French exile. For Walpole's enemies who remained in England, the reckoning was heavy. George II drove those who had raised the cry against the excise from their lucrative places. Walpole felt free to chastise the theater for its lampoons at his expense by enacting a law requiring all plays to be submitted to the lord chamberlain for approval.

The victory, however, was Pyrrhic. What Walpole gained in revenge he lost in respect. The Leicester House reversionaries needed only one strong issue after the excise, and that was provided by a growing demand for war with Spain. It is to his credit that Sir Robert's lifelong avoidance of war was seated in a conviction of its utter irrationality and needless destruction. The Patriots saw war as the road to glory and wealth. Walpole would have acquiesced in a Hanoverian military adventure if England pledged only money, but the Patriots clamored for an active expansionist contest with Spain and France on the high seas and in distant colonial climes.

The War of the Austrian Succession

Whereas five years before it had been "No excise," with the spring of 1738 the chant against Walpole became "No search." The issue was Spain's intensifying harassment of English ships in the Caribbean under the guise of searching for smugglers. Over two hundred English merchantmen had been stopped, some badly plundered, by licensed Spanish privateers. The *Rebecca* was totally stripped and the captain's ear slashed off with a cutlass and returned to him with a scornful order to give it to King George. Pulteney and the Patriots displayed Captain Robert Jenkins and his pickled ear before the House. They recounted the many atrocities in Spain's destruction of honest English trade. It now mattered little that Spanish grievances against England were weightier or that much of the clamor for war came from the small, but vocal, West Indian planters' lobby or that direct trade with Spain (worth £1 million annually) involved far more than did West Indian commerce. Jenkins' ear must be avenged! Of course, Walpole was as much the Patriots' target as were the Spanish. Being aware of this, he spent the winter of 1738 seeking compensation from Spain for the English merchants set upon by the Spanish coast guard. In the hasty negotiations of the Convention of Pardo,

Spain agreed to a reparation of £95,000. In return she decreed that the South Sea Company, which had been handling the *asiento* (the right to send one ship a year to Spain's empire), pay her a sum of £68,000. Since the issue of the right of search was completely ignored, the company refused to recognize the debt. Parliament overrode Walpole's strenuous objections and declared war on Spain on October 19, 1739.

Sir Robert found himself very much alone. The merchants he had protected, the king who had valued his policies, even Newcastle, who had fought every parliamentary division for him—each and all joined the outcry for bloodshed! George soon nudged England into a larger conflict already brewing, a contest in which England had only the barest interest, and though there was no formal declaration until 1744, the country joined with Austria against France in the War of the Austrian Succession. Walpole disconsolately presided over cabinet meetings, giving disheartened approval to all proposals. He brooded over the shambles the war was making of his twenty years of economic reorganization. Twice he tendered his resignation and twice was refused. In January 1742, with his majority in the House lost and his cabinet divided, he sadly informed His Majesty that there were no more services he could perform for him. George accepted his resignation with tears, but not before elevating him in gratitude to the earldom of Oxford.

The War of the Austrian Succession involved the country in a bewildering number of battle zones and tactics, some familiar repetitions, others makeshift innovations that were to come into regular usage in later contests with France. George II, the last warrior king in English history, commanded on the old battlegrounds of William III and Marlborough in the Netherlands and the Rhine Valley. At least in terms of casualties, the foremost battle since Blenheim was fought at Fontenoy in April 1745. Six thousand allied English troops were wounded or killed. While this would seem a victory for France, she too suffered staggering losses that crippled her capacity to pursue the war on land. Meanwhile, the English were using William III's diplomatic ploy to separate France from her allies. Although the war began with a western block headed by France against Maria Theresa of Austria, by 1742 the Prussians and Saxons had turned their backs on the alliance. Savoy defected and joined with the Austrians, and Naples withdrew her support of Spain when an English flotilla took the Bay of Naples and threatened to blow up the harbor.

All in all, England's central role in the war was more that of an organizer than an active campaigner. She furnished only a token land force on the Continent. Nearly £2 million was spent in subsidizing Hessian, Hanoverian, Dutch, and Austrian soldiers to keep the pressure on France. England's direct ventures were generally confined to the seas. She transported troops on a global scale, to Louisburg on Cape Breton Island, to Porto Bello on the

Panamanian Isthmus, to Madras on the coast of India. Her only substantial success was a spectacular circumnavigation of the globe (1740 to 1744) by Commodore Anson, during which he captured £1.25 million in Spanish treasure.

The event of the war most immediately affecting Englishmen was the "Forty-five," an attempt by Charles Edward Stuart (Bonnie Prince Charlie, the grandson of James II) to reinstate his family on the English throne. In 1744 the French launched a major invasion. It barely cleared the coast of France before the stormy Channel took its toll of men and supplies. In July 1745 they put Charles, the "Young Pretender," ashore in the Hebrides off the coast of Scotland with only seven followers and some crates of swords and muskets, largely as an elaborate decoy. Disenchantment with the Union of 1707, which made most Highlanders desirous of throwing off the English yoke, brought Charles 9,000 followers by his presence alone. In August he seized Edinburgh and proclaimed his father (James III, the Old Pretender) King James VIII of Scotland; in September he routed the English at Prestonpans; by late November he had occupied northern England. That winter his advantage slipped away with news that the 15,000 pledged French troops could not risk crossing the treacherous Channel. George II's younger son, the duke of Cumberland, relentlessly pushed the prince back into the Highlands, where at Culloden on April 16, 1746, the last Jacobite charge was launched into the mouths of eighteen English cannon. Charles gave the order to disband and retreated to France. Cumberland, "the Butcher," chased down every remnant of the tattered Scottish troops. In 1746 the Disarming Act outlawed the kilt, the garment of Scottish national identity, and a year later the clan system of the Highlands was abolished forever.

In 1747 the war with Spain and France slackened through mutual exhaustion. Both sides breathed sighs of relief at their narrow escape from defeat. The Treaty of Aix-la-Chapelle in October 1748 restored virtual prewar parity; the French returned Madras to the English, who returned Louisburg to the French. To the probable chagrin of Walpole's ghost, for he had died three years earlier, not one word of the Spanish right of search or of Caribbean trade was mentioned. Sir Robert Walpole had, however, lived long enough to witness the floundering of Pulteney and the Patriots in the morass of governmental detail that he had mastered so effortlessly for twenty years.

Chapter Nine
WILLIAM PITT, LORD CHATHAM, AND THE BRITISH EMPIRE

Major Personages

Carteret, John, 1690–1763; one of the ablest diplomatists of the century, successor to Walpole as chief minister; later the first earl of Granville (referred to here as Carteret)

Chatham, William Pitt, first earl of, 1708–78; greatest wartime minister, responsible for winning the Seven Years' War; styled the Great Commoner but an earl from 1766 (referred to as Pitt in this chapter and later called Chatham to differentiate him from his equally famous son)

Clive, Robert, 1725–74; conqueror of Bengal; Baron Clive of Plassey after his greatest victory, the Battle of Plassey

George III, 1738–1820, king of England, 1760–1820; most controversial monarch of the century; the last nine years of his reign under a regency (headed by his son) due to his mental stress

Pelham, Henry, 1696–1754; capable brother of the duke of Newcastle; first commissioner of the treasury, 1743–54

Wolfe, General James, 1727–59; brilliant commander who lost his life in the capture of Quebec

CHRONOLOGY

1746	Ministerial mass resignation crisis over Pitt's appointment to the cabinet
1756–63	Seven Years' War, concluded by the Treaty of Paris
1757	Battle of Plassey, the beginning of British territorial rule in India
1757–61	Pitt's great ministry
1759	"The year it rained victories":
	Capture of French West Indies
	Battle of Quiberon Bay
	Battle of Minden
	Capture of Quebec
1760	Death of George II

Rule, Britannia!

When Britain first, at Heaven's command,
    Arose from out the azure main,
This was the charter of the land,
    And guardian angels sang this strain—

Rule, Britannia, rule the waves;
Britons never will be slaves.

The nations, not so blessed as thee,
    Must in their turns to tyrants fall;
While thou shalt flourish great and free,
    The dread and envy of them all.

Rule Britannia, rule the waves;
Britons never will be slaves.

To thee belongs the rural reign;
    Thy cities shall with commerce shine;
All thine shall be the subject main,
And every shore it circles thine.

Rule Britannia, rule the waves;
Britons never will be slaves.

JAMES THOMSON, 1740[1]

The Man to Fill the Void

The administrative chasm that had opened with Walpole's resignation in January 1742 went unfilled by a man of comparable stature for fifteen years. It might be supposed that Pulteney, Walpole's erstwhile opponent, would fill the void in the treasurer's office; but during his fifteen years of active hostility to Walpole's ministry Pulteney had convinced his followers of the paramount need for a broad-bottomed cabinet (a ministry of shared leadership). Had he or any other single individual assumed Sir Robert's mantle, the identical charge of cultivating narrow and rotten foundations

[1] To the tune of "Rule, Britannia," by Thomas Arne. It first appeared in a musical (*Alfred*) of 1740. The musical was revived in 1756, and the song became so popular that it was nearly a second national anthem.

would have been revived. Instead, a figurehead replaced Walpole—Spencer Compton, the same cordial and inept gentleman who had briefly been granted the post back in 1727 in Sir Robert's stead.

Pulteney, by his aloofness, lost the opportunity to head his own ministry and gradually slipped from the center of power, but not before he and the Patriots had launched an inquiry into the last ten years of Robert Walpole's administration. They sought the dismissal of every minion who had served under the prime minister. The investigation, mired by the resistance of Walpole's steadfast friends, ground to a halt, and the king himself refused to sanction a clean sweep of the faithful, vowing, "I will part with no more of my friends."[2]

Because the War of the Austrian Succession was still raging when Walpole resigned, George II needed someone with a broad and knowledgeable diplomatic range. John Carteret, bumped from the cabinet in 1730, seemed just the man. For a year and a half, from 1743 into 1744, the king's new appointee directed the diplomatic intrigue against France, perfecting a system whereby England won allies by financing their staggering military debts. Carteret was well on the way to tying Europe into a series of treaties that might have made England the dominant Continental power when, to his complete amazement, he found himself accused of violating the broad-bottomed principle by becoming, as William Pitt charged, "sole minister." The fledgling prime minister, who had learned little from Walpole's error, declared, "Give any man the crown on his side, and he can defy everything."[3] He even held the good will of his ministerial colleagues lightly. On one occasion he loftily refused to meet with them in the Feather Tavern with the trite excuse that he never dined in taverns.

More the issue than Carteret's haughtiness was England's involvement in central Europe. The Patriots' clamor for war restricted to the high seas had now won Newcastle's adherence. Within the cabinet the powerful patron engineered a defeat of Carteret's proposal to subsidize Austria for the duration of the war. Newcastle's next step was to threaten resignation unless England drastically reduced her Continental commitments. He knew full well that without his connections the ministry could accomplish nothing. Consequently, Carteret plummeted from office in November 1744. Not content with this victory, Newcastle and the Patriots pushed for an ever broader-bottomed ministry to include not only Tory members, but also one of the king's antagonists, William Pitt. In February 1746 this demand precipitated the first trial of strength between a monarch and his ministers in modern English history.

[2] Derek Jarrett, *Britain, 1688–1815* (New York, 1965), p. 211.
[3] Quoted in Basil Williams, *The Whig Supremacy 1714–1760* (Oxford, 1952), p. 227.

William Pitt (who in 1766 was to become earl of Chatham), the man over whom this struggle for cabinet control was fought, represented a new breed of politician. Unlike Newcastle, he possessed no ancestral title. Unlike Walpole, he was no country squire. His grandfather, Thomas "Diamond" Pitt, had made the family fortune through interloping in the Indian trade. William's boyhood was colored by romantic stories related by this flamboyant relative of the glory awaiting England in the exotic Orient. A desultory training at Oxford, in Europe, and in the army was boring to the young Pitt (as it was to many boys coming of age in the comfort and opulence of early eighteenth-century England). The republicanism of the Civil Wars and the Jacobitism of the Glorious Revolution were alike preoccupations of ancient history. The House of Hanover was a despicably wasteful appendage with a value far below the worth of the country's holdings in America and India. What mattered now was England's destiny—to rule far-flung empires, to be the Venice of the world, to assume the global role once held by Greece and Rome.

Pitt had entered Parliament through the rotten borough owned by his family. In the House he earned a reputation as Walpole's incorruptible antagonist. When the great Sir Robert fell, Pitt's denunciatory speeches accompanied the prime minister's collapse. Then, during Carteret's regime, he decried what seemed a worse travesty—the selling out of England to Hanoverian interests. Pitt developed a voluminous international correspondence with merchants, seamen, and soldiers, became the leading expert on French overseas holdings, and unrelentingly called for a duel with France for mastery of the world. He proposed himself as the chief instrument of his program.

By 1746 Newcastle was equally sure of Pitt's indispensability, notwithstanding George II's aversion to that presumptuous gentleman who had attacked "miserable" Hanover for converting England into a "mere appendage." However, Pitt's enormous personal following in Commons, his demand that the Dutch shoulder a greater portion of the Continental war, as well as his detailed knowledge of France's colonial resources, made him eminently qualified to sit in George's broad-bottomed cabinet. When the beleaguered king acceded to Pitt's policies but balked at appointing him to the cabinet, Newcastle's ministry resigned to a man. The king irately reinstated Carteret, who could not assemble enough men willing to serve under him. Within two days Newcastle was recalled. His former ministry returned intact but now included William Pitt in the minor position of vice-treasurer of Ireland; Pitt was soon promoted to the more influential post of paymaster of the forces.

This first demonstration of ministerial solidarity, so much a part of modern English cabinet government, was but a token of Parliament's ability to make the monarch squirm. However, the technique of mass resignation was not used again for ninety years. Nonetheless, no minister could count solely on the king's confidence to keep him in office, nor could be expect to conduct any of the king's affairs without a substantial parliamentary following.

Their victory over the king once digested, from 1746 to 1756 the broad-bottomed coalition enjoyed ten years of relative peace. The Treaty of Aix-la-Chapelle, concluding the War of the Austrian Succession in 1748, freed the burdened budget from further military expenditures. Within the cabinet, animosities were so evenly matched that no single patron could dislodge another. When George II's son, Frederick, died in March 1751, leaving the king's thirteen-year-old grandson (the future George III) to inherit Leicester House, the perpetual reversionary threat to the administration momentarily evaporated.

With the normal infighting abated, there was even time for important reforms, not the least pressing being the management of the war debt, which stood at £79 million in 1749. Fortunately, Newcastle had in his brother, Henry Pelham, a lord treasurer with financial talents that nearly equaled Walpole's. Henry Pelham furthered Sir Robert's debt consolidation by easing out of circulation most of the government liabilities carrying interest charges over 3 percent. His most successful scheme for luring private investments into government coffers was the "consol" (the Consolidated Annuities program), all in all the safest of investments for a family of modest means.

The prime minister and his talented brother subsidized the first professional police force in the London area, the Bow Street Runners, at the modest sum of £400 annually. It was during the Pelhams' administration that the gin trade was brought under control and that the act abolishing secret marriages was put into law. The mood for enlightened legislation was further reflected in Parliament's repeal of all statutes against witchcraft. It also aligned the English calendar with the Continent's; in 1582 most of Europe had adopted the Gregorian calendar. England's anti-Catholicism had prevented her from following what was a pope's edict, and she had continued to reckon by the ancient Julian calendar. By the eighteenth century she was eleven days behind the Continent. In 1751 it was decreed that the day following the second of September 1752 should be the fourteenth rather than the third of the month. "Give us back our eleven days," demanded the unschooled, who believed that a week and a half of life had somehow been stolen through Parliament's ineptitude.

The serene decade from 1746 to 1756, probably the only period of relative internal and external peace in an otherwise turbulent century, terminated with the collapse of Newcastle's cabinet. The wisest voice in his assemblage was silenced in March 1754 with Henry Pelham's death. The first lord of the treasury was mourned by a king who somehow knew that he would have no more peace. It took only a few months for the old chemistry of political intrigue to dissolve the broad-bottomed coalition. The prime minister, Newcastle, reshuffled the cabinet, surrounding himself with ciphers. Pitt, jealous of his less talented colleagues, shifted his allegiance to the increasing strength of Leicester House (Prince George had declared himself of legal age at eighteen) and its patron, Lord Bute, George's tutor. A contest of major significance loomed, not only between Newcastle and Pitt, but also between England and France.

The Seven Years' War

Thomas Pelham, duke of Newcastle, whose only real talent lay in marshaling votes, might have retained office had Europe stayed at peace. He was undone in parts of the world of which he had no knowledge, by foreign threats he was totally unprepared to counter. Along the North American frontier English and French–Canadian settlements faced each other's thinly scattered lines of fortresses. In 1754 word came that the young Colonel George Washington's Virginia detachment had surrendered to French forces marching from Fort Duquesne. England had lost the fort to France a year earlier in one of the increasing numbers of border skirmishes. In 1755 General Braddock, sent to drive the enemy from its bastion on the Ohio River, was killed and his army slaughtered in an ambush on the banks of the Monongahela. The news in 1756 was starker. The island of Minorca had been under severe siege by the French for seventy days. Admiral Byng, sent to relieve the besieged English troops, considered the island irrevocably lost and after a brief sea encounter retired to Gibraltar. Minorca fell, and Byng, who according to the critics at his trial had retired too hastily, was executed on the deck of his own ship, a martyr to Newcastle's desperate search for a scapegoat. Now reports circulated that France intended a direct assault on England. The threat was then exaggerated, but Newcastle's impotence was exposed when a militia bill failed to muster the necessary majority to pass the House of Lords. Calcutta fell in India; Oswego on Lake Ontario capitulated to the French. There was little of the prime minister's pride intact when the government declared war on France in May of 1756.

Newcastle's one stroke of luck lay in maneuvering Frederick the Great of Prussia, France's old ally, into signing a treaty for mutual defense. Even that, the Treaty of Westminster (January 1756), was largely a product of Frederick's fear of a Russian invasion. The Anglo-Prussian alliance threw Austria and France into each other's arms, a diplomatic reversal from their roles in the War of the Austrian Succession. With these new and unfamiliar partnerships concluded, the Seven Years' War was launched.

When at last Pitt was commissioned by a grudging George II to form his own ministry in November 1756, it was at the expense of Newcastle's resignation. Soon the monarch was complaining that Pitt would not do his German business. It took only the refusal of the king's youngest son to serve abroad as long as Pitt held office to provide George with the excuse he wanted in order to overturn his own appointed prime minister. Newcastle was invited to return, but for ten harrowing weeks—with no leadership, no ministry—the nation poured out its hearty support for the ousted Pitt. Both camps finally realized that neither could achieve a thing without the other. At the end of June 1757, Pitt triumphantly returned to the head of the ministry, and Newcastle assumed his deft management of the vote in Parliament. Pitt and the king compromised on the "German business": unlimited English supplies and sumptuous English subsidies to Hanover and Prussia were to keep France perpetually preoccupied on the Continent by Frederick's superb army; meanwhile, England's manpower and her vast naval potential would be free to pursue the enemy everywhere else on the globe. "America was conquered in Germany," Pitt was to say later in praise of his own sagacity, and King George II, now assured of Pitt's willingness to protect Hanover, abandoned every shred of his old suspicion of the prime minister.

Not since Marlborough's single-handed generalship had England seen such a leader as William Pitt. Though he never commanded in the field, he was totally engrossed in the war, forever surrounded by maps, dispatches, and statistics. Each of his commanders looked to him for personal direction, with confidence that he knew precisely which man could take what military objective. Pitt promoted leaders, not by the old system's purchased commission or family connection, but by personal ability. Colonial militia officers, like Washington, were given rank equal to their counterparts in the regular royal command. Pitt shared the triumphs and failures in all military theaters with the public.

There were three major theaters in this mighty war: the Continental, under the general supervision of Frederick the Great; the Indian, commanded by Robert Clive; and the North American, managed by Pitt himself and regarded by him as the fulcrum of his world-wide operations.

Though the Continental exercises were seen by Pitt as diversionary, the diversions worked admirably. Pitt accepted the resignation of his earlier adversary, the king's youngest son, the duke of Cumberland, as military commander. He replaced him with Prince Ferdinand of Brunswick, whom he equipped with over a million pounds of supplies. Together with a token force of some ten thousand English troops, the Hanoverians kept the French off balance and gave flanking cover to Frederick the Great throughout much of the war.

In India, Pitt was able to reap the rewards and fame of an East India Company expansionism that had been pursued since the start of the century. The East India Company, endowed with a charter allowing it to maintain its own army and conduct treaty negotiations with local princes on the subcontinent of India, had been trading in the Orient since 1601. In 1623 the Dutch had driven the company's merchants from the wealthy East Indies (what is now Indonesia) in a bloody massacre. This forced the disconsolate English to interlope where they could in the declining Portuguese empire's enclaves along India's coasts. By 1700, after numerous bouts with Portuguese flotillas and local pirates, the East India Company secured the treaty ports of Bombay on the Indian west coast, Madras on the east coast, and Calcutta at the mouth of the Ganges River. The company's annual fleets brought home cotton, pepper, spices, and saltpeter for gunpowder. Then, in 1706, order disintegrated with the death of India's last emperor, the Great Mogul. England vied with France over the dismembered empire, at first by wooing local princes with money and firearms, then by overt seizure of Indian territory.

On the eve of the Seven Years' War, the East India Company possessed in Robert Clive an official whose command of the Indian situation had been proved by his success in reducing French influence in southern India. Clive's talents were tested in 1757 over the Black Hole of Calcutta episode, the victorious outcome of which redounded to Pitt's greater glory. Encouraged by the French garrison, the ruler of Bengal ousted the English from their stronghold at Calcutta. When the company force capitulated in June 1756, the 146 prisoners were stupidly crowded into a poorly ventilated cell eighteen by fourteen feet. By the next morning all but twenty-three had perished. Though not the calculated atrocity that it was portrayed in England, the episode understandably became a cause for revenge. Clive forcefully retook Calcutta in January 1757 and in June went on to the unheard-of feat of smashing the overwhelming forces of the Bengalese army at the Battle of Plassey. In one sweeping action, vengeance was satisfied, French influence was nullified, and England found herself direct ruler of an entire Indian state. Now freed from the confines of treaty ports, British expansion in India continued until 1947.

America: The First Priority

The empire in America, though differing from India in organization, extent, and productivity, was nonetheless also a creature of commerce. From Newfoundland to Georgia almost the entire east coast of North America was British. The colonial planners of the eighteenth century also thought of the island plantations stretching from the Bermudas and Bahamas, through the Virgin Islands, Barbados, St. Kitts, Montserrat, and

Antigua to Jamaica as part of the varied American complex. Unlike in India, there was no overall direction for America, no central authority. The settlements were unorganized, and highly diversified local economies proliferated. Some colonies, Rhode Island and Connecticut among them, had virtual self-rule; others, the Carolinas and Georgia in particular, had very little management over their own policies. All the colonies sent wide ranges of commodities to each other as well as to the mother country. From the north came furs and fish, as well as naval stores in such abundance that by 1750 England no longer relied on Scandinavian sources. The tar coming from New England amounted to over 100,000 barrels annually. Beams and masts from Massachusetts, measuring seven feet in diameter and over a hundred feet long, were drawn through the deep snows by teams of seventy oxen down to the coast. They were shipped to England or used by the local shipbuilding enterprises. From New England, too, came as much as 2 million gallons of rum per year. From New York to Pennsylvania a rich abundance of goods, from iron to barrel staves, from wheat to bacon, made its way overseas. Southern colonies specialized in tobacco. An annual average of £300,000 was gleaned by the colonists of Maryland and Virginia. The Atlantic and Caribbean islands contributed sugar, salt, and spices to the well-being of Englishmen.

North America's commercial activity represented an extraordinary amount of wealth. In 1755 Philadelphia was, after all, one of the largest cities in the empire. Its port saw as many as five hundred ships anchoring along two miles of wharves. Eleven out of twelve New Yorkers dressed in English-produced clothes, and yet New York in 1750 imported less from England than did Antigua and only half as much as Barbados. By 1760, with the American colonies accounting for £2 million worth of trade, it was little wonder that Pitt's foreign policies began and ended with colonial defense and expansion in mind.

Early in the war, in a series of circular letters, Pitt assured the "King's good subjects and colonies of North America" that their defense would be given priority over any other of England's holdings. The burdens of protecting America during the war years were carried by the home government to the tune of £1,275,000, about a third of the total cost of the wars.

The Year It Rained Victories

Seventeen fifty-nine was the "miraculous year," "the year it rained victories," the year, as Horace Walpole observed, "when we are forced to ask every morning what victory there has been for fear of missing one." Actually, as successful as were the broad campaigns, only a few major triumphs were achieved, but the average English subject heard daily reports of each phase of these prolonged engagements. The effect as each campaign mounted to a victorious climax must have been intoxicating.

The first of the exhilarating reports of the glorious year of 1759 came from the West Indies. A naval operation was designed to capture the competing French sugar islands. Initially Guadeloupe fell, followed by lesser French holdings. Now, two years after the rumors of an impending invasion first reached England's shores, it was learned that the largest invasion fleet the French had ever amassed was about to transport thousands of troops across the Channel. However, her ships never got under way because of an overpowering English blockade. Then, when the French armada made its move, the English Admiral Hawke pounced on the fleet before it lost sight of the coast of France, destroying seven ships and driving most of the balance onto the mud banks of Quiberon Bay. Next came news that the French invasion of Germany had been brought to a standstill at the Battle of Minden. The English wing of the allied armies had carried the day. But the most dramatic reports came late in the year. Young Admiral Saunders daringly escorted two hundred troop transports and twenty-two great ships of the line (the equivalent of today's battleships) up the St. Lawrence River in Canada to the French citadel at Quebec. General Wolfe and his army disembarked from Saunders' ships, but the French paid little heed, thinking he would be confined to the banks of the river long enough for the winter blizzards to wipe out the whole expedition. On the night of September 12, the dauntless Wolfe led his men noiselessly up an unguarded western slope to the Plains of Abraham outside the fortress at Quebec. He opened a surprise attack at nine the next morning and routed the entire garrison. Both Wolfe and the French commander, Montcalm, died of wounds. The war in Canada was virtually over.

Foreign Victories and Domestic Betrayals

The final four years of war brought ever more of France's empire under the British flag. Once Guadeloupe was lost, France's other West Indian holdings followed (Dominica, Martinique, Grenada, and St. Lucia). When Spain belatedly engaged the English in 1762 (the year before hostilities ended), she too was shorn of her island holdings (Cuba and the Philippines). Montreal surrendered in September 1760, ending the French–Canadian threat. In a joint land–sea operation in India reminiscent of the Saunders–Wolfe seizure of Quebec, Admiral Charles Steevens and General Eyre Coote bottled up the French in their last station in India (Pondicherry). After January of 1761 India was as British as Canada or the West Indies.

Had the king lived at least three more years, Pitt might have gone on to reduce France and Spain to beggary. As it was, he pushed the war to the enemy's home territory. In 1762 Belle Île, off France's coast, was taken. But in October 1760 George II had died, leaving the throne to his estranged grandson of twenty-two and his pompous tutor-adviser. George III and John Stuart, Lord Bute, were dedicated to ending what George described as the "bloody and expensive war" and dissolving the ministry that engineered it. Actually, a royal partnership between the new king and Pitt might well have been more amiable than the relationship between the monarch's grandfather and the prime minister. But George III held that Pitt had deserted him three years earlier by agreeing to do George II's German business. This had been a double betrayal to the former head of Leicester House (whom Pitt had courted), a breach of personal trust, and a disavowal of Pitt's lifelong opposition to English dependency on Hanover. George III felt no loyalty to the House of Hanover. He held himself to be the first native-born British monarch in two generations. He despised the prime minister for having sold his genius to the likes of Newcastle to gain support for imperial pretensions.

He also meant to end the old system of borough mongering and vote buying and to surround himself with honest gentlemen dedicated to fundamental reforms. Whatever the new king had in mind more specifically, no one was sure; but the hordes of politicians who had favored his grandfather's ministry were chilled by the sudden cold enveloping Pitt and Newcastle. Things were toastier in Bute's circle. Desertions from the prime minister's camp, even from within the cabinet, snowballed. Pitt could not even carry a vote to prolong the war. The king cut appropriations for Prussia in half, and as if by signal, the cabinet began to urge Pitt to sign a peace. Negotiations had been dragging since the victorious year of 1759. Bullheaded as ever, Pitt pressed to continue the war, until his brother-in-law, Richard Grenville, a member of the cabinet, was his only support. When it inevitably came in October 1761, the prime minister's resignation rang with a familiar rhetoric: "I was called by my sovereign and by the voice of the people to assist the state. . . . I will go on no longer since my advice is not taken. Being responsible I will direct and will be responsible for nothing I do not direct."[4] Newcastle, increasingly embarrassed, followed him into retirement six months later.

With Pitt, the chief obstacle, removed, the Treaty of Paris was judiciously concluded in 1763. The loss of some of his commanders' hard-won gains infuriated the former prime minister: in the West Indies, Guadeloupe, together with Martinique and St. Lucia, were returned to France, as was her coastal island, Belle Île; Pondicherry in India was restored under terms that the French guarantee that they would never rearm it. The loser retained remunerative fishing rights in Newfoundland. Cuba and the Philippines reverted to Spain. Yet the Treaty of Paris is a manifestation of England's

[4] Quoted in Williams, *op. cit.*, p. 347.

imperial growth prior to the era of the American Revolution: the immense assets of the new Canadian and Indian territories were complemented by Florida, which Spain reluctantly ceded to England in return for the restoration of her island holdings; the West Indian colonies were swollen by St. Vincent, Grenada, Tobago, and Dominica; Senegal, in Africa, completed the new aggregation.

Pitt prophetically attacked the peace on the grounds that the terms would leave France with enough strength to challenge the country again. He also called George III's desertion of Frederick and Prussia an act bordering on treachery, an assertion with which Germany—and Europe in general—concurred. Perfidious Albion had again deserted her allies. Mistrust of her motives were to hamper her diplomacy even to the eve of the Second World War.

As for Pitt, the country was not to see his likes again, or the glorious sense of heroic participation his leadership inspired. As Boswell was to recount years later, " Walpole was a minister given by the king to the people—Pitt was a minister given by the people to the king."

Chapter Ten
THE ERA
OF LORD NORTH

Major Personages

Bentham, Jeremy, 1748–1832; legal and social philosopher, founder of the utilitarian movement

Burke, Edmund, 1729–97; one of England's greatest statesmen; regarded as the father of modern conservatism

Bute, John Stuart, third earl of, 1713–92; George III's tutor, friend, and first chief minister

Fox, Charles James, 1749–1806; originally conservative, later famous as the century's most progressive politician

Grenville, George, 1712–70; successor to Bute, responsible for introducing government economies and extending taxation to the American colonies

North, Frederick North, second earl of Guilford, eighth baron, 1732–92; George III's chief minister during the Wilkes, East Indian, and American crises

Shelburne, William Petty, second earl of, 1737–1805; political patron of philosophical radicals, prime minister briefly after the fall of North

Smith, Adam, 1723–90; famed economic philosopher, professor at Glasgow University, author of *Wealth of Nations*

Wilkes, John, 1727–97; popular political leader whose various causes revived radical activism

CHRONOLOGY

1763–74	Height of "Wilkes and Liberty" agitation
1764	Sugar Act
1765	Stamp Act
1770–82	Lord North's controversial ministry
1772	Bankruptcy of the East India Company
1773	India Regulating Act
	Boston Tea Party
1774	American Continental Congress
1775–83	War of American Independence, concluded by the Treaty of Versailles
1780	Gordon riots

*I love the Americans because they love
liberty. The gentleman tells us that
America is obstinate, America is almost
in open rebellion. I rejoice that America
has resisted.*

WILLIAM PITT, earl of Chatham
Parliamentary speech, January 1766

George III was the most enigmatic personality to occupy the English throne since Henry VIII. Like his flamboyant forebear, he too was intensively groomed for kingship with the unexpected death of an heir apparent. But whereas his Tudor ancestor reacted against the severity of childhood training by later indulgences, George III never escaped his mother's incessant command, "George, be a king." His domineering parent and early tutors instilled in him an unnerving sense of inadequacy. He felt compelled to seek forever a surrogate with a strength and devotion to duty that might more adequately fill the post for which he judged himself imperfect. Only as "Farmer George," the devoted gardener, did he find a happiness and relaxation that eluded him in the pretentious London court.

The fault in this very conscientious monarch lay in his overhasty condemnation of opposition (which he facilely blamed on human perversity rather than on political conviction). He readily knew what he did not want but questioned his ability to discern the needs and desires of his people. Thus in late eighteenth-century England, with every facet of government and society faced with radical action—from America and France, from the English working class, even from religion and philosophy—a ruler as complex and confused as George III might well appear a tyrant.

His prolonged search for a satisfactory royal servant lasted from the resignation (October 1761) of his inherited prime minister, William Pitt, to the appointment of Lord North in 1770. In the nine-year interim England blundered chaotically from ministry to ministry. The first of the king's personal appointees was his friend of Leicester House days, John Stuart, earl of Bute. But however noble the sentiments of the monarch's ex-tutor, in the judgment of one astute observer, he would only "have made an admirable ambassador in any court where there was nothing to do."[1] The job was too much for Bute's limited resources; and after concluding the Seven Years' War (which pleased the public) and passing a cider tax (which alienated the public), both servant and master were less popular than at George's coronation. The prime minister's windows were smashed, his coach was vandalized, his nationality (Scottish) slandered. In April 1763 the much-maligned Bute plaintively implored his king, "having done my duty, and stood the hour of peril, every wish of heart . . . call[s] loud upon me to retire in quiet, and pass the autumnal part of life, unruffled by the little infamous scenes, the black ingratitude . . . that decorates every hour of my present situation."[2] George reluctantly accepted his resignation.

Possibly every minister of the next twenty years was to commiserate and share Bute's relief at resigning. None of them was to be successful in paying off the sizable war debt or in correctly estimating the proliferating costs of administering the new imperial holdings. The debt, standing at £79 million when the War of the Austrian Succession ended in 1748, passed £114 million in 1761. By then, the government's budget had tripled from prewar days, and its creditors were collecting £4 million annually in interest alone. The financial burdens of the new territories were soon to drive the formerly prosperous East India Company into bankruptcy and the king's American subjects into rebellion. Bad harvests plagued the land; high unemployment cursed the towns. Every minister of that aggravated period turned to expedients to increase revenue or reduce expenditures, but with each approach to solvency, another war obliterated the results.

Resentment over attempts by Bute to fatten revenue with a cider tax was inevitable, for here was the public's old enemy—an excise. His successor, the ambitious George Grenville, further alienated the nation by futile efforts to balance the budget; and because Grenville cut military expenditures to the bone, the country's ability to deal later with the American revolutionaries was disastrously impaired. To the dismay of the consumer at home, he multiplied the number and variety of goods under import duty until the English came to believe themselves the most overtaxed in the world. Rather than encourage that belief, Grenville passed on two assessments to the colonists to cover the enlarged costs of patrolling their frontiers—with the Sugar Act (1764) and the Stamp Act (1765). Actually, neither tax was his personal invention, but the first (related to the Molasses Act of 1733) had seldom been collected, and the second, requiring tax stamps for legal documents, had never before been imposed in America.

[1] Quoted in Charles Grant Robertson, *England under the Hanoverians* (London, 1948), p. 219.
[2] Quoted in V. H. H. Green, *The Hanoverians 1714–1815* (London, 1963), pp. 306–307.

A New Ascendancy

The general public was witnessing in Grenville's monetary policies more than just the machinations of another tax gatherer. He represented a new breed of expeditious economic reformer, one who equated government operations with those of a well-run private business. Thus when the minister calculated that £2,000 in American customs were costing England £8,000 to collect, he instituted the obvious reforms: tighter regulations, a clampdown on smuggling and the bribery of officials. But these remedial measures irritated the self-sufficient colonists into contemplating total independence. As R. J. White explains it, "The Americans wanted either free trade or unimpeded smuggling. Grenville gave them a high duty and an improved customs service."[3]

The English country squires were by then the prime minister's sole political support. Tired of financing the never-ending "merchants' wars" for trade and commerce, the gentry were delighted to pass on a share of the tax load to their American cousins. Had the decision lain only with that powerful group, Grenville's ministry might have endured; but the sovereign's view, "I would rather see the devil in my closet than Mr. Grenville," assured its collapse.

Part of George III's malevolence toward his prime minister was personal. After recovery from a nervous breakdown in 1765, the king called on his ministers to submit a bill providing for a regency should he be incapacitated again. When the cautious ministry excluded George's beloved mother on the grounds of her public unpopularity, the king all but choked on the insult. Then too, he found the business side of governing dull. He was to moan that "when [Grenville] has wearied me for two hours, he looks at his watch to see if he may not tire me for an hour more."[4] Their most rankling disagreement hinged on the prime minister's insistence that the monarch desist from soliciting the advice of Lord Bute. Grenville's ego, as well as his role as England's chief minister, demanded that he alone manifest the king's policy. No discussions, no letters, no appointments with any personage in government were to take place or be exchanged without his awareness—to this the king must promise! To this the king did promise for the sake of a unified governmental image. But from that degrading moment George III worked for a new cabinet. Although he succeeded in ridding himself of his antagonist, his weakness in the face of insolence emboldened future prime ministers to exact more control over their administrations.

Grenville's difficulties were increasing also from a totally unexpected quarter. Heretofore a ministry knew its enemies—sometimes the court, often Leicester

---

[3] R.J. White, *The Age of George III* (New York, 1969), p. 94.
[4] Quoted in *ibid.*, p. 81.

House, and usually one or more of the number of parliamentary cliques. Now a new ascendancy, the ordinarily unorganized electorate, harassed the office—and the crown and Parliament as well. The small landholders, the rapidly declining yeomanry, artisans, shopkeepers—middling men in all trades—were leery of the gigantic corporations, incensed by mounting taxes, and demoralized by an indifferent government. They suddenly found themselves a leader in John Wilkes, an arrogant and opportunistic renegade with a lusty private life (he belonged to a number of notorious gentlemen's organizations including the Hellfire club, in which he attended black masses and "orgies"). Yet "that devil Wilkes," as George was to dub him, possessed the appeal of such past folk heroes as Titus Oates and Henry Sacheverell in that he was a vent for public dissatisfaction. His political sagacity, however, outreached that of earlier popular leaders, and he was the sponsor of a number of genuine reform measures.

Wilkes was a member of Parliament and a minor functionary in the household of Pitt's brother-in-law when he was commissioned by Pitt's embittered followers to harass Lord Bute's administration. They felt Bute had betrayed their leader's wartime achievements. With their financial backing, Wilkes set up an opposition newspaper, *The North Briton*, which quickly became notorious in the court for its lack of royal reverence. In its April 23 issue (number 45) of 1763, Wilkes directly attacked the king for being a pawn of unscrupulous courtiers who were bent on reviving absolutism. He reminded His Majesty that "the king of England is only the first magistrate of this country, . . . responsible to his people for the due execution of the royal functions in the choice of his ministers; . . . [he is] equal with the meanest of his subjects in his particular duty."

It did not take long for the administrative ax to fall. Wilkes, together with forty-nine publishers and printers involved in the publication of "Number 45," was arrested on a general warrant. The first of many ensuing trials was short-lived, most of those particular charges being dropped; and Wilkes donned the mantle of an innocent citizen wronged for a devotion to liberty. He fought for the right to sit in a parliament that had tried to exclude him and, in a most unusual suit, successfully sued the secretary of state, collecting £1,000 in damages. In his prolonged career Wilkes' support knew no bounds. At one point the lord mayor and some aldermen of London went to prison in his cause.

Horace Walpole, Sir Robert's son, best described the Wilkes mania in a series of revealing letters to friends. In 1763:

> Well! we have had a prodigious riot. . . . It was so prodigious a tumult that I verily thought half the administration would have run away. . . . *The North Briton* was ordered [by Parliament] to be burned by the hangman at Cheapside, on Saturday last.

The mob rose; the greatest mob, says Mr. Sheriff Blunt, that he had known in forty years. They are armed with that most bloody instrument, the mud out of the kennels. . . . Numbers of gentlemen, from the windows and balconies, encouraged the mob.

Two years later he enlarged on the subject:

Williams, the reprinter of *The North Briton*, stood in the pillory today in the palace yard. He went in a hackney coach the number of which was 45. The mob erected a gallows opposite to him, on which they hung a boot [Bute/boot] with a bonnet [head] of straw. . . . In short, every public event informs the administration how thoroughly they are detested, and that they have not a friend whom they do not buy.

In 1768 Walpole added:

There have been constant crowds and mobbing at the prison, but on Tuesday they insisted on taking Wilkes out of prison [where he had been incarcerated as an outlaw by Parliament] and carrying him to parliament. The tumult increased so fast that the riot act was read, the soldiers fired, and a young man was shot. The mob bore his body about the streets to excite more rage, and at night it went so far that four or five more persons were killed and the uproar quashed though they fired on the soldiers from the windows of houses. . . . The coal heavers . . . have stopped all coals coming to town. The sawyers rose too, and at last the sailors, who have committed great outrages in merchant ships and prevented them from sailing.

Throughout these frenetic years the cry " Wilkes and liberty" bombarded the ears of king and court.

During his turbulent career the energetic John Wilkes was responsible for a number of significant decisions in civil liberties. The general warrant by which the books of *The North Briton* had been confiscated was declared illegal because the government had seized the papers to find evidence for charges otherwise impossible to substantiate. When the government pleaded the seizure on grounds of state necessity, the judge declared, "Public policy" was not an argument "in a court of law," and clearly implied that the law could not be used to sanction or punish political conduct, the law being above politics.[5] Wilkes is also credited with publishing the earliest accounts of parliamentary debates, thus breaking the rule of secrecy that protected parliamentary blunders from newspaper coverage. His early campaign against rotten and pocket boroughs and his espousal of universal male suffrage were to triumph after he had long departed from the scene. Wilkes also exposed the pretense that the House of Commons was a representative assembly; though he won three open

[5] See Goldwin Smith, *A Constitutional and Legal History of England* (New York, 1955), pp. 408–9.

elections, he was denied his seat each time by the pompous oligarchs who treated Commons as their private club.

Amid royal disfavor and growing public hysteria, Grenville quietly and gratefully relinquished his office to Lord Rockingham in July 1765. The new ministry, which resembled the old Newcastle broad-bottomed cabinet, scored no better than Bute's or Grenville's in ruling the ever more agitated empire. A New York meeting of nine colonies (the Stamp Act Congress) asserted that the home government had no tax jurisdiction whatever over them. When the still powerful William Pitt egged them on by announcing in Parliament, "I rejoice that America has resisted," Rockingham's group, under pressure, sponsored the repeal of the Stamp Act. But whatever good will the action gained was negated by the face-saving Declaratory Act escorting the repeal; it stated "that the said colonies and plantations in America have been, are, and of right ought to be, subordinate unto and dependent upon the imperial crown and parliament of Great Britain." Within a year of taking office, the Rockingham ministry disintegrated to the accompaniment of riots and boycotts by the colonists. The sugar duty was lowered, a parting admission of the failure of Rockingham's fiscal policies.

Pitt's Return to Office: A Mysterious Failure

George III, now on the throne scarcely six years and having witnessed the demise of three of his ministries, finally yielded to the general clamor: Invite Mr. Pitt to return! The king's personal animosity to the former prime minister had abated. He created Pitt earl of Chatham and appointed him lord privy seal in July 1766. But in peace Pitt lacked the decisiveness he had exhibited in the war years, and his imperiousness, which once passed as authority, now offended his cabinet, causing resignations. He treated America and India as though they were still under a French threat. His intractable cabinet colleagues, particularly the dissolute "Champagne Charley" Townshend, added to his anxieties. They humiliated him as well by bringing down upon the colonies the hated Townshend Act (a spate of import duties on lead, glass, paper, paint, and tea).

Pitt's inability to stop Townshend and master the cabinet is mysteriously tragic. It is said that Pitt had lost touch with his most ardent votaries. Because he had assumed the peerage, even his old popular title, the Great Commoner, had become outdated. The ravages of age showed on his face, gout had weakened his body, and at times his mind wandered. After March 1767 he was seldom seen. He spent hours sitting in the dark and refused to see anyone. He brooded in seclusion in remote Hampstead until his final resignation in October 1768. The flimsy remnants of his glory he bequeathed to a loyal colleague, the duke of Grafton. But because of the diversity of cliques, Grafton too could barely keep his ministry intact. America and Wilkes (then launching his six-year campaign over his right to be seated in Commons) made a shambles of Grafton's short tenure. The fifth of George's ministers wished heartily for the chance recovery of Pitt's mental health to keep the administration from running quickly aground. But when Lord Chatham did recover his reason, his caustic oratory was turned on his old friend in defense of Wilkes. The dispirited Grafton withdrew from office in January 1770.

Lord North and "the Evil at Home"

In February, Frederick, Lord North, began his ministry; its twelve years made it the most durable since Walpole's, but despite its comparative longevity it was by far the most controversial of the entire century. North was defamed then, as he occasionally still is, as the bumbler who lost America and as the willing tool of George III's wicked efforts to reassert royal absolutism. R. J. White provides a provocative insight into North's ill reputation:

> When the Americans became the successful people, they took over English history, imposing upon it their own peculiar myths, greatly to the disrepute of those who ever had the temerity to stand in their way. Among these, Lord North is the saddest, though not the most tragical, figure. His blown-out cheeks and goggle eyes have left him stranded on the shores of history like a deflated frog.[6]

Actually, North was no less equipped to rule an eighteenth-century English ministry than Newcastle or Rockingham or Bute had been. He had a moderate talent and had served in a number of ministries since 1759, neither distinguishing himself nor offending the great patrons. It seems that when Grafton relinquished his bloodied grip on the cabinet, no man favored by king, court, and country could be agreed upon. Thus Lord North, who had so miraculously survived eleven precarious years in public office, was probably chosen for his lack of notoriety. He was never comfortable in the post and tried frequently to resign for ten of his twelve years as prime minister, staying only on George's insistence. His course was not really as aimless as the negative results seemed to indicate. He did attempt to negotiate with the rebellious Americans, tried unsuccessfully to reform India's government, and futilely attempted to solve the curse of the ever rising national debt. He failed at all these efforts because it was forever beyond his comprehension that the occasional and piecemeal solutions of Newcastle's day could not effect cures for what had become total national problems. In the not-too-distant past a new customs duty, an eloquent speech (North was an excellent debater), or a well-placed bribe could

[6] White, *op. cit.,* p. 142.

reasonably readjust a political imbalance; in calmer times there were lesser matters (maintaining the fleet, correcting the calendar, mopping up after the gin mania) to concern the government. Now the costs of financing the vastly expanded empire were prohibitive. To increase taxes was not the answer, for the usual sources could not, or would not, be further bled. The gentry had forced the land tax down from four to three shillings. The Americans had burned the stamps England sent and had compelled the repeal of the Stamp Act. North never understood the reasons for these obstructions or for the other emergencies that vexed what was to him the unchangeable England of gentlemen's politics played for sport.

The domestic crises of North's dozen years initially swirled around the vortex of Wilkes' hurricane. A general deterioration in public morale during this period was manifest in a bleak opinion appearing in the 1775 issue of the relatively objective *Annual Register*: "It is no longer our task to describe devastation in Poland or slaughter on the Danube. The evil is at home." Numerous organizations were set up to expose the rights being denied, the corruptions being perpetuated. In 1769 the Society for the Defense of the Bill of Rights was founded; its first order of the day to collect £4,000 to erase John Wilkes' indebtedness. A year later the Society for Constitutional Information set out to uncover degeneracy in English public life. Parliamentary reform, especially for the disproportionate pull of the rotten boroughs, was the main target of these groups, though many of the members saw universal manhood suffrage as their worthiest objective. Both organizations were made up largely of urban and working-class people. The largest society for political agitation, the Yorkshire Association (founded in 1780) was composed largely of rural gentry, though it sometimes democratically joined the urban societies in joint demonstrations. Its leader, Christopher Wyvill, while put off by the depravity in Wilkes' private life, nonetheless sympathized with Wilkes' anger over vote buying and the wasting of tax money. Since the preponderance of corrupt parliamentary representatives came from the towns, Wyvill advocated expanding the rural electorate by a hundred seats. His theory that the honest God-fearing farmers could drive the moneychangers from the political temple seemed logical. At a mass meeting in London, a new ear-rending chant split the air—"Wilkes, Wyvill, and Reform!"

It is during this decade of intense social revaluation that writers began using the adjective "radical" as a noun denoting one who employed extreme methods for reforming a system that would not reform itself. Catherine Macaulay, intrigued by the arguments of her brother, a progressive London alderman, was among the first urging radical action in print. Another reformer, John Cartwright, in his *Take Your Choice* (1776), advocated the ballot and annually elected parliaments. But the most agitatedly discussed writer of the period was the mysterious "Junius," the pen name for an author still un-identified. It was rumored that this political phantom was Grenville, Pitt, Rockingham, Wilkes—the list of attributions lengthened to include nearly everyone. Junius' use of privileged information known only to a few well situated officials made his letters in the London newspapers sensational reading between 1767 and 1772. Whoever he was, Junius' attacks on the king's government were characterized by an audacity not seen in print since the Glorious Revolution:

> The name of Stuart, [he wrote] is only contemptible; armed with the sovereign authority [the Stuarts'] principles are formidable. The prince who imitates their conduct should be warned by their example; and while [George III] plumes himself upon the security of his title to the crown, [he] should remember that, as it was acquired by one revolution, it may be lost by another.

These broad references to 1688 were widely read. They were especially devoured by the Nonconformist clergy, the inheritors of the Puritans' revolutionary past, and by a small band of liberal Anglican sympathizers. The reformers of this period tended to be men of the cloth, as were Wyvill and Horne Tooke, founder of the Bill of Rights Society (both were parsons). Joseph Priestly, a Presbyterian minister–scientist, published his *First Principles of Government* in 1768, in which he revived an old Lockean principle: "The good and happiness of the members . . . of any state, is the great standard by which everything relating to that state must finally be determined." A considerably harder stance was taken by Dr. Richard Price, the popular Nonconformist preacher and economist. In his *Observations on Civil Liberty* (1776) he noted that the present political evil was coequal with the moral collapse of England:

> From one end of North America to the other they are fasting and praying. But what are we doing?—Shocking thought.—We are running wild after pleasure and forgetting everything serious and decent in masquerades.—We are gambling in gaming houses: trafficking in boroughs: perjuring ourselves at elections; and selling ourselves for places—Which side is providence likely to favor?

The radical clerics were infusing the reform movement with a moral fervor, even offering utopian expectations, as did Priestly, who promised, "Whatever was the beginning of this world, the end will be glorious and paradisiacal, beyond what our imaginations can now conceive."

But the present was decidedly gloomy. As Horace Walpole observed in 1771, England was "a gaming, robbing, wrangling, railing nation without principles, genius, character or allies; the overgrown shadow of what it was." A story made the rounds that the king would offer the renowned historian Edward Gibbon (whose *Decline and Fall of the Roman Empire* first appeared in

1776) a lucrative place if he agreed *not* to write the *Decline and Fall of the British Empire*. Against this somber background two of the century's greatest social philosophers, Adam Smith and Jeremy Bentham, produced their basic works, interestingly enough published in 1776, the same year that the Cartwright and Price books were issued.

These social reformers equated morality and politics with natural law. Adam Smith, in his *Wealth of Nations*, wrote that man would improve his condition without, or in spite of, human laws and restrictions:

> The natural effort of every individual to better his own conditions, when suffered to exert itself with freedom and security, is so powerful a principle, that it is alone, and without any assistance, not only capable of carrying on the society to wealth and prosperity, but of surmounting a hundred impertinent obstructions with which the folly of human laws too often encumbers its operations.

No artificial carrot-and-stick inducements would be needed:

> Every individual necessarily labors to render the annual revenue of the society as great as he can. He generally, indeed, neither intends to promote the public interest, nor knows how much he is promoting it . . . he intends only his own gain, and he is in this, as in many other cases, led by an invisible hand to promote an end which was no part of his intention. . . . By pursuing his own interest he frequently promotes that of the society more effectually than when he really intends to promote it.

Smith further thought he had discovered nature's eternal law of supply and demand, the regulator of the division of labor. He could not help applying the rule to the age of Grenville and North: no expenditure, however vast, could hold unwilling colonists; wasteful and vainglorious wars were follies—government policies that assumed otherwise should be abandoned in the name of economy, if not for the sake of the public good.

Jeremy Bentham's *A Fragment on Government* lifted from Priestly the idea that the true and simple object of government was to provide the greatest happiness for the greatest number of people. Any obstruction to this rule—tradition, archaic laws and customs, metaphysical and abstract moralities—must be quashed. His theory of utilitarianism stated that only the utility of an object, a law, an idea should be the measurement; utility was to be gauged by a pain-or-pleasure principle. Under such rational scrutiny it therefore must follow that the entirety of the English constitution was virtually useless convention since the English populace was obviously not happy. He was to write on in this vein throughout a career lasting close to sixty years, winning converts and revolutionizing English lawmaking under the banner of utilitarianism.

The budding careers of political reformers Lord Shelburne, Edmund Burke, and Charles James Fox illustrate the effects of radicalism on late eighteenth-century England. Polemist Edmund Burke, secretary to Lord Rockingham, opened his campaign in 1770 with his *Thoughts on the Causes of the Present Discontents*. "The power of the crown," he reported, "almost dead and rotten as prerogative, has grown up anew, with much more strength, and far less odium, under the name influence." With hindsight blurred by a zealous desire to castigate the "king's friends," he wrote as though George and Lord Bute had invented bribery, as if the great Whig families of the past had ruled honorably for the sake of the nation rather than for their own narrow interests. The message of the *Present Discontents* added to the swelling volume of demand against sinecures and places. However, Burke was less radical than many writers of the day. Being an aristocratic reformer of the old paternalistic school and a devotee of the Whig politics of 1688, he believed that if the constitution were safeguarded by a legion of honest gentlemen (Whig gentlemen, of course), the Tories around George III could be defeated.

Slightly left of Burke stood William Petty, earl of Shelburne, who employed Dr. Priestly as his librarian. His house at Bowood became an intellectual refuge for such as Cartwright and Bentham. Shelburne was one of the first political leaders to fall under the spell of Bentham's doctrine of utilitarianism and Smith's economic ideas. His slogan, "Measures and not men," was not only embraced by the aging Chatham but also by Chatham's son, William Pitt the Younger, and by the new school of reformers who intended service to the nation and not to its political patrons.

With the stuffy, statuesque Burke and the cerebral, philosophical Shelburne stood the dandified Charles James Fox in his red-heeled shoes and blue-powdered wig. Fox, the youngest of North's adversaries, looked more like a social caricature than a responsible politician. Yet, of the three, he was the activist. Attired in a blue suit that closely copied the uniform of General Washington's revolutionary army, he denounced the king from platforms shared with Wilkes and Price. Profligate, gambler, and spendthrift though he was, he was much more the people's image of a popular leader than either the remote Burke or the intellectual Shelburne. The three might have made up a powerful triumvirate; but since they were as critical of each other as they were of Lord North, North's ministry limped on.

North eventually allowed the entire Wilkes episode to lapse into a planned oblivion. John Wilkes was finally permitted to take his seat in Commons in 1774, where he was assiduously ignored by the prime minister. The ministry's general lack of initiative produced a program of retrenchment, an avoidance of European entanglements, and a restrained budget that, if nothing else, at least temporarily contained the debt. The government declined to oppose a number of bills to give Nonconformists relief from the Clarendon Code.

All these bills failed anyway, but in 1778 a restriction against Catholics holding military commissions was relaxed. The repeal of this restriction prompted the laŝt savage outbreak of anti-Catholicism in England. The Gordon riots of London, led by the irrational Lord George Gordon (who somehow linked North with an attempt to undermine Protestantism), exploded the first week in June 1780. As the mob progressed from looting Catholic homes to general mayhem, the distilleries became a favorite target, so much so that drunken rioters perished in the fires they had ignited and the London water supply tasted of spirits. The government, for the first time since James II, used its military power to quell Protestant rioters.

The only notable domestic measure sponsored by North's cabinet involved a royal family squabble. Because two of his brothers had married commoners, in 1772 George III instructed his ministers to hastily draw up the Royal Marriages Act to bar his relatives under twenty-five from marrying without his permission. As North's major piece of legislation, the act was understandably ridiculed for its insignificance: with the world in revolt the ministry could only assist the king in scolding the royal family. By 1779 Burke and the exasperated opposition were sponsoring large-scale programs on their own, as if the king's government were incapacitated, as in some respects it was indeed. On April 6, 1780, a John Dunning presented Parliament with a contemptuous explanation for the inept North's longevity in office. He introduced a resolution "that the influence of the crown has increased, is increasing, and ought to be diminished." To the government's discomfort the resolution passed by eighteen votes.

An Empire Spreading Thin

By the day of Dunning's Resolution, the prime minister was understandably exhausted, not so much from domestic as from imperial cares. Since the collapse of the East India Company in 1772 in the third year of his ministry, North had never regained control—and there had been ample warning of the company's failure. Clive had foreseen back in 1759 that with the conquest of Bengal, the territories in India might possibly be "an object too extensive for a mercantile company." But the company had continued to overextend itself. In 1765 its forces had defeated an Indian confederacy and extended its *raj* (overlordship) beyond Bengal. Its military arm, subsidized by government funds only during the Seven Years' War, was costing the organization £40,000 annually by 1771. This need not have disturbed its investors, except that after 1767 profits dropped by £400,000 a year. But these financial figures failed to shake the faith of speculators, and the price of shares continued to inflate. The company's problems were compounded by its own agents, who often plied a lucrative private trade with Indian merchants, usually in direct competition with their employer. The additional territories it now oversaw, the fact that the company grew too immense to be controlled by its three separate headquarters (at Madras, Bombay, and Calcutta), and a general trade depression in Europe had pushed the company into insolvency. The organization that was once capable of paying off a substantial part of the English national debt in 1772 had come, hat in hand, begging the government to save it from its declared bankruptcy.

At the time, North would have preferred a private understanding with company officials, but because its interests so immediately affected the country, a demand for a parliamentary inquiry forced the inequities into the glare of publicity. To his credit, the prime minister did save much of a bad situation by granting permission for the company's tea cargoes to bypass England and sail directly to America and by providing a government loan of £1.4 million. In the India Regulating Act of 1773, the three self-ruling districts were placed under the single direction of a governor-general at Calcutta. This official was to be advised by a four-man board selected jointly by the company and the government. Thus the British had belatedly gone into the business of ruling an empire that had been largely under private auspices for 175 years.

While direct interference may have salvaged England's position in India, it was her undoing in America. The machinery for nominal control over North America had existed since 1696, when the Board of Trade and Plantations with general supervisory powers was set up. The commissioners of the Customs and the Admiralty Board had handled trade regulations. The bishop of London had overseen all church matters. The restrictive trade laws imposed on America hindered her access to direct world trade. According to the Navigation Act of 1660, only ships that were British-built and -manned could carry American products. Some goods, called "enumerated" articles (sugar, molasses, tobacco, cotton, indigo and dyes, ginger, rice, naval stores, copper, furs, and iron), could be exported only to England or to another colony. Any hardware or cloth that competed with similar English goods was prohibited. The more recent declaration that no colony could make laws independent of Parliamentary approval, the short-lived Stamp Act tax, and the Townshend customs made the array of controls formidable. Actually, the colonies simply ignored most of these restrictions and directives and plied a bounteous trade in smuggling, falsifying papers, shifting cargo from ship to ship at night or on the high seas, or altering course to non-English ports in midpassage. The brief career of one customs officer exemplifies the problem of enforcement: he was so intimidated by neighbors' and relatives' threats that he would "be knocked on the head" if he meddled with the Oyster Bay smugglers that he resigned within a month of his appointment.

The sheer immensity of Britain's far-flung dominions also made policing of the borders impossible. Then too, by 1770 the Americans numbered some 2 million; they had been only 200,000 in 1700. In Queen Anne's reign the colonists had clustered around the shipping centers; now they were settling far inland, no longer dependent on the coastal ports, which few now ever saw. The cost of protecting the expanding frontier, rising from £370,000 in 1764 to £428,000 in 1767, was the financial problem that at last ended the era of "salutary neglect" and called America to the horrified attention of the home government.

The American Crisis

Four plans were proposed to defray the expenses of America's frontier patrols. One, for the selling of the interior lands to settlers, was quickly dropped because of the colossal surveys it would have necessitated. A second, union through confederation under the Albany Plan, was proposed in 1754. Benjamin Franklin favored this arrangement, which urged that the thirteen colonies come under the direction of a governor-general guided by a congress of colonial delegates; but rivalries among the participants at Albany engendered second thoughts once the enthusiasm of the New York meeting was left behind. The English parliament, suspicious of a republican flavor, also rejected the plan. Next, in October 1763 England tried to restrain her migratory subjects altogether by forbidding settlement beyond a "proclamation line" along the Alleghenies. This too proved impractical, for the enforcement of keeping Americans in would have been more costly than keeping Indians out. The fourth scheme resulted in Townshend's infuriating taxes and was to Americans the final exasperation in a long train of abuses. It forced on them an inferior status. As long as the duties were imposed in the name of trade regulation (and could be subsequently ignored), the Americans felt no more discriminated against than their smuggling English cousins in Devon or Cornwall. But it was common knowledge that these new abhorred duties were designed to raise tax revenue rather than to control the flow of commodities. In no time broadsides and chants ran, "Taxation without consent is tyranny."

From 1768 to 1773 the American crisis reached an equipoise between militants in ports such as Boston and the few reactionary hardliners in England intent on subjugating them. In the Boston Massacre in March 1770, five taunting demonstrators were shot by nervous king's musketeers. In 1772 a stranded customs ship was burned. These were but two larger incidents, but because these episodes were no more insurrectionary than what the English had encountered in dealing with domestic mobs, they received little note at home. Actually, much of American opinion in 1770 was summarized in the *New York*

Gazette's, "It's high time a stop was put to mobbing." In England, Lord North reacted temperately to the outbreaks, appointing boards of inquiry whose reports were quietly shelved. He did lift the obnoxious Townshend duties, retaining only a token custom on tea. Trade returned to normal, and for a time saner heads on each side of the Atlantic prevailed.

Then the near collapse of the eastern empire precipitated the total collapse of the western empire. The Tea Act of 1773, granting the bankrupt East India Company the right to ship tea directly to America, freed tea from a shilling's duty per pound. The company planned to pass the savings in shipping and handling on to the colonists, thus halving the price.

To Englishmen, what followed was inexplicable. Despite the steady pressure of pamphleteers in the colonies, most Americans had viewed the earlier impositions as honest errors committed in bureaucratic ignorance. It was generally held that Lord North did not intend malice, and it was common report how Mr. Burke and William Pitt, Lord Chatham, not to mention the hero Wilkes, had sided with America. There seemed less and less substance to the inflammatory letters of fellow colonists such as Sam Adams and John Hancock. Of course, the tea tax did remain in effect, but (thought the English) at the new price of ten shillings a pound, who would prefer smuggled Dutch tea to the now cheaper English tea?

Then in December 1773 a cargo of 298 casks, £11,000 worth of tea, arrived in Boston harbor. Trickery! Were Americans to forsake their liberty for cheap tea? The militants had been right—North grasped none of their grievances! On the night of December 16, 1773, a band of colonists dressed as Indians heaved the cargo into Boston harbor. A story had it that all along the coast—at New York, Greenwich, Annapolis, and Charleston—the seawater was tea-flavored. Now each side, the radical extremists in America bent on independence and the conservative extremists in England bent on punishment, had a cause behind which they could maneuver the moderate center into armed conflict.

Lord North moved to punish Massachusetts. He closed the port of Boston and threatened to keep it shut until reparation was made to the East India Company. English troops were quartered in the town; the Massachusetts Government Act virtually abolished self-rule. It had been North's intention not to chastise Massachusetts so much as to divide American unity by presenting an inducement to other ports to take over Boston's trade. But these penalties caused George Washington to question whether the colonists would wait to see one province after another fall prey to despotism. Washington's argument was persuasive, and the colonies united in a singularity of purpose.

In Philadelphia the Continental Congress of 1774, though it professed loyalty to the crown, stated clearly that it condoned the militant action at

Boston as a proper means of seeking redress. The proof of their defiance came in the spring of 1775 at Lexington, when an English attempt to seize American militia arms stored at Concord was stopped at a loss to the British of 273 of 800 troops.

The War of American Independence: Shifting Strategies and Attitudes

The ensuing conflict, more a civil than a revolutionary war, saw Englishmen in America fighting their brothers for the rights they would have enjoyed at home. But "rights" in the eighteenth-century idiom primarily meant the right to be left alone: to pursue one's own notion of happiness free from the government licenser, to seek one's own salvation free from regulation by a state church, to accumulate and enjoy one's property free of the excise man. This rather negative notion of freedom was embodied in the Declaration of Independence. The declaration's doctrine was one of the right to secession based on a natural law that bequeathed to all individuals the rights of life, liberty, and property. Should these rights be molested, both God and nature conferred on the oppressed the right to seek liberation. Thus the colonials had come to see themselves as already separated from Great Britain because she had transgressed from her proper role as beneficent guardian to that of wicked stepmother. As an English scholar writes, "It was not up to [the Americans] to win their independence: it was up to us to destroy it."[7] In a sense 1776 was for the Americans a replay of the Glorious Revolution of 1688.

The war of American independence consumed eight painful years. England was never sure whether to treat her errant subjects as recalcitrants who should be cajoled back into the family circle and sent to bed without supper or as a foreign foe to be conquered. Many Whig commanders were sympathetic and campaigned half-heartedly against the rebels. Never did the British forces have enough men or money; typically, at one crucial point General Howe asked for 20,000 troops and got 2,500. Foolish and paltry economies in the navy impaired fleet operations—decayed masts broke, rotten lines snapped. Strategy shifted from year to year: first, sea ports were blockaded; then there were prolonged forced marches through the interior. A concentration on seizing the cities changed to scattering tiny garrisons across the countryside. Whereas Pitt might have held America, North was not even consistent in a plan of attack. "The sooner Britain is out of this damned war the better,"[8] summarized his attitude and perhaps explains the ministry's failure to keep the colonies.

[7] Derek Jarrett, *Britain, 1688–1815* (New York, 1965), p. 306.
[8] Quoted in White, *op. cit.*, p. 143.

The war lumbered through two stages. The northern strategy (1775 to 1777) attempted to separate New England from the middle colonies; the southern strategy (from 1778 to the final surrender at Yorktown in 1781) tried to conquer Georgia, the Carolinas, and Virginia. Early in the hostilities the British established a preliminary foothold in Boston at an unnecessary cost of 1,054 men in the Battle of Bunker (or Breed's) Hill (June 1775). Throughout 1776 the ministry counted—on the basis of incomplete information, as it turned out—on pro-British sentiment in the middle colonies (New York, Pennsylvania, New Jersey, and Maryland). If it were possible to detach them from New England, separate negotiations with each individual colony might fragment the new-found American unity. Accordingly, General Howe evacuated his base at Boston and took New York. The English war council then proposed that two Canadian-based armies under Burgoyne and St. Leger would march from Lake Champlain and Lake Ontario, converge with Howe on Albany in the summer, and drive the desired wedge through the colonial center. But then St. Leger's western force was stopped at Oriskany (in central New York), and Howe's New York army foolhardedly swung south to take Philadelphia at a price of throwing away its opportunity to return to its base at the mouth of the Hudson River. Stranded in northern New York, "Gentleman Johnny" Burgoyne (a better playwright than militarist) was engulfed by General Gates and an entire countryside at arms. At Saratoga, New York, on October 17, 1777, Burgoyne's entire army surrendered.

Saratoga not only put heart into the Americans but also found its way into Benjamin Franklin's brief laid before the French in Paris. In February 1778 France declared her alliance with the colonies, sealing the bargain by dispatching 6,000 troops and two fleets to America. Additionally, the French again menaced the English coast, threatening invasion. A Spanish declaration of war, accompanied by a siege of Gibraltar, trebled England's woes. In 1780 she stumbled into a fourth engagement with the Dutch over their right to trade with the American rebels. The entire Atlantic community was now in arms over what England had foolishly considered a minor colonial administrative problem.

At this disenchanting juncture, North reconsidered peace terms he had offered separately to each of the colonies in 1775 and again in 1776. These terms had proffered little more than a return to the same dismal conditions that had precipitated the outbreak. After Saratoga he was willing to make the additional concessions of recognizing the Continental Congress and the colonies' right to levy their own taxes and elect their own governors. He even hinted that further deliberations might find a basis for colonial representation in Parliament. By the end of 1778, however, with the British evacuating Philadelphia, the Americans, recognizing their own strength, saw the negotiations as a symptom of North's weakness, a sapping of English resolution, and found hope for total victory.

Thoroughly harried in their northern strategy by Washington, the English vainly decided to invest their strength in the heart of the loyalist South, where the king's troops might find sympathetic support. Throughout 1780 British victories seemed to outweigh previous losses. Georgia fell in January, South Carolina in June, and North Carolina in August. The record was impressive at home, but every English commander in the field had come to realize that a string of ten victories could be erased by one colonial success: the land could not be held, and as His Majesty's wearied troops slogged from one engagement to another, the ground behind was swallowed again into the great, indifferent wilderness.

The one American victory to cancel Britain's ten came at Yorktown on October 18, 1781. General Cornwallis, conqueror of the Carolinas, amazedly found his 7,000-man force at the end of a peninsula. With Washington's 15,000 troops behind him and a French fleet on the sea, there was nothing to do but to relinquish his sword. With it went Lord North's office and the king's sovereignty over his American subjects.

North's final weeks, from February into March 1782, saw his ministry besieged by motion after motion to end the war. All the king's efforts at coercion provided the prime minister a flimsy majority of one vote in Commons. North could not end the war, nor could he wring from Parliament a farthing more to perpetuate it. On March 20, 1782, he resigned.

Protracted negotiations with England's host of enemies were concluded in the Treaty of Versailles in March 1783. Independence, with a boundary fixed at the Mississippi, was conceded to America; France regained the islands of Tobago and St. Lucia in the West Indies and Senegal in Africa, territories she had lost to England in the Seven Years' War; Spain recovered Florida and Minorca. The long-range impact of the treaty was devastating to England's colonial pretensions. For nearly a hundred years the attitude prevailed that colonies were an unnecessary burden on the home treasury, destined as they were to drop (in the favorite simile) like ripe fruit from the parent tree. Because she was burned so badly in the American experience, England's holdings in Canada, the West Indies, South Africa, Australia, and New Zealand later found relatively peaceful paths to self-rule.

The Renewal of Party Politics

During most of the eighteenth century, party affiliation had been of little consequence. Now party politics regained some of the former vigor as a result of the prolonged debate over America. Not since Queen

Anne's reign, when the Tories clamored for an end to "Marlborough's War," had the titles "Whig" and "Tory" been bandied about so vindictively in debate and press. But now the roles were reversed, for during North's twelve-year Tory ministry, his party had evolved into hawks and the Whigs had turned into doves. The opposition cheered the defeat at Saratoga. The prime minister's backing was more inclined toward Samuel Johnson's opinion that the colonists were "a race of convicts who ought to be thankful for anything we allow them short of hanging." The respected Johnson also found it ironic that a nation keeping slaves should so revere liberty. But in general the vast moderate center of Englishmen, experiencing relief at the news from Yorktown, sighed with North, "My God, all is over."

Chapter Eleven
THE ONSET OF REFORM

Major Personages

Hastings, Warren, 1732–1818; served the East India Company most of his life; the first governor-general of India; reform of imperial policy promoted by his prolonged trial for mismanagement

Pitt, William (the Younger), 1759–1806; son of the great wartime minister, Lord Chatham; responsible for launching England on its first era of modern reform

CHRONOLOGY

1783–93	Period of Pitt's major economic and political reforms
1783–1801	Pitt's great first ministry
1784	India Act
1786–96	Trial of Warren Hastings
1788	Australia settled
1791	Canada Constitutional Act
1793	Catholic Relief Act (for Ireland)

One would think there's not room one new impost to put
From the crown of the head to the sole of the foot.
Like Job, thus John Bull his condition deplores,
Very patient, indeed, and all covered with sores.[1]

The last thirty-two years of the Hanoverian era—dating from the ministry of Chatham's son, William Pitt the Younger (1783), to the end of the Napoleonic Wars (1815)—struck a balance between high purpose and deliberate cultivation of narrow self-interest. During the first ten of the young Pitt's seventeen-year administration, there were strenuous efforts to scrape the grime from the nation's electoral machinery, purge the corruptible placemen, trim the cumbersome administration, and effect a reasonable colonial policy. But this rigorous and idealistic momentum was brought up short by the French Revolution; and repressive legislation against labor, civil liberties, and radicalism came to dominate parliamentary programs until well after the critical years of the Napoleonic Wars.

From an Unbroken Mold: Pitt the Younger

England's experimental course through this first short-lived era of reform was steered by Pitt the Younger, who was born in 1759, the bright year of his father's victories. "He was cast rather than grew," Coleridge was to say of him. The son's incorruptible steeliness was a product of the mold the father had fashioned. The resolute young William absorbed knowledge, from the classics to the new economic theories of Adam Smith, with incredible ease. The precocious youngster authored a political play at thirteen, enrolled in Cambridge at fourteen, entered law at nineteen, and by age twenty-two sat in the House of Commons. The man-child (Master Billy to his opponents), wonder of the age and paragon of studied industriousness, had but two private vices that might endear him to this era of delight in wild indulgences—an addiction to port wine and a personal financial irresponsibility that necessi-

[1] This popular ballad lampooned the volume and variety of Pitt's new taxes.

tated a parliamentary intercession to wipe out his indebtedness at his death.

On the more positive side, it was his political impeccability that attracted George III's attention during the gray months after the collapse of North's ministry. Though Pitt had shown a devotion to Shelburne's and Fox's Whiggish opposition to the American war, he had more recently gravitated toward the liberal Tories. The king could thus overlook Pitt's youthful radicalism, especially when considering the baleful ministerial alternatives of 1782 and 1783.

For a few months George had unenthusiastically embraced the Rockingham Whigs, who were under Shelburne's management. That tenuous alliance produced a measure of reform, sponsored largely by Burke, which included deleting £50,000 worth of corrupt sinecures. During this period too, Ireland became the first dependency to benefit from the American lesson. Her trade and manufacturing restrictions were removed; and for the first time in hundreds of years, the Irish Parliament gained independence of Westminster. Despite this lofty record the Rockingham cabinet collapsed with the prime minister's death in July 1782. Shelburne, who by his radical actions had alienated the king, took over but graced the office for only eight months. As "the Jesuit of Berkeley Square" (the name given by his enemies) concluded peace with the Americans (Shelburne's only solid achievement), his majority in Parliament disintegrated.

A ministerial jumble again threatened. Shelburne was replaced by a most unlikely, but thankfully brief, combination of the resurrected Lord North and Charles Fox. The coalition, considered preposterous by some, a betrayal by others, and an insult to the crown in either case, had at best the virtue of pooling Whig and Tory strength into a formidable voting bloc. Yet the coalition ministry lived only ten months. When, in December 1783, George III discovered in Pitt a loyalty worthy of reward, he let the word come down that support for a Fox–North bill then pending in Lords would earn his displeasure. Despite grumbled charges of royal interference, the Lords defeated the measure, tippling the Fox-North ministry; and William Pitt, the king's chosen, was appointed first lord of the treasury.

At twenty-four Master Billy's endurance was, as predictions then ran, no more guaranteed than a Christmas pie. The strong Fox–North majority, now held together by resentment of George's play to make Pitt prime minister, embarrassed the new prime minister by voting down his every measure and censuring his every policy. Party politics had seldom been as vicious. By March 1784, however, Pitt had overcome his youthful inexperience and had shaved the opposition down to a one-vote majority. He stood accused, he claimed, of having nothing to his credit but a monarchical threat to punish his opponents and reward his supporters. Now let the public decide! He placed the issue between himself and the Fox–North bloc before the general electorate. For the first time within living memory, an election was fought over individual candidates and platforms. According to the old formula of bribery, outright ownership, and promises of peerages and other spoils, the number of boroughs considered safely in Fox's, North's, or Pitt's pocket before the election would have given Pitt a sound majority. But Pitt was returned to office by a landslide. Scrutiny of the election unearthed evidence that many constituencies, in a reversal of ordinary practice, had gone against the interests supposedly prevailing in their districts. Political conscience had triumphed! Fox carried his own home constituency but was then briefly kept from a seat in Parliament on a technical flaw. Other Foxites bitterly accepted defeat; the new popular chant was, "No Fox! No coalition! Pitt and the king forever!"

There was every appearance that Fox, once the darling of the people, had sold out to North, and Pitt, having already launched one bill for parliamentary reform (though it had not carried), was next in line for the role of public champion.

Pitt's prime ministry was in many respects unparalleled for the power he was able to exercise. There had been others, such as Walpole, Chatham, and North, whose positions also depended largely on monarchical favor; some, Newcastle in particular, had been able to impose terms on the crown because they commanded parliamentary majorities. Pitt's strength came to lie in both areas. Furthermore, he accepted the title of prime minister (still an insult) without apology and utterly ruled his cabinet.

" The First Minister "

The broad-bottomed cabinet system, once held to be a solution to the ministerial tyranny of such as Walpole, had degenerated, in the words of Burke, into "a piece of joinery crossly indented and whimsically dovetailed; a tesselated pavement without cement."[2] The earlier belief that each of the king's ministers should hold equal rank within the cabinet was also quickly losing validity. Pitt played on this opinion, curbing the independence of his colleagues by making his cabinet appointments from the Lords, thus holding the arena of Commons for himself. Furthermore, he confided in, and executed his own policy through, personally picked undersecretaries. Even Walpole had been forced to share his power with Newcastle; Chatham had lost control over his cabinet associates (especially Townshend), who undertook programs on their own. But Pitt brooked no opposition within the ranks, at one point even demanding that the king order the resignation of the lord

[2] Edmund Burke, "American Taxation," *Works* (Boston, 1884), vol. II, pp. 62–63.

chancellor, who had consistently voted with the opposition. Since Pitt's day prime ministers have happily embraced his view:

> There should be an avowed and real minister possessing the chief weight in council and the principal place in the confidence of the king. In that respect there can be no rivality [rivalry] or division of power. That power must rest with the person generally called the first minister; and that minister ought to be the person at the head of the finances.[3]

Pitt effected reforms in three areas—Parliament, finances, and the empire. He had declared in 1782 before taking office that he intended to eliminate corruption in Commons. With his pronouncement that "everyone ought to be governed by those laws only to which all have actually given their consent," he expressed his mistrust of the easily bribed borough constituencies. Augmenting the rural representation would counteract this bribery factor. But Pitt's attempt in 1785 to abolish thirty-six rotten boroughs was successfully blocked by the very forces he sought to demolish. The king allowed Pitt to introduce the bill, but he gave it no support whatever, not wishing to diminish his own role as patron. Although George would not then aid him in purging Commons, he later stacked the deck in Pitt's favor in Lords by rewarding eighty-seven faithful with new peerages. If Master Billy could not reform the lower house, he could at least pack the upper house.

Pitt's economic efforts were the most vigorous since Walpole's, but fifty years earlier there were far fewer claims against the budget. Then too, Walpole had had a leisurely twenty years to whittle away at the government debt. Back in 1735 the indebtedness had been little more than eight times the annual revenue of £6 million; in 1785, though income had not so much as trebled, the national liability, some £245 million, was sixteen times more than the government took in. A lack of faith in the ability to repay its loans had lowered government stock to nearly half of face value. Clearly the task confronting Pitt was not only to improve on Walpole's unparalleled record but also to concoct new taxes acceptable to the public.

Well over seven hundred worthless sinecures were abolished: some posts were simply left vacant at the incumbents' deaths, and other officials were bought off with lifetime incomes (as much as £7,000 annually) to smother their outcries of hardship. Those bureaucrats who survived were worked as never before under the strictest of supervision. Collections on old customs were tightened, and additional duties were added.

Wine and tobacco imports were the first to receive a new tax. Levies on consumer goods and luxury items exploited the well-to-do, with taxes on

[3] Quoted in E. Neville Williams, *The Eighteenth-Century Constitution, 1688–1815* (Cambridge, 1965), p. 132.

windows, dogs, hair powder, ribbons, clocks and watches, carriages and carriage horses, and even servants. In 1784 a national lottery capitalized on the current gambling craze and provided the government with ready cash. In 1786 Pitt, announcing that thereafter a million pounds in excess of budgetary needs would be commandeered, established a new sinking fund designed exclusively to repay the standing debt. Each year that million was to be automatically shifted to the sinking fund; each year the growing principal would be reinvested so that accumulated interest would eventually overtake the initial investment. Another of his projects, a 1786 trade treaty with France, foreshadowed later free trade movements. In return for reductions on English hardware, woolens, and cottons, the English reduced customs on French spirits. Another former foe, America, was lured by trade concessions in West Indian free ports. Within ten years of America's recognition, English exports to the United States were four times what they had been when the colonies belonged to the crown.

In 1788 Pitt weathered the only severe crisis of his innovative years. Like Walpole's office, his too was protected from the opposition not so much by cultivated majorities—his following was slimmer than Sir Robert's had been— but by placation of the king. The old Leicester House reversionary interest once doomed Walpole's incumbency when George I died in 1727. Now a new "Leicester House gang," under the twenty-six-year-old Prince George, was angling to follow the heir's gambling companion, Charles Fox, back into power. The occasion of the crisis was George III's first serious mental lapse in November 1788. For weeks Pitt stoutly upheld the queen's regency against Fox's and Burke's unrelenting demands that the young prince immediately replace the queen as regent. Pitt would have been forced to resign but for the king's chance recovery in March 1789. The monarch's gratitude for Pitt's loyalty and his contempt for his son's perfidy assured indefinite tenure for the faithful minister and prolonged political exile for Fox.

Estrangement in India

When Lord North had reconstructed the finances and organization of the East India Company in 1773, the enormous problem of ruling overseas possessions had been forced abruptly on Britain. North paid heavily for his rebuff in America; Pitt did not intend to suffer a similar fate for letting India slip from England's grasp. By now colonial troubles had assumed a classic three-dimensional nature: (1) the home government at Westminster imposed its fiat on distant colonial administrators (2) who in turn attempted to apply Westminster's dictates to the native situation (usually without success) (3) while at the same time they struggled to protect the frontiers with insufficient funds and an appalling lack of direction. These frontiers had once little concerned the company traders in the treaty ports; but since the Battle of Plassey in 1757, England's rule in Bengal had intruded her into India's ancient pattern of complicated territorial conflict. Under the able administration of India's first governor-general, Warren Hastings, the reformed East India Company acquitted itself to a degree by smashing the marauding Rohillas north of Bengal and the conquering Mahrattas to the west. Hastings might have received congratulatory accolades from Parliament—he had won the grudging respect, even the admiration of Indian rulers—but for the two company officials of his four-man council. They constantly worked not only against his reputation but also against his policies. One Philip Francis, who coveted the governor-generalship and whose seething jealousy even caused him to challenge Hastings to a duel, devoted much of his career to destroying his superior. Although Francis' assertions were true, though overdrawn—for Hastings had undoubtedly been high-handed—the governor-general had only played the game according to Indian rules. In England Edmund Burke, smarting from Master Billy's 1784 election victory and chafing at the Tories' close association with the East India Company, was gulled by Francis' charges of peculation and tyranny. Burke romanticized the Rohillas and the Mahrattas in an impeachment he initiated against Hastings in 1786. English society, concerned as it then was in extending justice to colonial peoples and anxious to wipe the blot of America from the record, made points at Hastings' expense through nine years of recriminatory trial. In the end Hastings resigned, though he was acquitted, but England had self-righteously lulled herself into the belief that downtrodden peoples could indeed count on British justice without resorting to Boston tea parties and declarations of independence.

Of more lasting consequence than this congratulatory self-praise was Pitt's India Act of 1784, passed during the years when Hastings' difficulties began feeding public debate. Government supervision of the Indian colonies was placed under the Privy Council in a six-man board of control, headed by a secretary of state and appointed by the king. While the revised office of the governor-general was under the new board, the power granted to it two years later gave it the right to override the revamped administrative council, now reduced to three members. The India Act was intended to end the factiousness nurtured by the former arrangement. By separating the officials from the company's business, they were effectively removed from the temptation to make profit out of company transactions. Together, Pitt's act and Hastings' trial produced a major change in the character of England's *raj*. The new rulers dispatched to Calcutta and Bombay hereafter safely observed the everyday life of the country from behind garrison walls. These imperious martinets viewed Hastings' involvement in the treacheries of Indian politics and business as demeaning to both his personal reputation and England's glory. However, this cultivated estrangement would come to prove more disastrous than the old entanglements pursued by Clive and Hastings.

Reform in Ireland

In another display of prudence Pitt turned to Ireland, where problems bore a similarity to those that had alienated America. " We are all Americans here," analogized the Irish Lord Middleton. The country's English Anglican ruling class considered the capital, Dublin, its private domain. Beyond the city's boundaries were thousands of Presbyterians, situated chiefly in Ulster (these were descendants of Scottish immigrants brought in by England in the seventeenth century largely to outweigh the country's Catholicism). The greater part of the population consisted of millions of native Catholics scattered throughout the rural countryside. They held meager land on which they grew their staple crops. Only the most powerful landlords, most of whom resided in England and who rarely participated in Irish affairs, enjoyed full political rights, which derived from their owning three-quarters of Ireland's farmland. They netted over a million pounds annually in rentals.

Of the four castes in Irish society—the absentee landlords, the Dublin English of the Anglican faith, the Ulster Presbyterians, and the native Irish Catholics—demand for change came first from the Dublin establishment. It controlled Ireland's wealth but was enslaved by the same discriminatory trading and manufacturing regulations that had caused Americans to revolt. Pitt attempted to alleviate these sore points in 1785. He would have promoted free trade between Ireland and England but for a burst of acrimony from English industrialists. They claimed that cheaper Irish labor would ruin both English manufacturer and workingman. A few Irish producers and tradesmen who profited from the old system added to the outcry, and the prime minister retreated.

On a second reform front, civil liberty for Irish Catholics, he had greater success, probably because he worked through the Irish Parliament rather than through the home government. He sympathized with the view of the Irish Protestant leader, Henry Grattan, that the Irish Protestant could never be free until the Irish Catholic ceased to be a slave. But Pitt misread Grattan, who had in mind the building of a stronger national base capable of wresting independence from England. Ironically, Pitt saw the reform as a means to reduce Irish revolutionary pressures. However, through their combined efforts the Catholic Relief Act of 1793 granted Catholics the vote and the right to bear arms, to sit on juries, and to hold minor civil and military posts, though they were still barred from Parliament and the central administration. But because these compromises barely altered the fundamental alienation between the countries, they only whetted the Irish appetite for total independence.

Conciliation in Canada

Pitt's constitutional overhaul of the empire went more smoothly in Canada. In retrospect, the reasons seem obvious. From the acquisition of the French colonies in 1760, the dominant French-Canadian populace had lived under a relatively lenient military rule. The predominantly Catholic population had been less rudely handled than in Ireland. Catholic toleration was allowed, Catholic church property was protected, and residents were not hindered from returning to their native France. In 1764 English civil and criminal codes had been instituted, and the Quebec Act of 1774 had replaced military rule with a governor and a nominated Canadian council. There were but a handful of English magistrates, and these generally dealt fairly with their frequently confused French-speaking subjects, despite the obscurity of when to apply old French law or English common law. But the relaxed relationship disintegrated after the influx into Ontario of some 60,000 United Empire Loyalists, staunch colonists who drifted north from the United States in order to retain their British citizenship. It was not long before the disenchanted Loyalists, considering themselves superior to the conquered French-Canadians, petitioned Westminster for greater participation in their adopted government. Pitt selected one of their proposals, making it the basis of his Canada Constitutional Act of 1791: the English- and French-speaking colonies were to be divided into two provinces, Upper Canada (English) and Lower Canada (French), jointly presided over by a governor-in-chief with two lieutenant governors, one for each province. Both provinces were to have nominated executive councils and representative assemblies elected by the landholders. These assemblies could control the levying of taxes, though they had little say in how that revenue was to be dispersed. Canada was the first of England's dominions to take a step in the long evolutionary process toward peaceful independence while remaining within the imperial fold. The initial success of separating the two nationalistic camps afforded the home government rare peace for many years.

The dispossessed American Loyalists indirectly inspired another significant colonial overture half a world away. Australia had been under English surveillance since the Dutch first scouted its commercial possibilities in the seventeenth century. But not until the British seaman Captain Cook's voyage of 1770 were the advantages of the continent's eastern shore made attractively apparent. When many repatriated Loyalists resettled in England, they became an embarrassment because, despite generous assurances of aid, no provision had been made for them. Australia then became an inviting alternative as a home for these loyal, but displaced, citizens. Initially, nothing came of this proposal, and the inviting eastern shore of New South Wales continued to breed fanciful schemes.

With the encouragement of Pitt's ministry, an idea gained momentum that with America and the West Indies now closed to felons (it had been standard punishment to ship them overseas as forced labor), Australia offered an advantageous site for a colony devoted exclusively to their exile. The beauties of nature and the redeeming toil were expected gradually to re-habilitate these outcasts. With humane purpose—and economy—in mind, 750 men and women prisoners were crammed aboard a ship, a cargo of misery bound for Botany Bay. They arrived in January 1788, just six days before the landing of a French fleet bent on claiming the same territory for Louis XVI. With a chivalrous gesture the French saluted and politely withdrew as the English commander was in the process of changing the base from Botany Bay to Sydney, which offered a better port.

The penal colony floundered for the next twenty years. It took strong governors, including the notorious Captain Bligh, formerly of the *H.M.S. Bounty*, to keep a modicum of order. The deplorable conditions, the constant hunger, the unchecked disease, and the ruthlessness of the more hardened criminals devastated all but the heartiest of England's deportees. As time passed, the criminal population languished and disappeared. Few contemporary Australians can trace their ancestry (even if inclined) to these wretched mis-creants. Sturdier free immigrants replaced them, taking advantage of the liberal land policies. In 1840 the last cargo of convicts was disembarked at Sydney, and when in 1849 the home government tried once more to dump its superfluous humanity, the more solid inhabitants turned the cargo back. However, western Australia received prisoners as cheap labor until as late as 1868.

The Reformist Momentum: A Western Phenomenon

In England the gathering momentum for reform continued with little impediment. Even sluggish King George III gave Mr. Pitt the patronage his measures needed. As long as the prime minister kept his re-formist tendencies restricted to administrative and fiscal mechanics, the king was mollified, though he warned Pitt that in his crusades against rotten bo-roughs and on behalf of Catholics and Nonconformists he would stand alone. Temperamentally, however, Pitt was no crusader. Though he was willing to risk royal displeasure for his practical aims, he fostered social reform as an adjunct to practical government, not in the name of humanity or justice.

Whatever its function, reform and its extreme manifestation, revolution, had come to dominate not only the English scene, but also the political attitudes of the entire Western world. Robert R. Palmer has called the period from 1763 to 1800 "the world revolution of the West,"[4] suggesting that what began with John Wilkes' protests and the Stamp Act crisis in America soon spread across all portions of the Atlantic community. For England it inspired the generation that produced Fox and Pitt and kindled independence in the Irish. In 1789 it became France's turn, and the clamor for reform would, by 1793, plunge Europe into a revolutionary war with more dire consequences for England than those Lord North had faced from America.

[4] Robert R. Palmer, "The World Revolution of the West," *Political Science Quarterly*, LXIX (1954), 1–14.

Chapter Twelve
FRANCE, REVOLUTION, AND NAPOLEON

Major Personages

Addington, Henry, 1757–1844 (later Viscount Sidmouth), prime minister between Pitt the Younger's two administrations

Nelson, Horatio Nelson, Viscount, 1758–1805; England's most spectacular admiral, commander in the most critical sea encounters against France

Wellington, Arthur Wellesley, first duke of, 1769–1852; commander who defeated Napoleon in Spain and at Waterloo, later prime minister (1828)

CHRONOLOGY

1789	French Revolution begins
1793–5	War of the First Coalition
1794	Habeas corpus suspended
1795	Treasonable Practices and Seditious Meetings Acts
1796–8	Period of Irish religious civil war
1798	Battle of Aboukir Bay; Napoleon's Egyptian army isolated
	Income tax inaugurated
1799	Combination Acts against collective bargaining
1799–1800	War of the Second Coalition
1800	Act of Union with Ireland
1801	Battle of Copenhagen, defeat of Armed Neutrals
1802	Peace of Amiens
1803–15	Napoleonic Wars, concluded by the Treaty of Paris
1805	Napoleon's threatened invasion
	Battle of Trafalgar, the defeat of combined French-Spanish fleet; death of Nelson
1806	Death of Pitt
	Death of Fox
	Napoleon's Continental System
1807	Abolition of slave trade
1808	Battle of Vimiero opens Peninsular campaign
1812–14	War of 1812 with America, concluded by the Treaty of Ghent
1813	Battle of Vitoria, Napoleon driven from Spain
1814	Congress of Vienna
1815	Battle of Waterloo, final defeat of Napoleon

Bliss was it in that dawn to be alive,
But to be young was very heaven! O times,
In which the meagre, stale, forbidding ways
Of custom, law, and statute, took at once
The attraction of a country in romance!
When Reason seemed the most to assert her rights
When most intent on making of herself
A prime enchantress—to assist the work
Which then was going forward in her name!

. . . Europe at that time was thrilled with joy,
France standing on the top of golden hours,
And human nature seeming born again.

WILLIAM WORDSWORTH
The Prelude, 1805

Good Will Toward France

By 1789 the kingdom of France, then purportedly the most enlightened, certainly the most powerful and the most often emulated, had strained the limits of her financial assets. While she gave every appearance of enviable wealth, most of the income of the numerous noble class was beyond the grasp of the government because aristocratic immunity from taxation was carefully guarded. A small merchant class thrived, but through government neglect the buying power of the average French worker shriveled during the eighteenth century. France, like England, staggered under an enormous standing debt; though the debt was only half as large as England's, solvency could only be a fantasy under the creaky makeshifts of French royal finance. There were no new sources of taxation to be tapped; no sinking funds to be gleaned from surpluses, which never materialized; and after the country's involvement in the American Revolution demolished the treasury, no one would loan Louis XVI a solitary sou.

By that year, 1789, a monetary crisis compelled Louis to summon the equivalent of the English Parliament, the Estates General. This action, assiduously avoided by the monarchy for 175 years, brought on a wave of public optimism and engendered a surge of loyalty for the inept king, who apparently had, after years of flagrant mismanagement, come to his constitutional, as well as his fiscal, senses. But by the end of June, hope again turned to despair as the court attempted to stifle the representation of the Third Estate (lawyers, merchants, bankers, artisans) and to rule with only the First (the church) and the Second (the aristocracy) Estates. The beleaguered Third Estate responded by declaring itself a national assembly. It was militantly backed by the Parisian workers, who made their loyalty grimly apparent by assaulting the Bastille and killing its commander and the mayor of Paris. Within three violent years the victorious masses abolished feudalism and the church, issued a Declaration of the Rights of Man, gave France a constitution, and, after tortuous contention, erected a republic (August 1792). The execution of the king and the institution of a bloody reign of terror rounded out the revolutionary cycle.

Such a fury of change had never before buffeted the leisurely world of the European upper class, nor had the scope of revolution ever been so total. The French Revolution was an accomplished fact within a three-year span, whereas the English had consumed twenty years of the seventeenth century muddling through their revolutionary experience and the Americans' march to freedom from Lexington to Yorktown had taken six. Also unlike France, neither the English nor the American republics departed substantially from the earlier constitutions, nor were their social changes sanguinary. Charles Fox, who among England's ruling order seems to have been the first to realize the enormous energy unleashed by the violence of 1789, described the fall of the Bastille "as how much the greatest event that ever happened in the world, and how much the best." Stimulated by the tricolor, Fox's small band continued to agitate for reform long after Pitt, fearing that the revolutionary excesses in France might incite English radicals to overt acts, abandoned reform as dangerous.

In 1797 Charles Grey, a disciple of Fox, proposed the democratic notions that anyone maintaining a home (not merely forty-shilling freeholders) should be entitled to vote, that rotten boroughs be abolished and rural representation increased and that the country revert from septennially to triennially elected parliaments. Had it not been that England was again at war with France (as of 1793), the country might have judged the bill fairly; instead, it failed, largely because of the fear of radicalism. Grey had to bide his time for over thirty years, until his own prime ministry, when his Great Reform Bill of 1832 finally succeeded.

Until the latest engagement with France opened, the reaction of the English public to the turmoil in France was enthusiastic. How splendid, it thought, that the French were at last remodeling their institutions along such obviously English lines: a prescribed monarchy, a middle class franchise, and a restored parliament—or so it seemed in 1791. Now the aggressive policy of the old tyranny would be repudiated and the interminable wars would end, because the restructuring of French society would divert her old imperial ambitions. Pitt accordingly trimmed the army from 17,000 to 13,000. Less than a year before revolutionary France declared war on England, he confidently predicted that "there never was a time in history of this country when . . . we might more reasonably expect fifteen years of peace than at the present moment." Instead there followed some twenty years of war.

Pitt was not alone in his optimistic view. At the time of his assessment, few of his contemporaries possessed the vision to see how the abundant good will toward France could diminish. England, having just concluded its centenary celebrations for the Glorious Revolution of 1688, was understandably sympathetic. Newly formed corresponding clubs (the Society for Constitutional Information, the Society of the Friends of the People, the London Revolution Society) sent deputations to France to observe the marvelous happenings and mailed thousands of brochures in praise of French action. Old Dr. Price epitomized this enthusiasm in his highly publicized sermon of November 5, 1789:

> Be encouraged, all ye friends of freedom . . . . Behold, the light you have struck . . . after setting America free, reflected to France, and there kindled into a blaze that lays despotism in ashes. . . . Tremble all ye oppressors of the world! Take warning all ye supporters of slavish hierarchies! . . . Restore to mankind their rights; and consent to the correction of abuses before they and you are destroyed together.

While some conservative rejection could be anticipated, it came, oddly, from a high Whig source. Edmund Burke surprised and dismayed his contemporaries by publishing a rebuke to Dr. Price's sermon. The values and the objectives of the English Revolution were diametrically opposed to those now pursued by France, argued Burke in his *Reflections on the French Revolution* (1790): in 1688 England struggled to preserve her ancient laws; but the present French conflagration would destroy every vestige of the past in a false belief that, by doing so, it corrected the folly of countless generations. As for Dr. Price, the man, in Burke's opinion, was wholly ignorant of English history: the Glorious Revolution was planned and directed by England's aristocracy, not by the populace, and never, as Price had suggested, included a provision that the people could discard their monarchs as they might their worn-out shoes. The quality of a nation's genius, Burke concluded, depended, not on votes or rights, but on a dedication to tradition, and this in France had been best served by Louis XVI's court, the noblesse, and the church.

At the publication of the *Reflections*, there was wide speculation over the author's intent. The work seemed a compromise. Had Burke sold out? Had he defected from his former reform tenets? More likely there is no inconsistency, for he had always been an advocate of aristocratic privilege. Yet it seemed to the public that he had forsaken the liberal sentiments he championed in the American cause. Tom Paine, the radical author of the working class, in his *The Rights of Man* (1791), criticized Burke for taking what Paine saw as the tyrants' part. Whatever the case, said Paine, the Revolution of 1688 was a poor defense because it had merely perpetuated aristocratic privilege; the Bill of Rights was really the "bill of wrongs" inasmuch as no one received the vote who had not had it before. He expressly faulted Burke for proclaiming, "We . . . do now wish to derive all we possess as an inheritance from our forefathers." Paine saw each generation as facing problems so unique that the imposition of laws passed by men long buried lay a dead hand on the present.

Disillusionment and War

As the French Revolution moved on to the violence of the September Massacres of 1792, the execution of Louis XVI in January 1793, and the reign of terror, Burke's continuing tirades gathered larger, more sympathetic audiences. It was natural to want freedom but license bred mob murder, ran a now common aphorism. Church attendance increased as atheism across the Channel, in the view of many Englishmen, assumed the face of true evil. Then, when France declared war on Britain the month after Louis' death, even some of the corresponding societies reversed their stand— the London group going so far as to offer to raise a military contingent to fight the now abominable French. The philanthropist Hannah More caught much of English middle class disillusionment in her popular *Village Politics*, (1792) a dialogue between two fictitious workers:

> *Tom:* I'm a friend to the people. I want a reform.
>
> *Jack:* Then the shortest way is to mend thyself. . . .
>
> *Tom:* Pooh! I want freedom and happiness, the same as they have got in France.
>
> *Jack:* What, Tom, we imitate them? We follow the French! Why, they only began all this mischief at first, in order to be just what we are already. . . .
>
> *Tom:* What do you mean by that? Aren't the French free?
>
> *Jack:* Free, Tom! Aye, free with a witness. They are all so free, that there's nobody safe. They make free to rob whom they will, and kill whom they will. If they don't like a man's looks, they make free to hang him without judge or jury, and the next lamp post does for the gallows; so then they call themselves free, because you see they have no king to take them and hang them for it.
>
> *Tom:* Ah, but Jack, didn't their king formerly hang people for nothing, too? And besides, weren't they all papists before the revolution?
>
> *Jack:* Why, true enough, they had but a poor sort of religion, but bad is better

than none, Tom. And so was the government bad enough, too, for they could clap an innocent man into prison, and keep him there, too, as long as they would and never say with your leave or by your leave, gentlemen of the jury. But what's all that to us?

Tom: To us! Why, don't our governors put many of our poor folks in prison against their will? What are all the jails for? I say; all men should be free. . . .

Jack: I'll tell thee a story. When Sir John married, my lady, who is a little fantastical, and likes to do everything like the French, begged him to pull down yonder fine old castle, and build it up in her frippery way. No, says Sir John. What, shall I pull down this noble building, raised by the wisdom of my brave ancestors; which outstood the civil wars, and only underwent a little needful repair at the Revolution [of 1688]; and which all my neighbors come to take a pattern by—shall I pull it all down, I say, only because there may be a dark closet or an inconvenient room or two in it? My lady mumpt and grumbled; but the castle was let stand, and a glorious building it is, though there may be a trifling fault or two, and tho' a few decays may want stopping; so now and then they mend a little thing, and they'd go on-mending, I dare say, as they have leisure, to the end of the chapter, if they are let alone. But no pull-me-down works. What is it you are crying out for, Tom?

Tom: Why, for a perfect government.

Jack: You might as well cry for the moon. There's nothing perfect in this world, take my word for it.

The French revolutionists cried, "Liberty, equality, fraternity," while the English spoke and thought in terms of law, order, and tradition. The French saw the war as a means to extend their revolution to the benighted masses of the world, while Pitt saw, not an ideological, revolutionary threat, but merely a continuation of ever-present commercial rivalries. It mattered little, he averred, what form of government the French chose; but if they began a march to the Rhine, international law and order would be endangered, and England must in that case, as in the past, adopt a policy of containment. In this spirit of neutrality toward the revolution itself, not in reactionary malice, he pushed through repressive measures against domestic insurrection. To enable speedy apprehension of spies, habeas corpus was suspended in 1794. The Treasonable Practices and Seditious Meetings Acts, which gave local officials discretionary powers to confine anyone even remotely suggesting revolution, followed in 1795. Newspapers were curbed and in 1799 a Combinations Act outlawed collective bargaining. By this time Charles Fox, leader of the "new Whigs" (dubbed "conscienceless rebels" by Burke), was alone in his anguished plea that England not abandon reform and liberty at home because of tyranny abroad.

The war against France was to rage far beyond Pitt's initial prediction of a few campaigns; indeed, it was to burgeon into four phases, one on the heels of another, that would take their toll on his health. The War of the First

Coalition lasted from 1793 to 1795; the War of the Second Coalition, from 1799 to 1800; there was a spinoff war from December 1800 to April 1801 against the "armed neutrals" (Denmark, Sweden, Prussia, Russia), who were encouraged by Napoleon to harass England for her maritime pretensions in the Baltic; the grand climax, an all-out engagement with Napoleon's Europe, was to lumber on from 1803 to 1815. England fought the last of these debilitating wars under embargo. The entire war period, during which each of her allies tasted defeat, even included a diversion against America in 1812.

The first of the four wars was lost by England because of Pitt's short-sighted overconfidence. As early as mid-1791 Austria and Prussia declared their intention of intervening in French internal matters for the sake of preserving the monarchy. Initially their armies cleared Flanders of Lafayette's vanguard (he had returned to his country after fighting in the American Revolution). But as the Austrians crept ponderously along the road to Paris, the French began their lengthy list of victories at Valmy (September 1792). The Valmy battle gave the fledgling republic not only breathing space, but also a degree of confidence to draw from, for the immediate future boded ill for it. With Louis XVI's execution in early 1793, French Royalists countered by temporarily seizing and holding large sections of western France, including the port city of Toulon; even the victorious commander of Valmy deserted to the Austrians.

It was at this crucial juncture that Pitt brought England into the war. Typically, his buoyancy overran his judgment, and with greater confidence than was shared by his allies, he predicted a swift and sure victory. He knew—or so he thought—that France was bankrupt. But he underestimated the young republic's resolve. Within a year, over 700,000 French troops, thrice the military capacity commanded by the old monarchy, were marching to defend their country's frontiers. Hitherto untapped resources of wealth (likely wrung from the formerly exempt aristocracy) backed the defenders. Within two years the allies—(Britain, Prussia, Austria, Spain, and Piedmont (northern Italy)—were repulsed where they had not been decimated. The Prussians withdrew entirely in 1795, signing a separate peace that gave France control of all the land south of the Rhine. By 1796 France had erected a puppet republic in the Netherlands and imposed a defensive alliance on the humiliated Spanish, who were forced into a declaration of war against England in October. The French sent a small invasion army to Ireland, where bad weather proved a most effective enemy. The flood of English misfortune continued, and in 1797 Austria deserted the coalition after having forfeited five armies in Italy to the republic's brilliant young commander, Napoleon Bonaparte. Ignominiously, the English cabinet at this miserable juncture found itself capitulating to its own navy. The sailors, striking for better conditions, refused to put to sea until their demands were guaranteed by Parliament. Pitt capitulated, even to having a document of the king's pardon rowed out to each ship. By the final days of 1797 the prime minister was lamely suggesting that the situation for the country, bereft of victories and allies, could only improve, since it could not possibly worsen.

Between the dissolution of the first coalition beginning with Prussia's defection in 1795 and the start of the War of the Second Coalition in 1799, European diplomacy became an adjunct to the career of Napoleon Bonaparte. It was Napoleon who drove an English fleet out of Toulon, Napoleon who smashed the Austrians in Italy, and Napoleon who now dominated the French Republic. With his next commission, to train an army to invade England, the island's luck improved. Bonaparte changed the government's intention in favor of an exotic expedition to Egypt. He intended that country as a springboard for an Olympian thrust at England's empire in India, from which France had been expelled forty years before.

Meeting the Threat of Napoleon

This grandiose plan could have been executed only by a Bonaparte; it would take a flamboyantly daring equal to halt it. Lord Horatio Nelson was that complement, for what Napoleon could accomplish on land, Nelson could match on the seas. By 1798 Nelson, whose motto was "Not victory but annihilation," already bore the scars of his fanatic dedication. He had lost an eye attacking Corsica in 1794 and an arm in combat with the Spanish at the Battle of Santa Cruz in 1797. This bulldog of the British navy was picked to track Napoleon's Egyptian expedition. Nelson barely missed the French fleet as it departed from Toulon in May 1798, pursued it to Malta, scoured the coast of Syria, and then, at the end of July, sighted it near the entrance to the Nile in Aboukir Bay. The impetuous admiral, never seeing the point of encounter unless total mastery was the object, daringly charged into the dangerous shallows on his enemy's unarmed flank. Napoleon's fleet was obliterated and he and his Army of the Nile were stranded in Egypt. This daring feat of valor raised Nelson to the House of Lords.

The Battle of the Nile convinced England's wayward allies that a second coalition might bear fruit. That fruit was to turn bitter. Napoleon miraculously escaped his arid prison, returned to take command at home, and proclaimed himself First Consul of the French Republic. English subsidies to Austria and Russia, far exceeding any in the past, went down the drain when Napoleon again smashed the Austrians at Marengo in 1800 and imposed a peace on them. The Russians, now under the neurotic Czar Paul, who ardently admired Napoleon, made England's presumptuous search for contraband in the Baltic

NELSON AT THE BATTLE OF ST. VINCENT.
Courtesy The Bettman Archive.

Sea a pretext to withdraw from the coalition. The czar, enticed by the first consul's promises of English booty, wheeled on his ally and revitalized the League of Armed Neutrals (Russia, Denmark, Sweden, and Prussia). From December 1800 to April 1801, England fought a Baltic foe while France enjoyed momentary calm on the high seas.

It took the "Nelson touch" to save the day again and to impress all of Europe with the island's resolve. Nelson, second in command, in March 1801 sailed for Copenhagen, the western stronghold of the armed neutrals. The port's shoals and formidable defenses appeared so impregnable that his superior hoisted a signal ordering withdrawal. Nelson vouched that with his blind eye he did not see the signal. In a repetition of Aboukir Bay, he drove savagely over the undefended shallows into the enemy's line, shredding it where it least expected. The result was the capitulation of the armed neutrals and greater honors for Nelson, now created viscount and supreme commander.

The threat of a Franco-Russian entente was terminated with the assassination of Czar Paul (by his own officers) even as Nelson canceled out the Danish fleet. The short War of the Armed Neutrals was, all in all, little more than a diversion. But the worst lay ahead, for the formidable Napoleon would soon have to be met on his terms, and this could mean none other than a land contest.

For the moment, however, England had something to show for her eight years of intermittent combat. She was absolute ruler of the seas. The Baltic, like the Mediterranean, might well have been an English lake. Every colony held by Napoleon's compatriots had been ripped from its Continental parent and dropped into England's imperial bag: Trinidad, Ceylon, the Cape of Good Hope, Minorca, Malta, the Spice Islands, the French West Indies. England garnered some satisfaction too from the fact that in 1800 Napoleon, recognizing the island's superiority on the seas, had approached Pitt with peace in mind. The overture had been spurned on the bizarre grounds that only the restoration of the French monarchy could guarantee England's security. Two years later, negotiations produced the Peace of Amiens: England returned all her booty except Trinidad and Ceylon; France withdrew from southern Italy and agreed to respect the independence of the puppet republics she had erected in the Netherlands, Switzerland, and northern Italy. Amiens and the Treaty of Lunéville, which France had signed with Austria the year before, produced a calm only fools took to be permanent.

The least fooled was Pitt, who was denied participation in the Amiens negotiations—he had been forced to resign a full year before the treaty was signed in March 1802. The political mood of the country had altered in the seventeen years of his ministry (1783–1801). Pitt's earlier pursuance of the war, and especially his laws against collective bargaining, spies, and rioters, had been considered proper patriotism. But his pursuit of Napoleon, particularly after the consul's peace overtures of 1800, was considered to have metamorphosed into warmongering when it produced a tax scale that pleased no one. When Napoleon effectively closed the Rhine trade and stopped 75 percent of all grain imports from the Baltic, Pitt, feeling the pinch, decided against financing the war with more loans; but the alternative required him to treble existing taxes on the already taxed windows, houses, servants, and carriages. Most obnoxious of all, in 1798 Pitt invented a graduated tax on earnings of £60 annually and up, which rose to as much as 10 percent of incomes exceeding £200. The income tax had come into being.

As long as King George valued his minister's practicality, Pitt could outrun the grumbling opposition. However, at any display of humanitarian reform, George would withdraw his support and let the school of political sharks have him. It was Pitt's earlier Irish Catholic emancipation efforts that came to produce just such an irreconcilable rupture.

Trouble at the Back Door

At Pitt's Catholic Relief Act of 1793, there had seemed good prospects for strengthening Irish self-government while keeping Ireland within the empire. The sympathetic Pitt had concurred with Grattan that final legislative independence and full civic (as well as religious) liberty were close companions. But a leisurely resolve of these involved problems was denied the well-meaning prime minister. The crucial questions of time and tactics, influenced by the French Revolution, rose more rapidly than anyone could have conjectured.

The Irish radical Theobold Wolfe Tone, in the pamphlet *A Northern Whig* (1791), was one of the early voices exhorting Protestant and Catholic alike to break the connection with England. Had the militant lawyer from Belfast combined with Grattan's more timid, but like-minded, following in a common cause of Irish independence, Mr. Pitt might have embraced his early reforms less eagerly. The internal religious enmity prevented all three—Pitt, Grattan, and Tone—from seeing fruition of their hopes, though each approached the problem and saw the outcome differently.

English methods and timing were bungled from the start. The viceroy sent to Dublin in 1795 precipitately implied that Catholic participation in Irish affairs would soon be fact. Catholic leaders rejoiced and Protestants quaked. As the viceroy was recalled to England for jumping the gun on the prime minister's long-range plans, Catholics despaired and Protestants exulted. The ingredients of religious war—suspicion, envy, betrayal—were in the pot. Tone helped fire them. In 1795 he left Ireland for America, where he and

French agents concocted a plan to invade Ireland that was to be carried out the following year. He next surfaced in Paris to accept a commission in the French army. Meanwhile, at home his Society of United Irishmen was formulating plans for open rebellion. Between 1796 and 1798 the dream of Catholic-Protestant unity completely fell apart. Protestant leaders, fearing a Catholic rebellion armed by French republicanism, harried, tortured, and even exterminated Catholic populations. The Catholics responded in kind. Too impatient to await a promised French invasion, they amassed a badly equipped army of out-and-out rebels bent on independence, which they hurled against English troops at Vinegar Hill in Southern Ireland (June 1798). They were easily destroyed by the authorities. When the French squadron belatedly arrived, it too was captured, as was Tone, who evaded execution for treason by committing suicide.

With Napoleon triumphant on the Continent, Ireland became cause for additional concern. She was England's back door, ajar to an adventurer who did not hesitate to project his armies as far from France as Egypt. Ireland therefore must be pacified, perhaps, as Scotland had been a hundred years earlier, through union with the English crown. Pitt used every available English pound to buy the votes of the Irish Parliament. Where money failed, he offered promises; as soon as union was effected, he would push through the English Parliament what the Protestants of Dublin and Ulster would never yield on their own—full Catholic emancipation. In 1800, shortly after Irish acceptance, the Act of Union went into effect. A hundred Irish members were slated for the English Commons, thirty-two Irish peers for Lords. With the political problem supposedly eased, Pitt now had to make good on his religious commitment. It was this issue that lost George III's favor and toppled Pitt from office. The prime minister's further plan for political toleration for Irish Catholics was leaked to the monarch by members of Pitt's own cabinet. The king reacted by calling it the most "Jacobinical"[1] thing he had ever heard. Pitt acquiesced to this overbearing prejudice not only by resigning, but also by promising not to oppose the new ministry or to ever again introduce Catholic emancipation. He relinquished his office to the safe and stolid Henry Addington in March 1801.

France: A Threat Redoubled

It was Addington who signed the Treaty of Amiens. During the little more than two years of peace that followed, which all but the dullest realized was actually a truce, Addington blithely reduced armaments, abolished

[1] Not to be confused with "Jacobitical," having reference to the followers of the deposed Stuarts. The Jacobins were French radicals.

the income tax, and made plans to pare the debt. The English tourists who flocked to Napoleon's court quickly weighed the chances of permanent peace more wisely. Though they were impressed by the demoniac energy of the first consul and fascinated by his alternate exhibitions of grandeur and coarseness, his petty jibes at English expense were a source of concern. They sent back accounts of continuing French hostility. Merchants complained that France had closed not only her own markets to them but also those of the Netherlands. Accounts of coerced ties with the Netherlands and Switzerland, of the activities of anti-English agents in Italy and Ireland, of French emissaries drawing detailed plans of English port facilities, and of the rapid rearming of the French fleet combined to create a growing uneasiness at court. When the English embassy itemized the scores of infractions of the treaty, Napoleon arrogantly berated it for meddling. Dejected and more than a bit frightened, the new prime minister feared that unless he seized the initiative, Napoleon's armies could strike at England's throat within the year. He made a declaration of war in May 1803.

Napoleon had little to fear: in Addington's largely defensive version of warfare, the French were not to be antagonized on the Continent, the English navy was to sit blithely in the Channel, daring the enemy to transgress past her forest of masts, and an augmented militia would be responsible for home defense. But when thousands answered the English government's call to arms, there were few weapons. The income tax was reimposed at half the former rate. Addington was obviously not the man to overwhelm Napoleon. Nor was Pitt, who, a victim of his promise to the king, had disaffected many of his old supporters by his self-imposed silence. Conditions worsened early in 1804, when George suffered another of his frequent mental lapses. Despite his recovery and Pitt's reappointment as prime minister in May, dreary days lay ahead. Fox's clique had always opposed the hostilities with the French. Addington's moderate majority continued to trust in low taxes and home defense. Thus Pitt, anxious to activate the war, found himself bedeviled by parliamentary dissension. Even his friends were attacked. Henry Dundas. Lord Melville, first lord of the admiralty and the administrative genius who had given Nelson his fleet, was ruined by petty charges of mismanagement of naval funds. Pitt's promise that Melville would resign was unsuccessful in fending off his colleague's impeachment. Fox next maneuvered the prime minister into having to reject Catholic relief. Few measures could have been dearer to Pitt's heart, and his promise to George must have made his opposition to Fox's token bill doubly taxing.

However, what England lacked in wartime unity in those factious years of 1804 and 1805 she made up in good fortune, despite the fact that the French emperor (Napoleon had crowned himself in 1804) found little to divert his aggressive attention from her puny belligerence. With an avowed intention of hurling a French "Army of England" across the Channel, Napoleon amassed nearly 100,000 troops in the Boulogne region and built 2,000 troop transports (actually little more than barges) for the crossing. As English coastal villages were being evacuated, George III made arrangements to personally lead the militia against the anticipated invasion. But the questionable formidability of English defenses was not to be tested. Napoleon dallied his most favorable months into oblivion, and by the time the ultimate militarist realized that the barges were not about to float over to England on the tide, it was too late to concert a convoy of the French navies at Brest and Toulon. Then, in August 1805, Austria launched its bid to stop the French emperor, and he had to deploy his Army of England from the Channel coast to the Danube. The October chill seemed to waft happier news from the sea as reports of the abandoned camps around Boulogne reached England.

Lord Nelson had been playing cat-and-mouse with the Toulon fleet throughout the summer. The French, hoping to deceive him into thinking they had sailed off to the West Indies to capture Jamaica, crossed the Atlantic, then veered back to Europe. Although Nelson rose to the lure and followed, he made up in speed what had been lost in advantage. When he discovered the trick, he hurried to Spanish waters, where the French fleet had linked up with the Spanish at Cadiz. Although the augmented fleet was now as blockaded as it had been in Toulon, the superior number—some thirty-four ships—made an encounter with Nelson feasible. As the combined fleets formed a crescent-shaped battle line off Cape Trafalgar, Nelson raised a final signal, an extension of his own creed—"England expects every man to do his duty." On October 21, 1805, he drove headlong into the enemies' line, scattered their vessels so that the largest could never engage in battle, and destroyed or captured half the fleet. But a well-placed shot felled the great Nelson; he survived only long enough to learn of his consummate victory.

The Battle of Trafalgar ensconced Nelson as England's greatest naval hero; his name has been perpetuated by a mammoth monument, Trafalgar Square, as great as any king's shrine. In gratitude his brother was made an earl and given £6,000 annually, his sisters were granted £10,000, and a sum of £100,000 was provided for an estate. After Trafalgar the seas of the world became England's. Her supremacy remained unchallenged until 1916 and was not lost until the Second World War.

Pitt's joy at the news of Trafalgar was considerably lessened by Nelson's death, and when, in December 1805, reports of the defeat of the combined Austrian and Russian forces at Austerlitz reached his ears, his despair was total. At forty-six he probably sensed that he could not live the ten years he felt he now needed to stop Napoleon. As he died on January 23, 1806, the tormented Pitt is said to have moaned, "Alas, My country! How I leave my country."

It is a measure of his stature that a coalition, a "ministry of all talents," was needed to fill his post. William Grenville, the son of George Grenville (the minister of 1763 who had precipitated the American Revolution), became lord treasurer; Addington returned; and after a twenty-three-year absence, Charles Fox resurfaced in the ministry as foreign secretary. The old friend of the French Revolution was confident he could negotiate peace. The wars against the French Republic, Fox had often maintained, were the contrivance of English reactionaries. Napoleon entertained Fox's emissaries but, after his stunning victory at Austerlitz, was in little hurry to negotiate. Fox, like Pitt, lost hope of having peace in his own time.

His despair was probably doubled by the knowledge that he would not likely survive the year, much less the war, for he was seriously ill. Despite his limited energies he introduced a bill reflecting his personal program—the abolition of the slave trade. For all his former frivolity Fox was honestly dedicated to humanitarian reform and sympathetic to the Society for the Abolition of the Slave Trade. He intended now to use his office on the society's behalf. Though he died in September 1806, his successor, Grenville, had little difficulty overriding the vocal West Indian planters' opposition to Fox's re-formist memorial, and the abolition act became law in 1807. Twenty-six years later, slavery as well as slave trade was outlawed throughout the British empire.

The patchwork ministries succeeding Grenville's (which crumbled in March 1807) produced only two men of notable talent: Foreign Secretary George Canning and Secretary of War Robert Stewart, Viscount Castlereagh. Both were to play important roles after the war, though their mutual hatred nullified any effect they might have had on the cessation of hostilities. In fact, their strained relations brought them to a duel in 1809. This was but one incident in the continual bickerings that disrupted ministry after ministry. The accommodating duke of Portland, whose government housed the in-compatible Canning and Castlereagh, held his ministry together from 1807 to 1809. Spencer Perceval, prime minister from 1809 until his assassination in 1812, was safe and stodgy and perhaps deserves the epithet of the nineteenth-century political scientist, Walter Bagehot: "Hardly any fact in history is so incredible as that . . . England was ruled by Mr. Perceval."[2] It was Lord Liverpool, successor to Perceval, who saw the war to its conclusion. Not one of these leaders reached the heights of the supernal Pitt.

Adding to the void in political leadership was George III's final departure into the dark world that frequently overtook him during these emotional decades. After the death of his beloved youngest daughter in 1810, he was

[2] Quoted in R. J. White, *The Age of George III* (New York, 1969), p. 94.

seldom lucid. He once asked whether Lord North had called. To humor him, he was told yes. The king revealingly responded,

> He might have recollected me sooner. . . . We meant well to the Americans; just to punish them with a few bloody noses, and then to make bows for the mutual happiness of the two countries. But want of principle got into the army. . . . We lost America. Tell him not to call again; I shall never see him.[3]

North had been dead since 1792. In 1811 the Regency Act gave titular power to the son who was to become George IV on his father's death in 1820. In the meantime, the confused parent spent his days reviewing imaginary troops and holding imaginary conversations.

After the 1805 disaster of Austerlitz, Europe was Napoleon's. Prussia fell in 1806, Russia was neutralized by the Treaty of Tilsit in 1807; and poor Austria, in a fourth feeble challenge, was all but dismantled in 1809. The remainder of Europe was absorbed by decree; or, as in the case of Spain, by the placement of one of the French emperor's relatives on its throne; or, as in the case of the Papal States, by imprisonment of the pope. France's bloated borders stretched from Hamburg to Rome; her "Grand Empire" included the balance of Germany and Italy, as well as Poland and Spain; Napoleon's intimidated allies included Austria, Prussia, Russia, Denmark, and Sweden. His relatives ruled the Netherlands, Spain, Westphalia, and Naples. When he implanted his brother Jerome into southern Germany as king of Westphalia, Napoleon typified his unchallenged control over Europe in a dispatch: "You will find enclosed the constitution of your kingdom. . . . The benefits of the Code Napoleon . . . will be so many distinctive features of your monarchy."

It was fortunate for England that the emperor concentrated on the Continent, for had his invincible army crossed the Channel, England might have had a Bonaparte ruling in Whitehall. As it was, Napoleon's forces were too widely spaced ever to pose a direct threat, his energies too scattered to focus on the island; and so little England escaped.

Rather than direct assault, both empires had conducted the war by blockade and embargo. Napoleon's "Continental System," issued under the Berlin Decree of 1806, tightened the already rigorous restrictions imposed against British shipping in 1803: vessels from any British holding were denied entry into the ports of French-controlled Europe. In 1807 Russia and Prussia were forced into compliance, and in November the Milan Decrees further forbade any ship stopping in Britain to land on the Continent on pain of confiscation as a privateer. England retaliated with orders in Council declaring that vessels trading with France left themselves open to capture, though this might be

---

[3] *Journals of Madame Papendieck* (London, 1887), p. 97.

avoided if they sailed by way of a British port, there to pay duty and secure a license.

The war of commercial recrimination, costly to both sides, perhaps canceled any advantage either antagonist sought to gain. French farmers suffered the loss of export moneys they had formerly received from grain shipments to England. English textile manufacturers were forced to shut down their plants or go to half time, and French factories, needing English equipment and raw materials, closed altogether. English merchants watched their receipts plunge from £13 million to £2 million between 1805 and 1811: bankruptcies abounded as Continental trade fell into the hands of neutrals, especially the Americans. The success of the embargo is documented by the fact that in 1807 44 percent of all ships sailing from Britain were under foreign flags.

The War of 1812

It was as much against the neutrals as against Napoleon that the search and seizure orders in Council were issued. The Americans felt particularly victimized, all the more so because England refused to recognize her subjects' right to become naturalized American citizens. Despite protests, even passport proof of their new allegiance, untold numbers of seamen were dragooned to serve aboard British men-of-war. The *Chesapeake* affair brought these grievances to a head. The commander of the British *Leopard* fired on and boarded the American naval frigate *Chesapeake* and lightened her by four purported English deserters. In retaliation President Jefferson supported the American Embargo Act against European shipping, aimed more at Britain than at France. To their mutual disadvantage England and America drastically curtailed their trade with each other and aggravated injury with further incidents on the high seas. But by 1811 England's shaky economy, effectively crippled by the double squeeze of French and American embargoes and plagued by two years of bad harvests, forced her to relax most shipping restrictions, not only against America but against the Continent as well. In June 1812, as the orders in Council were rescinded, America, now under the spell of the "War Hawks" (who clamored for a Canadian conquest) forced the search and seizure issue to the battlefield with a declaration of war against England.

The War of 1812, an additional distraction for the English, was carried on with what meager forces they could spare. Naval duels were little more than individual ship-to-ship encounters. The American fleet was soon bottled up behind a blockade, preventing any further sea clashes. The Americans' vaunted invasion of Canada quickly collapsed, though their Captain Perry's victory on Lake Erie had secured control of the Great Lakes. An English force burned Washington and retreated; the Americans took redress at New Orleans with a British rout (a battle famous for having been fought after the peace was agreed upon). The Treaty of Ghent, signed in December 1814, put an irresolute end to this half-hearted skirmish by placing the combatants in the approximate positions they had occupied at the onset.

Of far greater import to England's survival than this nuisance war was Napoleon's growing territorial greed. Had he patiently outwaited her ability to endure his embargo, he might have bankrupted the island. But in 1807 he committed himself to the invasion of Portugal, ostensibly to bring the Portuguese under the yoke of the Continental System. He seized a fortuitous opportunity in 1808 to remove the Spanish monarch and place his brother Joseph on the Bourbon throne. His act had less pretense of right than Louis XIV's bestowal of that crown on his grandson a hundred years earlier. But unlike his French predecessor's interventionism, the emperor's attempt ignited a national furor not anticipated; before long the entire Iberian Peninsula was mottled with insurrection.

The French army in Portugal was halted by English forces at the Battle of Vimiero in August 1808, and the tenuous foothold was safeguarded (though the English commander temporarily in charge accommodatingly allowed the beaten French to withdraw). The English failed to take immediate advantage of the Portuguese victory because the cabinet viewed the Netherlands as the best assault route into Napoleon's fortress. It sent a futile expedition to the Netherlands (perhaps recalling the glories Marlborough once secured there). Within six months the toll from disease convinced the War Office that Portugal was the best doorway to France after all. Having proved his coolness and precision, Arthur Wellesley (Lord Wellington as of 1809, duke of Wellington in 1814) was given command of the Portuguese front. He had taken Vimiero and had a complete knowledge of Iberia. Because Napoleon's armies were spectacular and reckless in movement, and because Spain and Portugal were mountainous terrain requiring a mapmaker's expertise, Wellington had every mile of his campaign charted beforehand. French troops lived off the land and had to move quickly to find new food supplies; Wellington established food depots wherever his army might march. The French preferred mass encounters; Wellington dodged and wove in the Spanish guerrilla fashion, wearing down his opponent by sheer activity. Napoleon's armies were a foreign horde; the English commander posed as the deliverer of Portuguese and Spanish honor. He paid for his supplies promptly, spoke the language, and familiarized himself with the native customs. With these well-thought-out advantages, though Napoleon's armies once numbered 250,000, Wellington managed with 30,000.

In 1811 he again stopped the French with an ingenious network of defenses around Lisbon's hills, the Torres Vedras lines, in their second bid to take Portugal. The French, with 25,000 casualties, nursed their wounds back to Spain. There, for the next two years, in eroding the enemy's defenses, Wellington repeatedly took two steps forward, one backward. Then, in June 1813, he caught the retreating army of Joseph Napoleon at the Battle of Vitoria. The French masters of Iberia fled, leaving behind their artillery and treasury. Wellington now assembled maps for the climactic encounter in France.

During 1812 and 1813 Napoleon's fruitless campaigns in Spain and Portugal depleted his treasuries. But what most compelled him to terminate the Continental System was his ambitious plan to invade Russia in June of 1812. For this venture he amassed the largest army (700,000 troops) ever assembled for a single expedition. The costs forced him to lift the embargo against England, though he still exacted exorbitant customs. By the end of 1812 English commerce to Napoleon's Europe had increased 28 percent over the previous year, even equipping his armies with English blankets, coats, buttons, and boots. The trade volume might have been greater except that in the crunch of the embargo England had shifted much of her export surplus to the new markets of South America. There she would dominate trade for the next century.

In the summer of 1812 Napoleon marched his 700,000 into Russia and oblivion. By the following spring the rugged winter and Russian tenacity had taken 500,000 of his troops. The emperor was reduced to commanding young boys and old men in the last of his major engagements, a carnage of three days' duration, the "Battle of the Nations," fought in Germany in October 1813; this battle marked the end of Napoleon's empire. While Napoleon was learning of defeat, Wellington was scoring victories in central France. Bordeaux fell in February 1814; Toulouse capitulated in April. That month the English commander joined the allies in Paris to toast the formal abdication of the French emperor. The exiled Napoleon was granted the rule of the tiny island of Elba in the Mediterranean (hardly sufficient to contain his ambitions), and France was restored to the Bourbons under Louis XVIII.

Napoleon launched one final thunderbolt from his principality, shattering the temporary peace in the ordeal of the Hundred Days. After ten months' exile in Elba, he returned to the mainland, gathered 6,000 stalwarts, and tested the resolution of the victors, who were already bickering over the peace settlement. The fantastic magic of the man entranced 170,000 more to his side. The plan was to attack the Belgian frontier in a new attempt to retake Europe. But the allies, however much they mistrusted each other, were resolute in denying the Prince of Elba a second chance. At Waterloo (in Belgium) in June 1815, a combined English and Prussian army dislodged the last of Napoleon's legions and sent him scurrying to Paris.

The Congress of Vienna

A series of conferences culminated in the Congress of Vienna from September 1814 to June 1815 and at last brought peace to Europe after twenty-two years of hostilities. Though France was included in the deliberations, it was tacit that she would never again encroach on her neighbors. Her borders were fixed to those of 1790, her puppet kingdoms were dismantled, and she was charged indemnity for allowing Napoleon's hundred-day fling. More immediate to English interests, as a buffer to future territorial pretensions, an enlarged kingdom of the Netherlands was created. As the other signatory powers redrafted the map of Europe consonant with their ideas of restoration and legitimacy, England looked to the oceans for her rewards. She took the Danish island of Heligoland; from the Dutch she exacted Ceylon, the Cape of Good Hope, and Guiana; and from the French, Tobago and St. Lucia in the West Indies.

In England the festivities during the Congress of Vienna were unrestrained. Little wonder—the effects of the embargo, the costs of the war (£830 million), the dizzying inflation, the resulting starvation and labor riots might now pass into oblivion. In 1814 optimism caused Sir Patrick Colquhoun, the author of *The Wealth, Power and Resources of the British Empire*, to assure his readers that "an era has arrived in the affairs of the British Empire . . . which [has] excited the wonder, the astonishment, and perhaps the envy of the civilized world."

But the sunny world of 1815 preceded a darker storm: foreign markets found English imports beyond their means, business slumped as wartime government contracts were terminated, and the ranks of the unemployed swelled with the return of 400,000 warriors. This brought more riot and despair and a suicide rate exceptional for the age. Troops that once rode against the French were soon charging into demonstrators at London and Manchester. Although England had approached the environs of her grandest age with the defeat of Napoleon, the social dislocations were so great in 1815 as to prompt J. H. Plumb to close his volume, *England in the Eighteenth Century*, with these words:

> In 1815 Great Britain seemed on the edge of bankruptcy and social revolution. Starvation was driving the poor to wreck the machinery which seemed to them to be the cause of the misery, and the government, without wisdom and without foresight, repressed brutally what in its turn it could not comprehend. To thinking men the horizon was dark and foreboding. After a century of war France had been defeated in the struggle for commercial empire, and at last the ports of the New World were open. India was ours. But what a racked and distracted Britain might make of these long-sought opportunities was hidden in the future; in 1815, at the end of long endurance, there was fear, and envy, and greed, but little hope.[4]

[4] J. H. Plumb, *England in the Eighteenth Century* (Harmondsworth, 1950), p. 214.

Chapter Thirteen
NATURE AND NATURE'S LAWS: THE ENLIGHTENMENT

Nature and Nature's laws lay hid in night:
God said, Let Newton be! *and all was light!*

ALEXANDER POPE
epitaph intended for Sir Isaac Newton

Manifestations of Nature

The builders of the English Enlightenment were smugly aware that they had left behind the dark shores of mysticism and superstition of the Middle Ages. They thought their Enlightenment consisted of having discovered that to know the secrets of nature was to know the works of God. Consequently, the study of nature and natural law came to be as compelling in the seventeenth and eighteenth centuries as the search for divine providence had been in the Middle Ages.

That is not to say that the study of natural law was new to England; it had been just as prized in medieval and renaissance times. Back in the thirteenth century Thomas Aquinas had declared that nature was as much an avenue for God's will as revelation (Scripture and church doctrine). In the seventeenth century, nature gradually came to supersede revelation as the primary source of divine truth. One should not be content with Biblical authority alone when "natural revelation . . . communicates to mankind that portion of truth which [God] has laid within the reach of [man's] natural faculties," wrote the philosopher John Locke. What concerned these theologians of nature was not the possibility that traditional religion was false or misleading but the possibility that many of the truths revealed in scripture were unverifiable through common observation of scripture alone.

The leaders of the Enlightenment denigrated what they called "enthusiasm" (blind flights of religious mysticism). A true religion, they affirmed with Archbishop Tillotson, must establish itself as workable, provable, and natural: "All the duties of Christian religion . . . are no other but what natural light [insight] prompts men to." Conversely, false religions proved their fallaciousness by their outlandish myths, absurd rituals, and reliance on pure magic. Said Charles Blount, "All faiths have been shaken but those only which stand upon the basis of common reason." Thomas Burnet, who attempted to square Biblical accounts of the creation, the flood, and the final judgment with natural science in his *Sacred Theory of the Earth* (1689), fretted at first how the entire earth could have been inundated by a mere forty days and forty nights of rain. He solved the apparent discrepancy by allowing oceans of ground water to break forth coincidentally with the downpour. The fiery final judgment, Burnet said, would come also through natural agents, and when volcanoes and meteors ignited its coal deposits, England would be a particularly hot spot. Little wonder the Enlightenment prided itself on works with such titles as *Christianity not Mysterious* (John Toland) and *The Reasonableness of Christianity* (John Locke).

What nature itself was, no one precisely knew. A modern scholar of the Enlightenment has catalogued sixty different definitions of the word as it was then used. Thomas Hobbes, though he lived prior to the height of the Enlightenment and was disowned for supposed atheism, called nature "the art whereby God hath made and governs the world." Most of his successors would have agreed, but each would have emphasized a different manifestation as the heart of nature, according to his own tenets: the scientist, the astral and planetary nature; the farmer, the nature of weather, crops, and cattle; the social philosopher, human nature; the poet, the nature of mountains, vales, and heaths; the artist, an emphasis on natural symmetry, form, and color. Although most saw order as nature's paramount attribute, there were those who allowed nature to be luxuriant, exotic, even chaotic—but full expression of this idea would have to wait until the blossoming of romanticism at the end of the eighteenth century.

Hobbes also revealed something else about the Enlightenment's preoccupation with nature; it was invariably thought of as a body of laws, though those laws, like nature, were ambiguous:

> They are called the laws of nature, for that they are the dictates of natural reason; and also moral laws, because they concern men's manners and conversation one towards another; so are they also divine laws in respect of the author thereof, God Almighty; and ought therefore to agree, or at least, not to be repugnant to the word of God revealed in Holy Scripture.

Thus natural law, which was supposed to be rational, moral, and divine all at once, seemed to be a justification for any course of thought and action. But what about violent murder, brutalizing war, earthquakes, and pestilence? Is whatever happens natural? Shakespeare's audience would have said no; but the Enlightenment was not as positive. Alexander Pope tried to explain away chaos in his *Essay on Man* (1734). Natural harmony exists even if we do not see it:

All nature is but art, unknown to thee;
All chance, direction, which thou canst not
    see;
All discord, harmony not understood;
All partial evil, universal good:
And, spite of pride, in erring reason's
    spite,
One truth is clear, WHATEVER IS, IS RIGHT.

Questioning Natural Law

There were a few, however, who thought otherwise. Jonathan Swift was not one of those easily mollified by a sweet reasonableness in natural law, or, especially, by man's ability either to know or follow that reasonableness. At one point in his *Travels Into Several Remote Nations by Captain Lemuel Gulliver* (1726), the captain arrives at an island of sorcerers who are capable of conjuring the dead back to life. Gulliver, through them, reviews all past history and concludes:

How many innocent and excellent persons had been condemned to death or banishment by the practising of great ministers upon the corruption of judges and the malice of factions. How many villains had been exalted to the highest places of trust, power, dignity, and profit: how great a share in the motions and events of courts, councils, and senates might be challenged by bawds, whores, pimps, parasites, and buffoons. How low an opinion I had of human wisdom and integrity when I was truly informed of the springs and motives of great enterprises and revolutions in the world, and of the contemptible accidents to which they owed their success.

Bernard Mandeville went one step beyond Swift in unmasking an adverse reasonableness in natural law. In his *Fable of the Bees* (1714) he declared that civilization thrived on vice, vanity, and folly. How else could armies of tailors, shippers, builders, and servants be kept scurrying to satisfy their desires? "The fire of London [1666] was a great calamity," to be sure, he says, "but if the carpenters, bricklayers, [and] smiths" who rebuilt the city "were to vote against those who lost by the fire, the rejoicings would equal, if not exceed the complaints." Reason and happiness are therefore incompatible, for nature seems to thrive as well on vice and chaos as it does on virtue and order.

The skepticism that Mandeville brought to natural law achieved its highest expression through the Scottish historian-philosopher David Hume. In a series of essays, treatises, and dialogues, he diverted the inquiry from nature of nature into one of what we are capable of knowing of nature. Man can never really discover anything substantial about natural law inasmuch as he is depen-

dent on what he *thinks* he has witnessed. What others would call scientific observation Hume chose to call subjective observation. In other words, we do not
know what we have seen, only what we think we have seen. Thus Hume's
essays abound with words like "opinion," "sentiment," and "self-interest."

It appears evident that the ultimate ends of human actions can never, in any case,
be accounted for by reason, but recommend themselves entirely to the sentiments
and affections of mankind without any dependence on the intellectual faculties.
Ask a man why he uses exercise; he will answer because he desires to keep his health.
If you then enquire, why he desires health, he will readily reply, because sickness is
painful. If you push your enquiries farther, and desire a reason why he hates pain,
it is impossible he can ever give any. This is an ultimate end, and is never referred to
any other object.

Thus, although we can never know anything beyond what we believe (or want
to believe), our belief acts as a kind of natural law. If pressed, Hume would have
said that all actions have a kind of utility; and usefulness, especially if it provides
pleasure, is a sort of reason unto itself, at least for mankind if not in nature.

A dramatic reaction to the "Whatever is, is right" school came early in 1750
when two severe earthquakes rattled London, driving many into the surrounding fields in their "earthquake gowns" (robes made of bed sheets) to await a
prediction by a deranged soldier that the city would be destroyed on April 4.
The great destruction came, but not until 1755, and then it shattered Lisbon
in Portugal, not London. If natural law were so beneficently ordered, many
asked, what was its purpose in having blindly destroyed thousands of Portuguese? There was bewilderment throughout Europe. In England George II
ordered a national fast day for the repentance of the sins that had brought
down the wrath of God. Scores of books questioned the rationality of natural
law. One of the more effective, by John Wesley, called attention to a growing
religious revival within the Church of England (*Serious Thoughts Occasioned
by the Late Earthquake at Lisbon, 1756*).

Critics claimed that the Anglican Church had been slipping into secularism
for decades; that many of its clerics were no better than the "Vicar of Bray"
who, according to the old ballad, facilely altered his theology to please whatever party was currently triumphant at court. Some reproved Archbishop
John Tillotson's popular sermons (published in William of Orange's reign),
in which he intimated that the gulf of original sin no longer separated man
from God. The bishop of Bangor scandalized even more of England's populace
by declaring in 1717 that the church ought not to hold any privileged place
in either the constitution of the land or in the conscience of the individual
Christian. While most churchmen in the eighteenth century plied their callings
diligently, the impression conveyed by those who neglected their charges for

the hunt, business, scholarship, or politics was demoralizing to many parishioners, but especially so to John Wesley, the founder of Methodism.

Wesley's intellect was shaped more by the residual pietism of the seventeenth-century Puritans than by the intellectual currents of his own day. A tutor at Oxford, around 1730 he there organized a club for intense devotionalism. He sailed as a missionary to Georgia, but after his return to England, he received in 1738 what he regarded as a direct divine experience. From that moment he energetically preached the doctrine of salvation by fundamental faith. His methods were direct, noninstitutional, and emotional. They ignored the hidebound formal parish framework of Anglicanism. Inevitably, he was barred from preaching by his superiors, who felt that his practices demolished normal decorum and appealed to the raw emotionalism of his followers. Undeterred, Wesley took to the road, sometimes covering as many as seventy miles in a single day to deliver four or five sermons to gatherings in streets, shops, and fields. Over the fifty years of his ministry, his tens of thousands of adherents built chapels outside the Anglican establishment. They financed what became, by the end of the century, the Methodist church, though Wesley had never formally broken with the Church of England.

Though he ignored all the tenets of Enlightenment philosophy, Wesley inadvertently shared some of its features. He was suspicious of systematic theology, and he decried rank mysticism, favoring a common-sense school of moral goodness. His Christianity stressed virtue, thrift, self-help, and hard labor. As an intuitive Tory, he advocated abject obedience to king and country, which he carried down through lords, squires, and employers. Perhaps it is little wonder that Methodism later throve in industrial areas where subjection to factory rule was difficult to enforce. Probably no power since Puritanism had so galvanized a group into a sense of belonging to a meaningful world community. During the early years of the Industrial Revolution, the multitude of workers who were enlisted in Methodism came from diverse regions and backgrounds. They were probably given their first sense of social cohesion by affiliation in a local Methodist chapel.

Most "gentlemen," however, were able to resist the power of Wesley's enthusiasm. An exception was the Countess of Huntingdon, who gave her devotion and fortune to the Methodists. The religion of fashionable society in the eighteenth century consisted of bland rectitude, of having the "heart in the right place." The "religion of nature," or "deism," the upper-class belief, emphasized the total compatibility of everything—for God had created a self-regulating universe that could neither destroy, much less sin against, itself. Although there was a worship of science (thanks to Newton's discovery of the law of gravity), deism's major ingredients were social awareness, everyday good fellowship, and a helpfulness to others:

Thus God and Nature fixed the general frame,
And bade self-love and social be the same.

As revealed in the Royal Society's proceedings, the scientists of the day
quested not so much for the abstract qualities in matter as for projects that
would enhance the good life, such as;

Whether diamonds and other precious stones grow again after three or four years
in the same places where they have been dug out? What river is that in Java Major
that turns wood into stone? Whether there be a tree in Mexico that yields water,
wine, vinegar, oil, milk, honey, wax, thread, and needles?

The Enlightenment in England, though it stressed the primacy of natural
law, departed from the European Enlightenment in its avoidance of mathematical and systematic certitudes. Alexander Pope summed up the English
intellectual's suspicion of dehumanized science:

Know then thyself, presume not God to scan;
The proper study of mankind is man.

Go, wondrous creature! mount where science
    guides,
Go, measure earth, weigh air,
    and state the tides.

But when his own great work is but begun,
What reason weaves, by passion is undone.

The French philosopher Voltaire noted the English aversion to the study of
abstract physical analysis when he wrote of John Locke in his *Letters on the
English*:

This great man could never subject himself to the tedious fatigue of calculations,
nor to the dry pursuit of mathematical truths, which do not at first present any
sensible objects to the mind; and no one has given better proof than he, that it is
possible for a man to have a geometrical head without the assistance of geometry.

Some Enlightenment figures, particularly the earl of Shaftesbury (grandson
of the Whig politician), made an even greater leap from the theory that held
reason itself to be a source of knowledge independent of the senses. His
followers hated the uniform proofs that seemed to rob nature of its creative
spontaneity. Common-sense experience, they felt, provided the rational
intellect with everything it required: in fact, it was dangerous to sever oneself

from empirical observation in favor of ideas perfected in the mind without the verification that everyday life alone could provide. Thus John Locke, perhaps the Enlightenment's most influential thinker, praised experience as the teacher of mankind in his *Essays Concerning Human Understanding* (1690):

> Let us then suppose the mind to be, as we say, white paper, void of all characters, without any ideas:—How comes it to be furnished? Whence comes it by that vast store which the busy and boundless fancy of man has painted on it with an almost endless variety? Whence has it all the materials of reason and knowledge? To this I answer, in one word, from EXPERIENCE. In that all our knowledge is founded; and from that it ultimately derives itself. Our observation employed either, about external sensible objects, or about the internal operations of our minds perceived and reflected on by ourselves, is that which supplies our understandings with all the materials of thinking. These two are the fountains of knowledge, from whence all the ideas we have, or can naturally have, do spring. . . .

Classical Models: The Augustan Ideal

The recovery of so-called pure nature forever eluded eighteenth-century intellectuals, for they could not agree upon what form nature took. Instead, each sought the forms through which he assumed nature was supposed to work, and for these each had a supposed model. By far the most accepted model was that of the ancient Roman world of the first century. Thus in the eighteenth century education was largely based on Roman thought as well as its Greek antecedents; Roman forms were slavishly copied in architecture and writing, and Roman history became the example both for heroic emulation and the inculcation of patriotism. That the Romans had been in particular harmony with nature was a conception predating the Elizabethan Renaissance. Classicism gathered more and more adherents, until by the reign of Anne a new Augustan age was thought to have arrived.

John Dryden, writing his *Of Dramatic Poesy* in 1668, had opened the classical door by suggesting that in her drama England approached the shores of classical greatness. Nonetheless, he was aware that a gap in form still existed:

> Those ancients have been faithful imitators and wise observers of that Nature which is so torn and ill represented in our plays; they have handed down to us a perfect resemblance of her [nature]; which we, like ill copiers, neglecting to look on, have rendered monstrous, and disfigured.

For the next two generations a battle raged between "the ancients" and "the moderns." If for no other reason than that the most talented writers of the period, notably Jonathan Swift and Alexander Pope, sided with the classics, the ancients momentarily triumphed. Few thought to go against the genius of Pope when, in 1711, he advised in his *Essay on Criticism*

Hear how learned Greece her useful rules indites,
When to repress, and when indulge our flights:
High on Parnassus' top her sons she showed,
And pointed out those arduous paths they trod;
Held from afar, aloft, the immortal prize,
And urged the rest by equal steps to rise.

.   .   .

Learn hence for ancient rules a just esteem;
To copy nature is to copy them.

True, he noted the ancient Roman and Greek authors frequently exceeded their own stylistic boundaries.

But though the ancients thus their rules invade,
(As kings dispense with laws themselves have made)
Moderns, beware! or if you must offend
Against the precept, ne'er transgress its end;
Let it be seldom, and compelled by need;
And have, at least, their precedent to plead.

Pope concluded this essay with what was to become the eighteenth century's favorite historical theme:

Learning and Rome alike in empire grew,
And arts still followed where her eagles flew;
From the same foes, at last, both felt their doom,
And the same age saw learning fall, and Rome.

Supposedly the Dark Ages (the term was invented in the eighteenth century) had witnessed a swarming of vandals and superstitious monks who encouraged ignorance. Then the Renaissance had come to the rescue in the person of the Dutch humanist Erasmus, who "drove those holy Vandals [the monks] off the stage." Others, said Pope, furthered the work of uncovering Rome's greatness:

But see! each muse, in Leo's[1] golden days,
Starts from her trance, and trims her withered bays;
Rome's ancient genius o'er its ruins spread,
Shakes off the dust, and rears [its] reverend head.

[1] Pope Leo X, 1475–1521, patron of the arts.

Dryden and Pope thought themselves the conveyors of Roman excellence. Dryden went on to translate Ovid, Juvenal, Persius, Virgil, Horace, Lucretius, and Theocritus, and Pope repaid his indebtedness to the classic muses by spending five years translating Homer's *Iliad* (1715–20).

Although the Augustan ideal had begun to fade from literary circles by the time of Pope's death in 1744, classicism's greatest architectural monuments were still to be erected in George III's reign. Classical tastes continued to tantalize the Georgians, though perhaps Dr. Johnson's aversion to "*that* stuff," his phrase to describe Roman history, was a symptom of the moderns' impatience with the tyranny of the ancients:

I know not why any one but a school-boy in his declamation should whine over the Common-wealth of Rome, which grew great only by the misery of the rest of mankind. The Romans, like others, as soon as they grew rich, grew corrupt; and in the corruption sold the lives and freedoms of themselves, and of one another.[2]

But by the time Johnson penned this opinion, neoclassical influences had effectively stabilized the English language. Before Dryden's involvement in classical regulations, the written word floated on a sea of bombast, localism, and crude invention. Early in the seventeenth century Francis Bacon had spent many of his last years translating his works into Latin, fearing they might otherwise lose their meaning. But the Latinate copies made by the Augustans changed this. The demand grew for English to become standardized. Possibly Pope's use of the rhyming heroic couplet and his imitators' reliance on inflated poetic diction ("the finny tribe" for "fish") made English poetry too stilted, but to English prose neoclassicism at last brought the clarity and precision that had long been lacking.

Classicism also reinforced an older tendency in English literature—didacticism. Prose and poetry could not merely divert; they had to provide moral elevation, or at least some universal truth about man. Probably the most ambitious work of the seventeenth century, Milton's *Paradise Lost,* and that of the eighteenth century, Pope's *Essay on Man*, had as their professed objectives the enlightenment of man's relation to God and the universe.

On a less intellectual plane, the average public's experience with the classicists' compulsion for social commentary was gained in the theater of the comedy of manners. This dramatic school of social propriety (or impropriety) had begun with Ben Johnson's comedies of humors (based on characterizations dominated by one of the four humors, or ruling passions) in James I's reign. It had withered as a result of the Puritans' aversion to the theater during the Interregnum, only to blossom again under French influence during the Restoration and reach fruition under Oliver Goldsmith's and Richard

[2] Quoted in Joseph Wood Krutch, *Samuel Johnson* (New York, 1944) pp. 75–6.

Sheridan's direction early in George III's reign. Fast-paced and full of favorite stock characters, these comic farces were outfitted with complicated plots and sub-plots, crammed with political and social allusions, and salted with such personages and titles as Sir Foppling Flutter and *The Comical Revenge; or Love in a Tub*. But the comedy of manners really belongs to the Restoration. After the Glorious Revolution its coarseness and raciness, its topical allusions, and its aristocratic flavor were condemned as reflections of the dissolute world of the Stuarts, and a neo-Puritan movement demanding moral reform engulfed the theater. When, in 1698, the Reverend Jeremy Collier blasted the playwrights with his *A Short View of the Immorality and Profaneness of the English Stage*, there was a headlong retreat from ribaldry and sophisticated farce. One popular author, George Farquhar, who had previously contributed his share to the theater's comedy of manners, set the new tone in his plays by professing to write them "so they be not offensive to religion and good manners." Throughout the eighteenth century the English stage maintained some of its former popularity but lost much of its liveliness.

The Rise of Romanticism

The new post-Revolution style that came to dominate not only the stage, but poetry and prose as well, was that of the sentimentalists. The canons of sweetness and sentiment published by Shaftesbury in Queen Anne's reign were reflected in a variety of influential forms. Scores of sermons written by Archbishop Tillotson on the love of God, the benignity of the universe, and the goodness of the soul found homes in hundreds of private libraries. Daniel Defoe's novels of moral suasion, particularly his charming classic depicting Robinson Crusoe's virtuous triumph over shipwreck, isolation, pirates, and cannibals, tapped the new vogue. Samuel Richardson's novels of virtue brought him great financial reward. His saccharine heroines, Pamela and Clarissa (these are also the names of the novels for which he is generally remembered, published in 1741 and 1748) are of two simple girls trying to make their ways through a world of lechery and betrayal. His audience doted on what critics since have called Pamela's "hothouse morality" and "aggressive chastity" as she flees pathetically, yet calculating, from one narrow escape from seduction to another until she finally trades in her chastity for a wedding ring.

By the end of the eighteenth century, sentiment was to cultivate deeper moods within playwrights, poets, and novelists. Quiet pastoral settings such as those portrayed in James Thomson's *The Seasons* (1730) came on the scene. Writers consciously avoided an urban wit in favor of loving descriptions of animals and forests. Passing from pastoral nature to pastoral man, writers now

explored the uncluttered sentiments of servant girls, plowboys, and unsophisticated country parsons. Oliver Goldsmith's *The Vicar of Wakefield* (1766),
the most uniquely romantic production of the eighteenth century, eulogized
the unencumbered motives of countryfolk. Primal moods were explored
in Horace Walpole's *The Castle of Otranto* (1764), which has as its setting a
pseudomedieval world of ghosts, gloom, supernaturalism, and villainy, and
which gave birth to a new fashion for the "Gothic." Moreover, the genius
of the folk culture of preclassical man lured eighteenth-century writers to
uncover lost ballads and epics. Dr. Thomas Percy published his *Reliques of
Ancient English Poetry* in 1765, giving rise to a popular search for Saxon and
medieval verse. The charms of rustic spontaneity and domestic common-
places were best expressed in the works of Robert Burns, the "poetical
plowman." The passion for physical nature, for emotional outpourings and
lyrical sentiment, had reached the point, when Burns published his first book
of poems in 1786, that the nation lionized him as a pastoral genius for im-
mortalizing Scottish dialect with his power and poignance. "Auld Lang
Syne," "The Cotter's Saturday Night," and "Tam o' Shanter" made the
colorful Scot the soul of romantic expression. Finally, with the publication of
Wordsworth and of Coleridge's *Lyrical Ballads* (1798), the earlier school of
sentiment had blossomed into an identifiable movement—that of romanticism. Wordsworth issued the romanticists' manifesto in his famous preface to
the *Ballads,* announcing that the "humble and rustic life" was chosen as the
theme for their poetry

> because, in that condition, the essential passions of the heart find a better soil in
> which they can attain their maturity; because in that condition of life our elementary
> feelings coexist in a state of greater simplicity, and . . . because in that condition
> the passions of men are incorporated with the beautiful and permanent forms of
> nature.

It is doubtful that Dryden and Pope and the Augustans of fifty years earlier
could have agreed. The forms in which nature had been expressed in the early
years of the English Enlightenment had been abstract, classical, and constrained;
now nature was earthy, personal, emotional, and, in Wordsworth's phrase,
"the very language of men."

The change in taste—from the courtly to the commonplace, from the
classical to the sentimental—can be attributed to the rise of a popular culture
in England. Dryden and Pope labored largely for a grateful elite. By the end
of the eighteenth century the public had become the writer's master. The
aristocratic wells of sponsorship and patronage were running dry, and in their
place money for publication was wrung from middle-class subscribers who
provided the capital for a book before it was even finished. By 1800 subscrip-

tions were giving way to commercial publishing houses as the dominant source of an author's remuneration. Nowhere could the expanding taste for print be seen more pointedly than in daily, periodical, and serial literature. Weekly newspaper circulation in 1705 was estimated at 44,000; six years later the estimate reached 200,000. London had sixteen newspapers in 1724, only two less than in 1782. Outside the capital there were no papers whatever in 1700, whereas 130 were counted in 1760. Such growth meant the emergence of an army of anonymous scribblers to feed the presses. These were badly educated for the most part, certainly untrained in the increasingly remote language of court etiquette, Latin, and Greek. It was at an audience trained to the casual, simple language of the press that ambitious authors now aimed. Wordsworth and Coleridge may have philosophically chosen to ennoble the humble swain and the common man, but in a new world based on industry, utility, common sense, and mass production, did they have a choice? The nineteenth century was to retain a respect for the classical image of Augustan natural law, and was even to blend it into part of the romantic ideal, but people under the strains of an industrial society were to find refuge more often in romantic vistas and Gothic piles than in austere classical temples.

$\mathscr{Bibliography}$

Chapter One THE TWILIGHT OF AGRARIAN ENGLAND

When it is completed, the master reference for agrarian social history will be that of H. P. R. Finberg, ed., *The Agrarian History of England and Wales*, Cambridge: Cambridge University Press, 1967, of which volume 4, covering the period 1500–1640, edited by Joan Thirsk, has appeared. Essays by experts on all aspects of life on the land are included.

For a superb single volume by a major social historian, see Christopher Hill's *Reformation to Industrial Revolution: The Making of Modern English Society, 1530–1780*, volume 1, New York: Pantheon, 1967.

Special studies on the roles of the politician, the merchant, the churchman, and the artist by advanced scholars such as J. H. Plumb, Jacob Viner, and G. R. Cragg are in *Man Versus Society in Eighteenth-Century England: Six Points of View*, edited by James L. Clifford, Cambridge: Cambridge University Press, 1968.

An unusually lucid study of the everyday world of preindustrial man, including intriguing chapters like, "Did the Peasants Really Starve?," is Peter Laslett's *The World We Have Lost*, New York: Scribner, 1965.

A fascinating discussion of the impact made by agricultural writings is that of G. E. Fussell, *More Old English Farming Books From Tull to the Board of Trade, 1731 to 1793*, London: Crosby Lockwood, 1950.

A classic reference for agricultural changes is Roland Prothero, Lord Ernle, *English Farming Past and Present*, 6th ed., Chicago: Quadrangle, 1962.

The customs, fads, and fashions of polite society are entertainingly discussed in A. S. Turberville's *English Men and Manners in the Eighteenth Century*, Oxford: Clarendon Press, 1929.

London receives a superb biography as the capital of English public life in Dorothy Marshall's *London Life in the Eighteenth Century*, Oxford: Clarendon Press, 1929.

Chapter Two   THE GATHERING OF FORCES

The master reference for this period is the Oxford History of England's ninth volume by Godfrey Davies, *The Early Stuarts, 1603–1660*, Oxford: Clarendon Press, 1959.

The multitude of causes preceding the Civil Wars is summarized in Philip A. M. Taylor's *The Origins of the English Civil War*, Boston: D. C. Heath, 1960.

There has been a prolonged debate over whether the Civil Wars were a class conflict between a declining aristocracy and a rising middle class. Some of the key works in this controversy are two books by Lawrence Stone, *The Crisis of the Aristocracy, 1558–1641*, Oxford: Clarendon Press, 1965, and *Social Change and Revolution in England, 1540–1640*, London: Longmans, 1965; see also J. H. Hexter's *Reappraisals in History*, London: Longmans, 1961.

Constitutional aspects of the entire century are treated through the documents themselves, republished with critical commentary in J. P. Kenyon, *The Stuart Constitution, 1603–1688*, Cambridge: Cambridge University Press, 1966.

Other works dealing with the purely constitutional conflicts preceding the Civil Wars are J. G. A. Pocock, *The Ancient Constitution and the Feudal Law*, Cambridge: Cambridge University Press, 1957; J. R. Tanner, *English Constitutional Conflicts of the Seventeenth Century*, Cambridge: Cambridge University Press, 1928; and M. A. Judson, *The Crisis of the Constitution*, New Brunswick: Rutgers University Press, 1949.

Religion, particularly the struggle between the Puritans and the church, has received excellent analysis in William Haller's *The Rise of Puritanism, 1570–1643*, New York: Columbia University Press, 1938; Christopher Hill's *Society and Puritanism in Pre-Revolutionary England*, New York: Schocken, 1964; and J. F. H. New, *Anglican and Puritan*, Stanford: Stanford University Press, 1964.

A broad sketch of the intellectual antecedents to the Civil Wars may be had in Christopher Hill's *Intellectual Origins of the English Revolution*, Oxford: Clarendon Press, 1965.

Finally, superb biographies of the leading figures in the pre-Civil War years are C. V. Wedgwood, *Strafford, 1593–1641*, London: J. Cape, 1953; J. H. Hexter, *The Reign of King Pym*, Cambridge: Harvard University Press, 1941; and H. R. Trevor-Roper, *Archbishop Laud*, London: Macmillan, 1962.

Chapter Three   THE GREAT REBELLION

Master references for this period are Godfrey Davies, *The Early Stuarts, 1603–1660*, Oxford: Clarendon Press, 1959 (ninth volume of the Oxford History of England); Samuel Rawson Gardiner, *The History of the Great Civil War, 1642–1649*, London: Longmans, 1893, 4 volumes; and C. V. Wedgwood, *The King's War, 1641–1647*, London: Collins, 1958.

The special attention that the Independents and Levellers have richly earned is found in Leo Solt, *Saints in Arms*, Stanford: Stanford University Press, 1959; George Yule, *The Independents in the English Civil War*, Cambridge: Cambridge University Press, 1958; G. P. Gooch, *English Democratic Ideas in the Seventeenth Century*, Cambridge: Cambridge University Press, 1928; D. M. Wolfe, *Leveller Manifestoes of the Puritan Revolution*, New York: Nelson, 1944; and Christopher Hill, *Puritanism and Revolution*, New York: Schocken, 1958.

The wars themselves are well explained in A. H. Burne, and Peter Young, *The Great Civil War*, London: Eyre and Spottiswoode, 1959; and Austin Woolrych, *Battles of the English Civil War*, London: Batsford, 1961.

Chapter Four   THE PURITAN COMMONWEALTH

Volume nine of the Oxford History of England should be consulted: Godfrey Davies, *The Early Stuarts, 1603–1660*, Oxford: Clarendon Press, 1959.

Other master references are Samuel Rawson Gardiner, *The History of the Commonwealth and Protectorate, 1649–1656*, London: Longmans, 1893, 4 volumes; C. H. Firth, *The Last Years of the Protectorate*, London: Longmans, 1909, 2 volumes; and Maurice Ashley, *Financial and Commercial Policy Under the Cromwellian Protectorate*, New York: Kelley, 1962.

The variety of reforms within and reactions against the Commonwealth is discussed in David Underdown, *Royalist Conspiracy in England, 1649–1660*, New Haven: Yale University Press, 1960; Stuart Prall, *The Agitation for Law Reform During the Puritan Revolution, 1640–1660*, The Hague: M. Nijoff, 1966; Wilhelm Schenk, *The Concern for Social Justice in the Puritan Revolution*, London: Longmans, 1948; Maurice Ashley, *Cromwell's Generals*, London: Cope, 1954; and Godfrey Davies, *The Restoration of Charles II, 1658–1660*, San Marino: Huntington Library, 1955.

Biographical literature of Oliver Cromwell abounds. Among the best is John F. H. New, ed., *Oliver Cromwell, Pretender, Puritan, Statesman, Paradox?* New York: Holt, Rinehart and Winston, 1972; Christopher Hill, *God's*

Englishman, New York: Dial Press, 1970; Maurice Ashley, *The Greatness of Oliver Cromwell*, New York: Macmillan, 1958; and Charles Firth, *Oliver Cromwell and the Rule of the Puritans in England*, London: Putnam, 1901.

Chapter Five FROM THE HAPPY RESTORATION TO THE GLORIOUS REVOLUTION

The master references for this period are George Clark's *The Later Stuarts, 1660–1714*, Oxford: Clarendon Press, 1955 (volume 10 of the Oxford History of England); two books by David Ogg, *England in the Reign of Charles II*, 1934, and *England in the Reigns of James II and William III*, 1955, both published in Oxford by Clarendon Press; and Thomas Babington Macaulay, *History of England From the Accession of James II*, London: J. M. Dent, 1906, 4 volumes.

A number of special studies have focused on the growth of parliamentary opposition in Charles II's reign: Clayton Roberts, *The Growth of Responsible Government in Stuart England*, Cambridge: Cambridge University Press, 1966; Douglas R. Lacey, *Dissent and Parliamentary Politics in England, 1661–1689*, New Brunswick: Rutgers University Press, 1969; D. T. Witcombe, *Charles II and the Cavalier House of Commons, 1663–1674*, New York: Manchester University Press, 1966; Maurice Lee, *The Cabal*, Urbana: University of Illinois Press, 1965; J. H. Plumb, *The Growth of Political Stability in England, 1675–1725*, London: Macmillan, 1967; and Keith Feiling, *A History of the Tory Party, 1640–1714*, Oxford: Clarendon Press, 1924.

Chapter Six THE DEFENSE OF THE REVOLUTION SETTLEMENT

The most complete references for this period are David Ogg, *England in the Reigns of James II and William III*, Oxford: Clarendon Press, 1955; and G. M. Trevelyan, *England Under Queen Anne*, London: Longmans, 1930, 3 volumes.

Superbly detailed analyses of party politics for the period can be found in Robert Walcott, *English Politics in the Early Eighteenth Century*, Cambridge: Harvard University Press, 1956; Geoffrey Holmes, *British Politics in the Age of Anne*, London: Macmillan, 1967; George Every, *The High Church Party, 1688–1718*. London: SPCK, 1956.

Among the multitude of studies on the Revolution of 1688 are G. M. Trevelyan, *The English Revolution, 1688–1689*, Oxford: Oxford University Press, 1938; Maurice Ashley, *The Glorious Revolution of 1688*, New York: Scribners, 1966; John Carswell, *The Descent on England: A Study of the English*

Revolution of 1688 and its European Background, New York: John Day, 1969; Geoffrey Holmes, ed., *Britain After the Glorious Revolution, 1688–1714*, London: Macmillan, 1969; Gerald M. Straka, *Anglican Reaction to the Revolution of 1688*, Madison: State Historical Society of Wisconsin, 1962.

The finest biography of England's warrior-statesman-king is Stephen Baxter's *William III*, London: Longmans, 1966.

The most complete biography of Marlborough is by his famous descendant Winston Churchill: *Marlborough: His Life and Times*, London: Harrap, 1933–1938, 4 volumes.

Chapter Seven THE DAWN OF INDUSTRIAL ENGLAND

Master references for the economic history of eighteenth-century England are Christopher Hill, *Reformation to Industrial Revolution, the Making of Modern English Society, 1530–1780*, volume 1, New York: Pantheon, 1967; E. J. Hobsbawm, *Industry and Empire, the Making of Modern English Society, 1750 to the Present*, volume 2, New York: Pantheon, 1968; M. W. Flinn, *An Economic and Social History of Britain Since 1700*, London: Macmillan, 1963; T. S. Ashton, *An Economic History of England, the Eighteenth Century*, New York: Barnes and Noble, 1955.

The causes of the Industrial Revolution have been under considerable analysis recently, and a superb introduction to them may be had in R. M. Hartwell, ed., *The Causes of the Industrial Revolution in England*, London: Methuen, 1967; P. A. M. Taylor, ed., *The Industrial Revolution in Britain*, Lexington: Heath, 1970; T. S. Ashton, *The Industrial Revolution, 1760–1830*, London: Oxford University Press, 1948; Charles Wilson, *England's Apprenticeship, 1603–1763*, New York: St. Martin's, 1965; G. N. Clark, *The Idea of the Industrial Revolution*, Glasgow: Jackson, 1953; W. W. Rostow, *The Stages of Economic Growth*, Cambridge: Cambridge University Press, 1960.

The effects of industrialization on Britain are treated in M. Dorothy George, *England in Transition*, London: Penguin, 1953; E. P. Thompson, *The Making of the English Working Class*, London: Gollancz, 1963; J. L. and Barbara Hammond, *The Town Labourer, 1760–1832*, New York: McKay, 1925.

Chapter Eight THE ERA OF ROBERT WALPOLE

An old master reference for the entire eighteenth century is W. E. H. Lecky, *A History of England in the Eighteenth Century*, New York: Appleton, 1879–90, 8 volumes; but it should be augmented by more recent scholarship reflected in Basil Williams, *The Whig Supremacy, 1714–1760*, Oxford: Clarendon Press, 1962; Dorothy Marshall, *England in the Eighteenth*

Century, London: Longmans, 1962; Derek Jarrett, *Britain, 1688–1815*, New York: St. Martin's, 1965; and E. N. Williams, *The Eighteenth-Century Constitution, 1688–1815*, Cambridge: Cambridge University Press, 1960.

A superbly lucid presentation of Hanoverian party politics is found in Robert A. Smith, *Eighteenth-Century English Politics, Patrons and Place-Hunters*, New York: Holt, Rinehart and Winston, 1972.

Two biographies of the era's leading statesmen are Basil Williams, *Stanhope, a Study in Eighteenth-Century War and Diplomacy*, Oxford: Clarendon Press, 1930; J. H. Plumb, *Sir Robert Walpole*, London: Cresset, 1956–60, 2 volumes.

The Jacobites receive full treatment in Charles Petrie's *The Jacobite Movement*, London: Eyre and Spottiswoode, 1959.

Chapter Nine WILLIAM PITT, LORD CHATHAM, AND THE BRITISH EMPIRE

The master reference for this period is Basil Williams, *The Whig Supremacy, 1714–1760*, Oxford: Clarendon Press, 1962.

Special studies for the period include two additional books by Basil Williams, *Carteret and Newcastle: A Contrast in Contemporaries*, Cambridge: Cambridge University Press, 1943; and *William Pitt, Earl of Chatham*, New York: McKay, 1913, 2 volumes; also, John B. Owen, *The Rise of the Pelhams*, London: Methuen, 1957; and O. A. Sherrard, *Lord Chatham*, London: Bodley Head, 1952–58, 3 volumes.

The indispensable reference for the growth of the empire is Lawrence H. Gipson's, *The British Empire Before the American Revolution*, New York: Knopf, 1958–??, 14 volumes when completed.

Chapter Ten THE ERA OF LORD NORTH

The master references for this period are J. Steven Watson, *The Reign of George III, 1760–1815*, Oxford: Clarendon Press, 1960; Lewis Namier, *England in the Age of the American Revolution*, New York: St. Martin's, 1962; and R. J. White, *The Age of George III*, New York: Anchor Books, 1969.

Significant political analyses are found in Lewis Namier, *The Structure of Politics at the Accession of George III*, New York: St. Martin's, 1957, 2 volumes; John Brooke, *The Chatham Administration, 1766–1768*, New York: St. Martin's 1956; Lewis Namier and John Brooke, *The House of Commons, 1754–1790*, Oxford: Oxford University Press, 1964, 3 volumes; Ian R. Christie, *The End of North's Ministry, 1780–1782*, New York: St. Martin's, 1958; and John M. Norris, *Shelburne and Reform*, London: Macmillan, 1963.

The controversial political role played by George III is studied in Earl A. Reitan, ed., *George III, Tyrant or Constitutional Monarch?* Boston: Heath, 1964; Richard Pares, *King George III and the Politicians*, Oxford: Clarendon Press, 1953; and Herbert Butterfield, *George III and the Historians*, New York: Macmillan, 1959.

The Wilkes crusade has sparked a number of intriguing studies: Raymond Postgate, *That Devil Wilkes*, New York: Vanguard, 1930; George Rude, *Wilkes and Liberty*, Oxford: Oxford University Press, 1962; and I. R. Christie, *Wilkes, Wyvill and Reform*, London: Macmillan, 1962.

The crisis in the empire is studied in Lucy S. Sunderland, *The East Indian Company in Eighteenth-Century Politics*, Oxford: Clarendon Press, 1952; and John C. Miller, *Origins of the American Revolution*, Stanford: Stanford University Press, 1959.

Chapter Eleven THE ONSET OF REFORM

The major reference is J. Steven Watson, *The Reign of George III*, Oxford: Clarendon Press, 1960.

Detailed political studies are Donald Grove Barnes, *George III and William Pitt, 1783–1806*, Stanford: Stanford University Press, 1939; J. W. Derry, *The Regency Crisis and the Whigs, 1788–1789*, Cambridge: Cambridge University Press, 1963; and also by Derry, *William Pitt*, London: Batsford, 1962.

Imperial developments are described in V. T. Harlow, *The Founding of the Second British Empire, 1763–1793*, London: Longmans, 1952–64, 2 volumes; E. P. Moon, *Warren Hastings and British India*, London: British Universities Press, 1947; and K. E. Knorr, *British Colonial Theories, 1750–1850*. Toronto: University of Toronto Press, 1944.

Chapter Twelve FRANCE, REVOLUTION, AND NAPOLEON

The major reference is J. Steven Watson's *The Reign of George III, 1760–1815*, Oxford: Clarendon Press, 1960.

Politics of the period will be found in Philip A. Brown, *The French Revolution in English History*, London: Lockwood, 1918; Carl B. Cone, *Burke and the Nature of Politics*, University of Kentucky Press, 1957–64, 2 volumes; and Michael Roberts, *The Whig Party, 1807–1812*, London: Macmillan, 1939.

The Napoleonic Wars are considered in Carola Oman, *Nelson*, London: Hodder, 1947; Piers Mackesy, *The War in the Mediterranean, 1803–1810*, London: Longmans, 1957; and Godfrey Davies, *Wellington and His Army*, Oxford: Oxford University Press, 1954.

Chapter Thirteen NATURE AND NATURE'S LAWS:
THE ENLIGHTENMENT

Still the most comprehensive presentation of England's Enlightenment is the classic by Leslie Stephen, *History of English Thought in the Eighteenth Century*, London: Murray, 1902, 2 volumes; but close seconds in concept and scope are Basil Willey's two books, *The Seventeenth-Century Background* (1934) and *The Eighteenth-Century Background* (1940), both published in London by Chatto and Windus.

Special studies in intellectual history are W. H. G. Armytage, *Heavens Below: Utopian Experiments in England, 1560–1960*, London: Routledge, 1961; Carl Becker, *The Heavenly City of the Eighteenth-Century Philosophers*, New Haven: Yale University Press, 1959; Herbert Butterfield, *The Origins of Modern Science, 1300–1800*, London: Bell, 1949; Elie Halévy, *The Growth of Philosophical Radicalism*, London: Faber, 1934; and Ronald Knox, *Enthusiasm*, Oxford: Oxford University Press, 1950.

Methodism and the church are discussed in R. F. Wearmouth, *Methodism and the Common People of the Eighteenth Century*, London: Epworth, 1945; William J. Warner, *The Wesleyan Movement in the Industrial Revolution*, New York: McKay, 1930; and Norman Sykes, *Church and State in England in the Eighteenth Century*, Cambridge: Cambridge University Press, 1934.

Social and political philosophy is considered in these studies: Wilfrid Harrison, *Conflict and Compromise: A History of British Political Thought, 1593–1900*, New York: Free Press, 1965; C. B. Macpherson, *The Political Theory of Possessive Individualism, Hobbes to Locke*, Oxford: Clarendon Press, 1962; and two books by J. W. Gough, *The Social Contract*, 1957, and *Fundamental Law in English Constitutional History*, 1955, both published in Oxford by Clarendon Press.

Index

A CERTAINTY IN THE SUCCESSION
BY GERALD M. AND LOIS O. STRAKA

GERALD M. STRAKA, Professor of History at the University of Delaware, has been teaching and writing since he received his Ph. D. from the University of Wisconsin in 1959. His wife, LOIS, has worked with him on all his projects, but this is their first full collaboration. Professor Straka, now of the University of Delaware, has studied at the University of Virginia, the University of Wisconsin, and the London School of Economics, and taught at Oakland University and Rice University. He has held Woodrow Wilson, Davidge, and Folger fellowships and a Fulbright Scholarship. Among his works are *Anglican Reaction to the Revolution of 1688* (1962), *The Medieval World and its Transformations* (1967), and *The Revolution of 1688 and the Birth of the English Political Nation* (1973).

A NOTE ON THE TYPE

THIS old face design, BEMBO 270, has such an up-to-date appearance that it is difficult to realize this letter was cut (the first of its line) before A.D. 1500. At Venice in 1495, ALDUS MANUTIUS ROMANUS printed a small 36 pp. tract, *Petri Bembi de Aetna ad Angelum Chabrielem liber*, written by the young humanist poet PIETRO BEMBO (later Cardinal, and secretary to Pope Leo X), using a new design of type which differed considerably from that of Jenson's. The punches were cut by FRANCESCO GRIFFO of Bologna the designer responsible six years later for the first italic types. A second roman face followed in 1499 and this type design, based on the first, and used to print the famous illustrated *Hypnerotomachia Poliphili*, was the one which, after adaptation by Garamond, Voskens and others, resulted finally in Caslon Old Face.